Tsm'syeen Sagas
Clan Claims and Clashes of the Pacific Northwest

Tsm'syeen

Dzo<u>g</u>a Tsm'syeen a <u>k</u>ala ksyeen ada 'na gyiyaaks. Gaba da hoon dił *helda wil liks gyigyeda wüünaya. <u>k</u>'piil di gupl wil büs baasxga galtsiiptsap. A 'na'na ganoonakit. Saigat txaalpxa p'deex wil ksi wit 'waat ga gyet Gispwudwada, <u>G</u>anhada, Laxsgiik, Laxgibuu. 'Na smhawksa da naxnox ada halaayt. Nago<u>g</u>a dmt dit wilaays ga smoogit ga laxaga'a. Dat ama doo wila waalm smoogyit, smgyigyet, liikagyigyet, ada łałuungyit. Gyaawin ła dzo<u>g</u>a Tsm'syeen a'na gwa'a* dił *'naka boson.*

The Tsimshian live along the Skeena river and sea coast, eating salmon and many other foods. They are divided into a dozen tribes ~ towns. Through their mothers, people belong to four *p'deex* ~ crests named Orca ~ Blackfish, Raven, Eagle, Wolf. They believe in *naxnox* ~ wonders and *halaayt* ~ privileges and became Christians. They are organized into chiefs, councilors, ordinaries, and slaves. Now Tsimshian live in Canada and Alaska.

Adaaw̱x̱ Chronology

Tsimshian of the North Pacific Coast of Canada and Alaska insist that *adaawx̱,* the term for one of their densely cultural epics, be translated as "real history." Each saga is firmly based in their matrilineal social structure (of houses, clusters, clans and towns) while also being intensely both private and personal within these matrilineal kinship networks. Despite massive depopulation and crushing outside pressures, Tsimshians have long committed themselves to perpetuating these "histories" because of their guarantees of renewing immortality, providing a sequence of at least fifteen episodic overlays across ten thousand years.

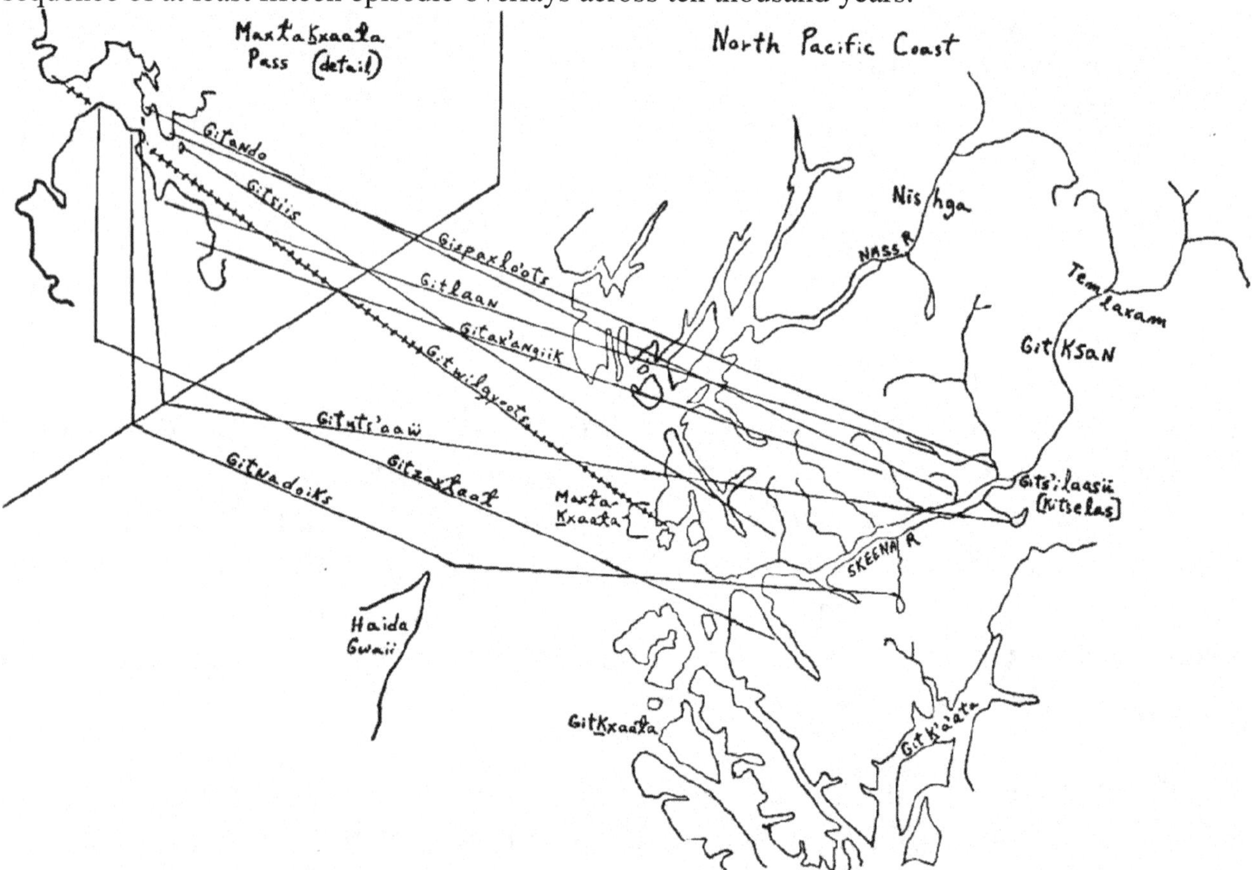

In the beginning was the word, and the word became a name, and the name became a story linking together places, people, and events into a culture.

Thus, from their own perspective, might begin a contemporary version of genesis and subsequent history for any number of Native American tribes. Unfortunately, popularly and dubiously regarded as "myths," these epics have often been slandered by the insensitive and slighted by scholars seeking to impose their own sense of detail and linear chronology on much more complex narratives.

Yet any truly Native (ethno) history must focus on the tribes' own profound sense of these events as both spiritually and temporally informed. While episodes of Euro-American history are sometimes abbreviated into the name of a significant individual involved, such as Washington, Pontiac, Lincoln, Sitting Bull, the events themselves — the American Revolution, French Defeat, Civil War, End of the Frontier — are understood to have been much more complex and complicated, sometimes even allowing for "the hand of God" in the outcome. These personal names, however, provide mere tags to events regarded by Euro-Americans as solitary and unique, [659] rather than, according to Native Americans, exemplary and worthy of repeated emulation, as these names are passed on to native family members in subsequent generations.

Within Native North American, the Maritime North Pacific ranks as one of its most complex culture areas. Yet at all times and places, relations with local lands and waters dominated all other sources for providing basic cultural understandings, as is well illustrated by recent insights among members of the Tsimshianic language family, speakers of an isolate composed in the interior of Nishga (*Nisga'a*) on the middle Nass River and of Gitksans (Gitxsan) on the upper Skeena River, and, near the ocean, of Coast and Southern Tsimshians. Neighbors to the north were the Tlingit, to the west were the Haida, to the south the Wakashan speakers, and to the east various Athapaskans, called *Ts'ets'awt* by Tsimshianic speakers. For thousands of years, these nations interacted through trade, warfare, ceremonial exchanges, and royal intermarriages, effectively overarching differences of town, tribe, or parent language.

With the publication of my holistic study of Tsimshian culture based in institutions metaphorically dealing with refracted light (Miller 1997), I return herein to the wealth of native sources to find an alternative way to represent the same information.[1] In my initial eagerness to assure an overview of the complexities of traditional Tsimshian religion, replaced by an enthusiastic Christianity for over a century, I avoided probing deeply into the *adaawx̱*,[2] the revered if "messy" histories fixed in time and space to be passed down with precision through the heads of noble houses (Boas 1916; Spier 1931). Indeed, the *adaawx̱*, along with clans (*p'teex*) and heraldic crests (Garfield 1966), survive quite well among modern Tsimshian, while the *naxnox* (masked wonders) and *halaayt* (elite privileges in four [660] orders or guilds) of the ancient religion do not.[3] In other words, the realm of women, the basis for matrilineality, has survived well into the present, while the realm of men, the basis for traditional religious expressions, has not, except as sometimes recast in Anglican ways.

---

[1] Though I was not always entirety gracious during this ordeal, I remain inexpressably grateful to Susan Marsden, John Dunn, Christopher Roth, Jean Mulder, Tanya Stebbins, Marjorie Halpin, Margaret Anderson, and, most especially, the Clifton, Hill, Gamble, Brown, Leighton, Wilson, and Neasloss families.

For years, Raymond Fogelson has been calling for such an ethno-ethnohistory, relying on native sources and interpretations of their own sense of history, more than just the blending of written and oral sources of the same events during colonialism. Simultaneously, Helen Tanner has reminded one and all that native history is ipso facto personal and family history. Moreover, this labor is dedicated to the memory of Alfonso Ortiz, who now gets his revenge for my avoiding Pueblo epics of clan migrations while he was mentoring my writing of a dissertation on the Keresans, southern neighbors of the Tewa. In parallel fashion, such migration epics of the Tsimshian and Pueblos lay out a vast but relative chronology from earliest times to the present which pays little if any attention to later European interlopers. For Tsimshian, moreover, reality is clearly specified by the presence of the word *SM*, as in *smgigyet,* the word for "chiefs" literally meaning "real people."

[2] In Tlingit, the term *at.oow* is equivalent to the Tsimshianic *adaaxw*.

[3] Indeed, William Duncan, famous missionary ro the Tsimshian, was explicit: "I have never interfered with the crest business. It was very helpful to me" (quoted in Usher 1974:153, note 14).

Through intermarriage these crests became shared by elite families in all Northcoast nations, regardless of language. Indeed, most royalty were multilingual. Nevertheless, Tlingits have been expanding to the north and south at the expense of neighbors, as have Wakashans along the central [661] coast. After a migration down the Skeena about 3,500 years ago (of the archaeologically designated Skeena complex), Tsimshianic seems to have developed along the sea, where it split into Coast and Southern dialects before Coast forms of language and culture spread back upriver, eventually influencing inland Athapaskans.

In general, the situation on the coast seems to have been dense and stable with prime lands long occupied by locals; while in the interior, with its varied terrain and climate, groups were highly mobile over time. On the coast, ancestral houses (in a corporate sense) were more important, while resourceful heros (in an individualistic sense) appear more often in the interior. Indeed, given that the coast had much greater prestige and resources, a variety of peoples were drawn to (or borrowed from) it, in contrast to the individuals in quest of adventure or trade (or both) who ventured upriver. For this reason, in seeming contradiction to this general pattern, when tracing one of three clusters of the Wolf clan among the Tahltan, George Emmons (1911: 16) noted, "They came first and collectively from the interior, and later and individually from the coast."

For Tsimshians, each crest represents a cluster of houses sharing an ancestry that remained distinct within the larger grouping of a clan. For example, Coast and Southern Tsimshians recognize four paired clans (semi-moieties) called *Ganhada* (Raven) + *Laxsgiik* (upon Eagle) or *Gispwudwada* (Orca, locally called Blackfish or Killerwhale) + *Laxgibuu* (upon Wolf). The inland Gitksan and Nishga use Frog for Raven, and Grizzly or Fireweed for Orca.

Between the house and the clan are more than one cluster of house groups tracing a common origin from a different place or spirit. These clusters derive from epic *adaawx̱* and account for subsidiary crests within each clan, such as *Gispwudwada* (Orca, Grizzly, Grouse, Mosquito, Stars, Sun, Fireweed), *Ganhada* (Raven, Frog, Sculpin, Starfish), *Laxgibuu* (Wolf, Bear, Crane, Owl), and *Laxsgiik* (Eagle, Beaver, Halibut, Octopus) (Miller 1997: 54). Such a sterile listing, however, does not recognize the basis for these eight major crests in the epics, which validate the house clusters given below (epics 2-11) and thus enrich our understandings.

Religious law insisted that respect was due all forms of life. Thus, while humans might use parts and pieces of other beings, the entire body could only be used by members of that particular species. The *adaawx̱,* therefore, carefully interdict the abuse of living things or their articulated skeletons, their source of eternal vitality.[4] Indeed, a primary duty of any chief, as with the leader of a species, was to become so "evolved" as to channel such vitality down his spine (or its representation in totem pole or cane) to fructify the land of his people. [662]

Within these larger units Tsimshian remain organized on the basis or the household, once a distinct and decorated dwelling covered by adzed cedar planks. Each house owned a corpus of immortal names, passed down through that matriline, with the leading name serving as the title of the house chief, who had the sole right to recite its *adaawx̱* — the dense, distilled, and concentrated essences of world-shaking and world-making events involved with that name. Beginning in a stark and wet world that is obviously postglacial, the most ancient *adaawx̱*

---

[4] For this reason, Tsimshian placed fish and animal bones in a fire to be consumed and reborn for the benefit of future life.

therefore span at least ten thousand years. Yet, as with the temporal sense of the Iroquois mentioned below, all these events do not happen simultaneously in a chaotic jumble, but, instead, sort themselves out as episodes in relative terms of what happened before and after each one. Because of these glacial conditions, remaining in alpine situations, and the endemic watery environment, however, flood stories reappear throughout the full chronology.

More important, each *adaaw̠x* is told from the perspective of that one house, so it is both personal and laudatory. Triumphs are therefore always reported, yet defeats rarely. To convey this highly localized sense of "grounding," I have added details from the Douglas Channel homeland of the *Gitga'at* (People of the Cane) where I was named. Though distinctly coastal, the Ecstall River Valley provided access to this region from the Skeena River, where the Coast Tsimshian majority have been confederated for about two millennia.

Where I most vary from a native perspective is in trying to present an account which interweaves, over time, as many crests as possible instead of specifying only the crest(s) of the house, and of related houses in that cluster, while ignoring or overlooking other houses, other crests, or foreign peoples who may have been there but have no longstanding or overt "claims on" or "relations with" a narrator.

Because the highest-ranking name holders were and are invited to the most feasts and potlatches, they were in a position to hear all the major epics recited in a public context. Their role, however, was to witness rather than to record or judge these "other" *adaaw̠x*, for only the master of a house had the unassailable right to recite its epic, personally or, with greater prestige, through a designated and "paid" narrator.

Those who have long avoided getting lost in the maze, as some have phrased it, of the *adaaw̠x* have now been provided with a brilliant ball of thread in the work of Susan Marsden (1996) of the Museum of Northern British Columbia in Prince Rupert.[5] Building on her insights at unraveling a relative chronology for middle-level events involving major clusters regarded as most significant by Tsimshian themselves, her useful guidelines allow for the identification of fifteen overlays, at least, within Tsimshian traditions, each associated with the famous name of a person or place. [663]

In presenting thumbnail sketches of each level, my intent is never to trivialize nor to slight these very significant and complex events.[6] Instead, within this overall guide, each layer

---

[5] Susan Marsden was educated as a philosopher and thus is mercifully free of the academic baggage detrimental to understanding the *adaaxw* in their own right and relational sequencing. Her greatest insight has been the recognition that this sequence fills thousands rather than hundreds of years of culture chronology and consists of actual "history," in the sense that these events involved real (biological) people, places, emotions, and motivations.

[6] At the core of each *adaaxw* is one or more song (*limk'oy*), often translated [672] "dirge" for its slow place, although "anthem" conveys more of its patriotism while "lamentation" suggests its religious tone. During moments of great crisis, such as a world cataclysm, an adaaxw will specify that sages met briefly to compose a song in case anyone survived and needed a reference point to explain its impact, often a fatal lesson in showing respect for all other life forms. Most *adaaxw* detail encounters with *naxnox*, spirits resident in the Tsimshianic landscape embodied in masks. In general, if the human were a male, he will acquire access to strengthening power;

represents a milestone along the route of Tsimshian narrative history. Each name should be regarded in the same way as anyone seeking to understand the "Matter of Britain" would regard the personage of Arthur as the key figure in events that also include Twelve Knights of the Round Table, with Lancelot, Guinevere, Merlin, Mordred, and a host of other named characters and places playing significant roles within the story of Arthur.

Similarly, the nearest Americanist equivalent is the "historic" chronology among Iroquoians recognizing three layers, each named for a foremost participant. Thus, the creation of the world after their mother fell from the sky involved Earth Grasper and his malevolent twin Flint. Next came the founding of the League of the Iroquois by Degandawida, aided by Hyanwentha (Hiawatha, "comber") and Jingonsasay (the Peace Queen), now generally dated to a lunar eclipse of 1350. In about 1800, Handsome Lake rose from his deathbed to preach the Good Word and revitalize Iroquoian religion.

For Tsimshian, however, the layering of chronological episodes is much more complex.

Laxha

This preexistence is and was inhabited by immortals known as *naxnonax* under the leadership of Heaven (*laxha*). Most naxnoxwere and are protean batrachian shape-shifters combining aspects of humans, fish, and frogs. Beings have names and families, but no institutional units larger than the house (*walp*).

More avian naxnox living along inland valleys included the Robins of Kitsumkalum (Gitsmgeelm) and the Wind Brothers, who traveled as Ducks from the Ecstall headwaters.

Txamsem

A naxnox comes to earth as a shining youth born to a noble Haida couple. Changed from an ascetic to a glutton, he becomes *'Wiigyet* (Big Man), also known as Txamsem, and goes to the Nass River, changing the world toward its present condition.[7] Coming upon a rock and an elderberry about to give birth, he quickened the bush so humans now die and these bushes grow on their graves. Only the hardness of fingernails and toenails reminds people that they might have lived forever like stones.

He stole the bentwood box(es) holding sun, moon, and stars from [664] Raven at the Head of the Nass and opened it with a blinding flash, creating present species and seasons, except for those who escaped to remain *naxnox*.[8] In recognition of his acts, the Ganhada matriclan with the

---

whereas if a woman, she will have a child with divine powers and the right to pass on crests associated with these and subsequent events.

[7] According to Sterritt and others (1995), the Nass River is the most ancient and complex homeland of Tsimshianic peoples, since its mouth was once occupied by Coast Tsimshians, middle reaches by Nishga, and upper reaches by Gitksans.

[8] This epic of the theft of the Box of Daylight was and is shared throughout the North Pacific, both American and Asian, and regarded as the "big bang" of creation that began the current progression and dimensionality of both time and space. In consequence, Raven took over

Raven Crest was instituted, along with its Frog variants. In particular, this Raven and Frog interlinkage is well illustrated on the Raven rattle so distinctive of North Pacific chiefship, particularly in its *halaayt* aspect.

Nagwinaks

On the coast a canoe from the Southern Tsimshian was taken under the sea into the elaborately decorated house of a resident naxnox, the chief of the Orca known as Gitnugwinaks. After four years, thinking they had been gone four days, the crew returned home with the right to build, carve, and paint a duplicate house and assume the names of *naxnox* from this spiritual abode. They became the *Gispwudwada* of the *Laxmoon* cluster within the Orca Crest, closely associated with the Kitasoo (*Gidestsu*) at Klemtu, who have long intermarried with *Gitga'at*. As the Raven and Frog were interlinked in the interior, so, on the coast, were the Orca and Wolf, both social carnivores organized into pods or packs, with Grizzlies sometimes added to the mix.

Ts'ooda

One of the first beings to travel up from the mouth of the Skeena into the Yukon and back through the Nass and Skeena was Ts'ooda and his slave Haalus. More *naxnox* than mortals, the behavior of each clearly indicated his class and rank. Ts'ooda was kind, considerate, and efficient, while Haalus was awkward, greedy, and insufficient. Ts'ooda and Haalus also appeared, respectively, as a brightly colored butterball duck and a dull one. Though primarily a Wolf, Ts'ooda's coastal origins also associated him with Orca. *Txamsem* (as Big Wings) built the first coastal house for him, setting the posts and beams with his claws, before sending a sister down from Heaven to be his wife and teach other women useful domestic skills. Later, Ts'ooda taught his own children the smelting of copper to make them rich and famous.

Sats'aan

One of the earliest gathering places in the interior was *Laxwiiyip*, on the plateau drained by the headwaters of the Stikine, Nass, and Skeena Rivers. An important name there was Niislaganoos (Grandfather + Tlingit [665] term for "hill of the chief"), using a hat topped with ten articulated disks symbolizing vertebrae.

Among the earliest out-migrants were a Raven group led by Sats'aan.[9] "While crossing a lake on a raft during a storm, a man drowned. His mourning sister later heard two songs and saw a frog and what looked a raven flying in the water (actually, a dark fish called a bullhead). These

---

responsibility for finishing the work of the Creator with not always satisfactory results.

[9] Among the Wet'suwet'sen (Bulkley River Carrier), a Raven artist became wealthy enough to potlatch and claim a formal seat using the name of *Sats'aan* because it was so venerable among the Tsimshian at nearby Kitselas. While he remained something like one of the Kwakwaka'wakw parvenus called Eagles, ranked between commoners and nobility, his daughter and later descendants became fully noble (Jenness 1943: 489-90).

laments and crests (Water Raven-Bullhead, Frog) were thereafter claimed by this cluster.

Gaw'a

A prince of the Raven village on the upper Nass was having an affair with a married woman in a village across the river, ruining her husband's hunting luck so he died impaled on a beaver dam. In revenge, his brothers killed the lover(s) and hid the prince's severed head. When the Ravens realized what had happened to their prince, they razed the other town. Only a girl (*Gaw'a*, *Gawo*) and her mother escaped. Pleading "Who will marry my daughter?" the mother accepted a son of the Sun, who then placed the mother inside a tree branch to produce arboreal creaking sounds and then took the girl into the sky to father Heavenly Children, often four sons and two daughters, one of them crippled.

Quickening their maturity, their grandfather Sun sent these youngsters back to the upper Nass, each son in a house with the first painted fronts and specialized crests, along with miraculous weapons used to destroy the Ravens utterly. Unrestrained, these brothers kept on fighting and killing until they met the beautiful women of the Babine River, who brought with them the Loon Crest. The sisters of these tamed warriors became the *Gisk'aast*, Fireweed Crest, after a miraculous encounter with this plant.

Temlaxam

A city called *Temlaxam* (prairie town, good land) grew up at the forks of the upper Skeena River near modern Hazelton, and its refined governance instituted the full flowering of culture, complete with clans, clusters, potlatches, and the moral law respecting all life. Among male religious institutions, displays of *naxnox* wonders and *smhalaayt* shamanism were specifically mentioned. As Temlaxam was the Tsimshianic center, so neighboring Dizkle was the Athapaskan hub.

Over time, however, the vast and growing population became wasteful, careless, and disrespectful. Several divine punishments ensued before a final one dispersed everyone. First, some boys abused a goat kid so [666] mountain goats lured everyone into the path of a rockslide that killed most of them. Second, some maidens used articulated trout skeletons on hats, playing frivolously with this integral source of life until a huge grizzly emerged from Seeley Lake to ravage the area. Third, after a young man insulted a salmon run, Heaven sent a blizzard that raged all summer long, until a bird with a berry in its beak warned *Ts'ibasaa* and his brothers *'Wiiseeks* (Big Seeks) and Seeks to struggle, each in turn, to the coast.[10] Fourth, some youths insulted a run of trout, so Heaven sent a flood to drown all but a few of those wealthy enough to have huge canoes to keep them afloat. From *Temlaxam*, a cluster of Nishga, Gitksan, and Tsimshian royal houses took up their historic locations, moving into towns long occupied by

---

[10] Relying on detailed ornithological knowledge, this bird is often identified as a bluejay because they are very localized. Seeing this bird with a berry, those trapped inside the house knew that it was now fall with real winter on the way.

locals but now bound into an extensive trade network through this dispersed royalty.[11]

Of particular note as corroboration toward dating these events, a massive Stikyooden landslide at Chicago Creek near Seeley Lake has been geologically dated to 3,500 years ago (Monet and Skanu'u 1991: 111).

Assembling as neighboring tribal winter towns along Metlakatla Passage, replacing Temlaxam, Coast Tsimshian thrived. Also, the various *Gisk'aast* and *Gispwudwada* royal houses, both inland and sea, conjoined. Some survivors also went to the Tlingit, Haida, and other tribes, where their common origin was indicated by shared crests, chiefly names, and cluster label as a *wilnaat'aał* = a house cluster grouping providing a loyalty and identity between between a clan and a house.

Near Temlaxam, the heavy snow of the summer blizzard crushed the log salmon trap of the royal Orca house of *Nta'wiiwalp*, who escaped near starvation with his wife down the Ecstall Valley. There she gave birth to a daughter who grew up to marry the local *naxnox* son of the North Wind. Because of the husband's affinity with ducks, the wife always gave birth to quadruplets, until these numerous offspring founded the first semihuman town at a protected river fork in the homeland, now known as Old Town.

Nta'wiiwalp's brother Gaaymtkwa briefly joined them there before moving on to settle at Kitkatla. Similarly, the Orca brothers *'Wa'moodmłk*, married a Raven woman, while *Gwinaxnuutk* went to Kitkatla and settled in that homeland. Later their sibling rivalry over the white Kermode Bear Crest led to the founding of Star House, where *'Wa'moodmłk* added the name of Raven Snare, while a war was averted by giving the crest to *Gwinaxnuutk*.

Gwisk'aayn

Strife with Ravens in the upper Stikine set off an extensive migration of Wolf clanspeople intermarried with Eagles. Over time, in addition to the [667] layering of events, this cluster (called the *Gwinhuut*, meaning fugitives, refugees, displaced people) leapfrogged over space, claiming places not permanently occupied or away from Tsimshian settlements. One of their leaders was Gwisk'aayn, whose Wolves sought protected inlets throughout coastal Tsimshian territory where they could entrench in a fort or stronghold. Among their affines were Eagle royal houses later associated with the high chief named Ligeex and another cluster headed by *Gitxon* (*Gyetxawn*, *Gyethoon*, Salmon Man).

Throughout the region, native houses are recognized as either "owners" or "others" (Miller 1981). Owners are those who saw the advantages of a place and pioneered its settlement

---

[11] Viola Garfield (1966: 34) argued that these royal houses were the result of resettlements at the fur trading posts, but the *adaaxw* insist that certain clusters arrived on the coast already royal because of the fame acquired via their lavish potlatching, stone crests, and international relations, much as members of the Russian nobility fled to Europe, keeping their "good names" if nor always the family fortunes and treasures. Among Northcoast people, however, royalty was even more a matter of intermarriage, since fathers and sons belonging to different clans contributed a cosmopolitanism to each other's rankings in a way that uncles and nephews belonging to the same clan could not.

and use after being empowered by a local *naxnox* assumed as a crest.[12] Others include various affines, friends, or visitors who reside in that locale with the approval of the owners. Thus, these fugitives wandered the coast seeking productive places where each could establish ownership, however briefly. By this time, however, most of the Tsimshian area had long been claimed by houses, so bitter fighting frequently ensued until victories, compromises, and all-important intermarriages settled these situations.

Of note, carbon dates from around Metlakatla indicate that more than twelve existing towns were abandoned in about A.D. 100, suggesting a starting date for this exodus when embattled Coast Tsimshian retreated to their tribal territories along tributaries of the lower Skeena. Of note, these towns had been widely dispersed with houses of uniform size, while those reoccupied after A.D. 400 were concentrated (confederated) along Venn Passage in the immediate vicinity of Metlakatla with houses of varying size and wealth. Clearly, conditions of warfare encouraged the rapid growth of a ranked society concentrated for its own defense (Archer 1996).

In the homeland, Nta'wiiwalp led an intertribal war expedition to clear the Wolves from Douglas Channel and then Lowe Inlet, albeit allowing intermarriage with the royal survivors.

Aksk

Eventually, after a brutal *Gwinhuut* attack on the Ecstall River, only a boy and girl survived and, vowing revenge, married although both were *Gispwudwada*. Thus, though often avoided in the *adaaw̲x*, Aksk married his mother's sister's daughter to father ten sons, more often called his "nephews," all trained to be skilled warriors.[13] By this time, many *Gwinhuuts* were being identified as Tlingit enemies, although still sharing a remote ancestry with Tsimshian house clusters from the Nass and *Temlaxam*. Their stronghold was near Dundas Island across from the mouth of the Nass. [668]

When his sons were grown, Aksk moved to Kaien Island and built a two-story fort. Wooden effigies were placed in the beds with kelp tubes to carry the sound of imitated snoring. Lured into the fort, attacking Tlingits plunged daggers into the manikins only to become trapped because the weapons, which were tied to their wrists, remained stuck deep in the wood. Victorious, Aksk and his family took all of the weapons, crests, and treasures of these slain enemies.[14]

---

[12] In *sm'algyax* (real language, Coast Tsimshianic), the phrasing is that owners have a place "where they could work the land" [*ndega dm di wil ha'li hałeeist*] (Ts'ibasaa 1916).

[13] Since *aks* means "water" and *-k* particularizes the meaning of a word (such as *gaws* [hair] becomes *gawsk* [thin]), his name may be "fetch water" with the sense of providing relief.

[14] Much earlier at this locale was the home of a chief whose daughter suckled a woodworm until it became a menace to the town and was killed. Though a Tsimshian epic set in their homeland, this crest is best known from the Whale House of the Chilcat Tlingit, where it is represented in an enormous carved feasting trough.

adaawx̱

Metlakatla

With the Tlingits driven north, the Coast Tsimshian tribes came out of the lower Skeena to resume winter festivities along Metlakatla Passage in territory now "owned" by *Aksk*'s tribe, the Gitwilgyoots (People of the Kelp), because they had successfully fought for and "invested in" that locale. By A.D. 1200, the region was densely and diversely occupied, with rankings presumably derived from the preeminent standing of the Kelp People.

Niishaywaaxs

A high chief of Temlaxam, *Niishaywaaxs*[15] of the Grizzly Bear *(midiik)* Crest took his people downriver to claim the Zymoetz River Valley and the gateway at Kitselas Canyon (Wright 1962), but they were bitterly opposed by local Ravens for many years. Recriminations were unceasing. Treachery and murder shattered brief truces or marriage alliances. One Grizzly princess was incinerated on her wedding night; one *Niishaywaaxs* was crushed to death in an elaborate show of hostility, and so on until these Wars of Midiik ended at a settlement feast where Ravens compensated for the initial death, and land claims were validated to confirm Grizzly control of the upper Skeena Canyon. {see following below Men of Medeek}

Ligeex

Building upon a vast array of marital ties, an Eagle chief of the *Gispaxlo'ots* (People of the Elderberry) rose to primacy among the Coast Tsimshian after 1800 under the titled name of Ligeex. In about 1500, the name had come from the Kitamaat via a marriage between a Raven chief and a *Gwinhuut Gispaxlo'ots* princess, whose daughter married Hamdziit, high chief at Heiltsuk (*Wutsdaa*, Bella Bella) and source of many *'wiihalaayt* (great *halaayt*) privileges. Via access to these secret orders and through strategic marriages by nephew heirs, the name *Ligeex* became allied with important houses over a wide area for several hundred years. By then, these [669] Elderberry People were the most numerous of all Coast Tsimshian tribes. Bitter wars were fought for direct access to the Gitksan fur trade through Kitselas Canyon, until dynastic marriages by *Gwinhuut* Eagles established the necessary links. After a devastating defeat, one Ligeex maneuvered to have the victorious *Niistaxho'ok* of Kitselas lead his flotilla against the Haida. Under Old Ligeex (died 1840), the most famous, intermarriages involved European institutions like the Hudson's Bay Company, who built their second Fort Simpson on a portion of his own land in 1834.

Duncan

Then, in 1857, a lay Anglican missionary named William Duncan arrived from England and spent a year learning to speak Tsimshianic from an Orca nobleman named *Clah* (*łaa*) before he began to preach and to convert. By 1862, he led fifty converts, soon joined by two hundred

---

[15] The name means 'Grandfather of *Haywaaxs*'.

more, back to ancient Metlakatla to found one of the most successful cooperative Christian communities in the world. The continued importance of the power of "light," together with identifying Duncan as "the chief," indicate that Christianity fit quite easily within the template of the traditional culture.

Deciding to join with other Tsimshian, *Gitga'at* families left their homeland to join Duncan between 1863 and 1873. In 1874, Methodists began a mission at Port Simpson which became the base of Reverend Thomas Crosby for twenty-three years.

New Metlakatla

A bishop was sent to Metlakatla to downplay the economic cooperative in favor of a religious community of avowedly Anglican form. Duncan refused both ordination for himself and the sacrament of communion for his converts, fearing that consuming the body and blood of Christ would be confused with the ancient cannibal *halaayt.* Conditions worsened until, in 1887, Duncan led about eight hundred Tsimshians to Alaska in quest of religious freedom under U.S. protection.

Deciding to return to their homeland, about thirty *Gitga'at* canoed south and founded a new town along Christian tenets at their ancient fall camp, since affiliated with the United Church of Canada.

As a result, Tsimshianic speakers now continue to live as Gitksan along the upper Skeena; Nisga'a along the Nass; Southern at Klemtu, Hartley Bay, and Kitkatla; and Coast at New Metlakatia, Lax Kw'alaams (Port Simpson), Kitsumkalum, Kitselas, and Old Metlakatla, the ancient Tsimshian bastion where a few chiefs stayed behind with Bishop William [670] Ridley after everyone else had left. Today, of course, most Tsimshian, like others involved in the cash economy, have moved to Prince Rupert and other Canadian and American cities.

Delgamuuk^w

Under their hereditary titled names to assert their lasting aboriginal rights, the chiefs of the Gitksan and Wet'suwet'en spent three and a half years (1987-91) in British Columbia provincial court to argue for their land claims, based in the *adaaw̲x*, only to be told by the chief justice that the province holds title by "virtue" of discovery by European ships (Monet and Skanu'u 1992). A decision on appeal was only marginally less insulting. At present, most native peoples of British Columbia are actively engaged in research in preparation for either court cases or treaty negotiations, which have been denied or resisted by officials of the province since the 1860s.

Currently, traditional uses and ownerships of the homeland are being documented, along with *adaaw̲x*, proving their ongoing vitality and strength. In the process, the *adaaw̲x* are more alive than ever, a varied topic of and for reference, discussion, and even debate.

Conclusion

Tsimshian say that people are given to the names rather than the reverse became the names are immortal and each can convey benefits to its "holder," who treats it with respect by leading an honorable and generous life. Names that are "older" in the overlays can be more famous, but that is not always the case because considerations of class remain vital. Thus, a royal name from Temlaxam should be more prominent than a more ancient one associated with a more remote context.

Yet more than antiquity or rank, names provide the basis of and for Tsimshian history because they are not just remembered, they are inherited to "live again" by another mortal body. Such recursiveness interweaves past, present, and future within an overall context of the immortal, the wellspring for cultural significance and understanding. Thus native history is a repeated and progressive viewing of glimpses of the immortal in ways that benefit the ongoing community through public events like feasts, ceremonies, and potlatches. So vital is this mortal-immortal connection that during and after the devastating epidemics, in the absence of suitable heirs, names were passed on to pets such as dogs or to the arms, legs, and other body parts of already overburdened "holders."

Tsimshian also say that "names feed people" because each is firmly [671] grounded in a portion of the landscape, conferring rights to all its resources. These rights were and are witnessed and validated at public events to make them "legal," provided that the holder and name are further enhanced (not tarnished) by generous sharing of that bounty with members of the house and with many guests. In this manner, the immortal sustains the mortal, both benefiting in the resultant prestige.

In keeping with the cultural elaboration of the North Pacific Coast, the recall of a few significant and "mythic" ancestors by many Native American tribes, such as the Iroquois and others,[16] is more complexly expressed by Tsimshian and their North Coast neighbors in terms of names stretching back to their very beginnings as a nation and leaning forward into the distant future. [672 endnotes now footnotes] [673]

References

Documentation for this chronology, of course, resides in the *adaawx̱* of the hereditary houses of the Tsimshianic chiefs, with relevant sources in the Tsimshian File assembled by Marius Barbeau of the Canadian National Museum with all-important help from William Beynon, a Gitlaan Wolf chief named for layer 5.

Archer, David
1996   New Evidence on the Development of Ranked Society in the Prince Rupert Area. Twenty-ninth Annual Meeting of the Canadian Archaeological Association, Halifax, NS.

Boas, Franz
1916   *Tsimshian Mythology.* Based on Texts Recorded by Henry Tate, Bureau of American Ethnology, Annual Report 31 for 1909-10: 29-1037.

---

[16]   Though discredited, the Walam Olum — purporting to be the Delaware account of their own migration from Siberia into the American Northeast — lists the sequence of chiefs who led them during various stages of this migration.

Emmons, George

1911   *The Tahltan Indians*. University of Pennsylvania Anthropological Publications 4 (1). Philadelphia.

Garfield, Viola

1966 *The Tsimshian Indians and Their Arts*. Seattle: University of Washington Press.

Jenness, Diamond

1943   *The Carrier Indians of the Bulkley River*: Their Social and Religious Life. Bureau of American Ethnology, Bulletin 133, Anthropological Paper 25: 469-586.

Marsden, Susan

1996   *Defending the Mouth of the Skeena*: Perspectives on Tsimshian Tlingit Relations. Twenty-ninth Annual Meeting of the Canadian Archaeological Association, Halifax, NS.

Miller, Jay

1981   "Tsimshian Moieties and Other Clarifications." Northwest Anthropological Research Notes 16 (2): 148-64.
1997 *Tsimshian Culture ~ A Light through the Ages*. Lincoln: University of Nebraska Press.

Monet, Don, and Skanu'u [Ardythe Wilson]

1992   *Colonialism on Trial*: Indigenous Land Rights and the Gitksan and Wet'suwet'en Sovereignty Case. Gabriola Island, BC; New Society Publishers.

Spier, Leslie

1931   Historical Interrelation of Culture Traits: Franz Boas' Study of Tsimshian Mythology. *Methods in Social Science: A Case Book*: 449-57. Stuart Rice, ed. University of Chicago Press.

Sterritt, Neil, Susan Marsden, Peter Grant, Robert Galois, and Richard Overstall

1995 *Tribal Boundaries in the Nass Watershed*. Gitanmaax, BC; Gitxsan Treaty Office. [675]

Ts'ibasaa, Joshua

1916 The Adawx of Garment of the Lightnings. Recorded and transcribed by William Beynon. Orthographic and poetics interpretation by John Asher Dunn. Manuscript.

Usher, Jean
1974   *William Duncan of Metlakatla ~ A* Victorian Missionary in British Columbia. Publications in History 5. Ottawa, ON; National Museums of Canada.

Wright, Walter NiistaKo'ok

1962 *Men of Medeek*. Will Robinson, ed. Kitimat, BC: Northern Sentinel Press.

{following next below}

Men of Medeek

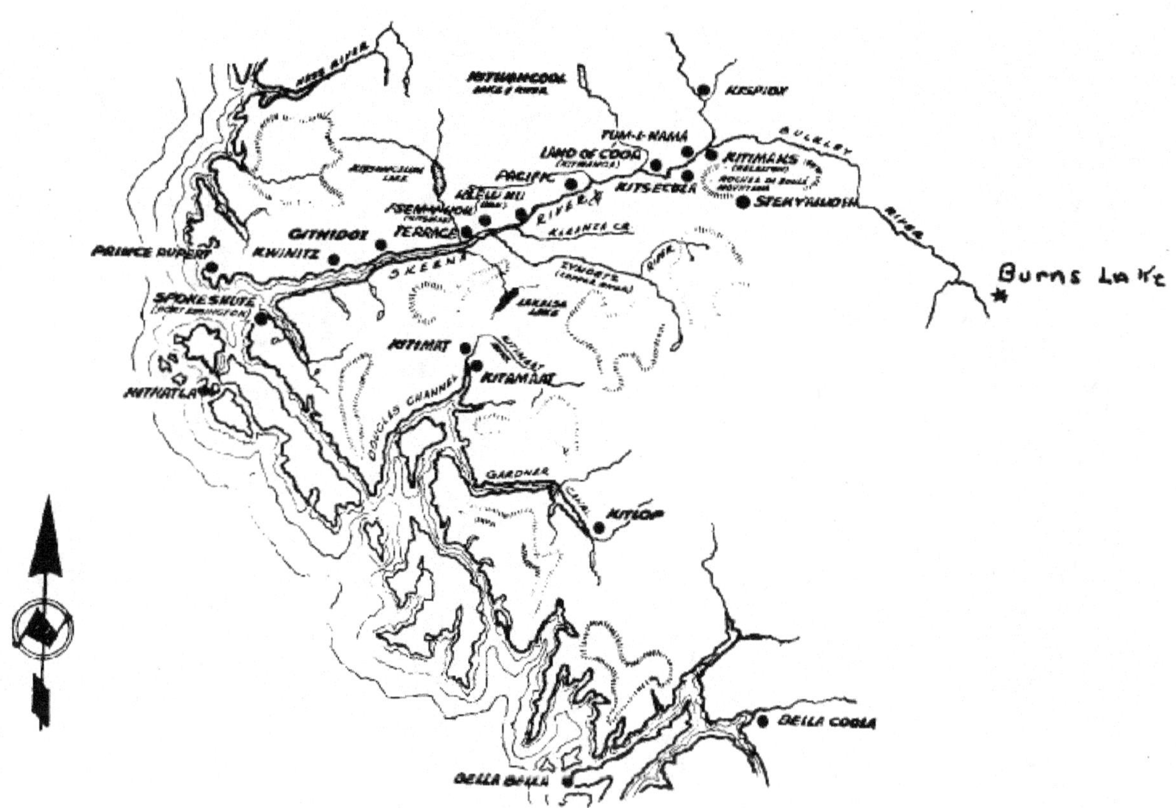

by Will Robinson as told by Walter Wright
Second Edition   Printed By The Northern Sentinel Press Ltd

Acknowledgements

"Men of Medeek" was written during 1935-36. Its author, Will Robinson, submitted the manuscript to several publishing companies, whose editors felt that its appeal was too limited. In 1953, Mr. Robinson died, and several years later Mrs. Robinson endeavoured again to secure its publication, but while editors showed interest, no company was prepared to arrange for its publication.

In May 1960, I heard about the manuscript from Terrace friends and read it. I was much impressed, and in order to reassure myself of its value, asked Mrs. Barry Blix and Gordon Robinson, Chief Councillor of Kitamaat Village (author of Tales of Kitamaat), to read it. They shared my enthusiasm.

I submitted it to yet another publisher, and after holding the manuscript for a year, they returned it feeling that it had a limited sales potential. Before proceeding further, I asked Mrs. Pixie Meldrum, editor of the Kitimat Northern Sentinel, to read it. Mrs. Meldrum's enthusiasm again re-affirmed my original resolve that "Men of Medeek" should be published.

Wiggs O'Neill of Smithers, George McAdams, Herb Spencer, Don Steele and Clair Giggy of Terrace and John Pousette of Kitimat all offered financial assistance.

G.A. Duncan of Terrace assisted in securing a picture of Walter Wright. Ron Baumeister of Kitimat produced a map depicting the area covered by the legends, and Sammy Robinson of Kitamaat Village carved the grizzly bear which appears on the cover. Max Patzelt of Kitimat is responsible for the photography. To all these interested people as well as the staff of the Kitimat Northern Sentinel Print Shop, who took such a personal interest in its publication, my grateful thanks.

Stan Rough   Kitimat, August 1st, 1962

Table of Contents

Preface

During the years 1919-1928, while residing at Prince Rupert, BC, my work brought me in contact with the Native People of British Columbia.

I found them an interesting folk, and such fragments of their history as came my way whetted my appetite for a deeper knowledge.

In those years I followed the work of Harlan I. Smith, Esq., Dominion Archeologist, and Dr. Marius Barbeau, Dominion Historian, with keen interest. A further insight was secured from a series of talks with Mr. Smith.

Coming to Terrace in 1928 I had cause to make certain inquiries in the matter of Native affairs. Friends suggested that I contact Chief [vii] Walter Wright of the Kitselas Band. I found him a man of marked intelligence — and shrewdness. He was willing to give information — up to a certain point. I sensed that he wished to know me better before he spoke more freely.

In the following years it was my lot to be of some slight service to him. I had the opportunity of travelling the Skeena River in a gas engined skiff. Chief Wright was the captain. On other occasions it was my lot to work with him on official matters. So friendship ripened.

And so, during these years, the Chief gave me more and more insight into the life and history of his people.

I was convinced, however, that pressing for information would defeat my objective. I had to bide my time and wait for Chief Wright to offer his confidence.

So, after some years, in September of 1935, the Chief came to my home one Sunday afternoon and told me the story of L - La - Matte — The Goat Feast.

That afternoon Chief Wright spoke for two and a half hours. When he left I wrote down what I could remember of the story. There, for the time, the matter rested.

During the months that followed the Chief told me he planned to tell me his "Story" so that it could be written down.

After several such promises the work began in September of 1936. The first half hour of his talk showed that a considerable task lay ahead. A system had to be evolved. It worked out in this manner.

As each session opened I established the Chief in a comfortable chair. On the table, close to his hand was a jug of water, a glass, and a dish of apples. Then work started. Across from him I sat with typewriter and paper.

When all was ready the Chief would take up the tale. He would recount an incident, or a part of one. He would come to a natural break in the narrative — and stop. Then, in turn I would record in precise narrative form what he had said. Periods averaged five minutes each. The system suited the need of the historian — and that of the recorder.

At times, when the meaning was not clear, I would call a halt and seek fuller explanation. Often some cross examination was needed. In order to make the story still more clear the Chief would rise from his chair and act the parts he wished to explain.

So night after night, and often on Sundays, the tale unfolded. Sometimes we worked two and three hours at a time. One Sunday we worked for seven hours with but a short rest.

So, when Christmas was close the story ended. I checked. I found my notes extended over 40,000 words. I had the history of Medeek from its beginnings in the dim ages of mythology down to some ninety years ago. [viii]

I had interpretations of all Native words used. I had Native place-names tied in with our modern ones. I had particulars of tribal laws and taboos; of intertribal laws; of codes of war; particulars of raw materials used for food, clothing, implements, and war; particulars of how these materials were worked, and of the finished products.

The history is in two parts. A natural break comes in the narrative. While chronology as we know it did not exist close questioning led to a reasonable assumption that the first part ended some 600 to 700 years ago.

The first part has been re-written under the title of "Men of Medeek". It deals with the basic myths, with life in the legendary city of Tum - L - Hama, with a westerly migration that ended on the rocky cliffs of the Kitselas Canyon, some 100 miles up the Skeena River from where Prince Rupert stands. "Men of Medeek" looks to the east; back to the land of the ancestors. Only once — the raid down the Pacific coast — does the narrative deal with the peoples of the sea-board.

"Wars of Medeek" still remains to be written.

The people of Kitselas, the Totems gathered on the canyon cliffs, held the narrow waters below them in a secure grip. Tsimpsians. from the coast traded with Gitsans of Kitwanga and with Carriers still further cast. The coast people carried herring eggs, dried clams, dried halibut, dried kelp and other sea foods to the interior. In exchange they received prime furs, fruits and berries.

The Men of Medeek held the toll gate. They exacted tribute from the traders who passed on the river.

So, human nature being what it is the world over, the peoples of the sea coast sought to break the grip and secure free passage.

Wars ensued. The leaders were the successive Legaics, Chiefs of the Flying Eagle Totem who came from Naha in Alaska and established themselves at Port Simpson.

Wars were fought. They extended over some centuries. Finally, about 90 years ago, when the impact of white civilization was beginning to be felt, the last war came and the history ended.

"Medeek" offers avenues for a variety of studies.

Of a religion that had no formal expression of ritual, yet had its impact in conservation and other ways on every phase of the life of the People; of a code of chivalry; of uses of the products of the forest and streams; of codes of morality; of social organizations in courtesy and modes of life.

All in all the laws of *Gyamk* the Sun God as promulgated by successive wise men plotted a way of life eminently suited to a people who lived in an arboreal state and whose sustenance came from the forests, the mountains and the streams.

WILL ROBINSON
Terrace, B.C. November 10th, 1941

Prologue

Neas - D - Hok is my name, and I am the head Chief of the Grizzly Bear People of Kitselas.

I have "Power" on both sides of The Big Canyon.

On the right hand side I have the power of my Chieftainship. For many generations Neas

- D - Hok has had that right.

On the left hand side I carry the "Power" of Neas Hiwas, for in my generation there is no Chief of that name.

When I was a boy my Grandfather, who was Neas Hiwas, taught [2] me the history of Medeek. His had been the duty of carrying it through his generation,

His was the responsibility of choosing one of The Royal Blood to keep it safe after he had died.

As a lad I sat at my Grandfather's feet.

Many times he told me the story. It is long. In the Native tongue it takes eight hours to tell.

So, several times each year, I sat at his feet and listened to our records.

I drank in the words.

In time I became word perfect. I knew all the story. I could repeat it without missing any of its parts.

So I became the historian of Medeek. So I took my place in a long line that had gone before me.

For so it is. In our land of Ksan there was no written word; the record had to be passed down from man to man by word of mouth.

Now my years are increasing. Now I have seen 65 summers.

When I was a lad few white men lived in our land. Now there are many.

And with the coming of the men whose skins are white like the peeled willow stick there have come many new modes of life.

The life of my People has left its accustomed ways. There is little time to learn the history of our People, Many things have drawn the minds of our young men from the habit of peacefully listening to their elders.

So, lest the record be lost, I tell it that it may be written down and preserved.

Thus may the Men of Medeek, now scattered in many places, read. Thus may they learn of the deeds that are recorded on their Totem Poles.

Thus may they come to have an honest pride in their lineage, and in the deeds performed by their ancestors. [3]

1. Ksan

A pleasant land was Ksan.

From the banks of the big river the forests marched in unbroken ranks. They stretched across the lowlands; they climbed the mountain slopes. Thousands of feet above the valley floor they gave way to tundra, and rocky crests.

High, over all, the peaks glistened with the eternal glaciers that, in the hot months, fed their waters to the river's flow.

In the land of Ksan food abounded.

Each year, with the fulness of the late springtime, the salmon came up the river. They came in a silver horde, millions of fish; running against the swift waters to reach their ancestral spawning grounds.

From this migration the People of Ksan took their toll.

With great traps they caught such fish as they needed. They dried them, and smoked them; preserving them against the winter's need of food.

In the forest wild creatures lived. Caribou, deer, and rabbits, and groundhogs.

On the mountain slopes the hoary marmots had their homes. In the high peaks the mountain goats fed on the alpine meadows.

Grouse flew in the lowlands; ducks and geese had their homes on the lakes. Big grouse — the blue ones, and the ptarmigan whose coat is white in winter — dwelt in the lands of the high peaks.

And in the creeks the trout swarmed.

Truly a pleasant land where food abounded.

Each summer, when their seasons came, the wild berries ripened, Of their abundance the People took for their winter stores.

Roots grew in the forests. On the low lands wild carrots could be gathered.

Other roots provided medicine to cleanse the body; to heal diseases. [4]

Still others furnished long, supple threads with which the people sewed their baskets.

The skins of the wild animals provided clothing and blankets.

From skins of deer, and caribou, carefully dressed, they made fine buckskin for leggings and coats and robes.

Fishers and martens, mink and weasels gave their glossy furs against the winter need. So warm clothing and soft blankets were made under which the People enjoyed their sleep.

It was a good land, and a pleasant land: a land where *Gyamk* the Sun God gave lavishly to his People.

2. Tum-L-Hama

PLEASANT was the land of Ksan.

But choicest of all that ancient country was the city of Tum - L - Hama.

It lay on the north shore of the big river — The Skeena — and had its western outpost where Carnaby now stands. Along the river's front ran the Street of Chiefs, reaching to where Hazelton has been built at the joining of two rivers, the Skeena and Bulkley. Thence northward ran that street until it came close to the bounds of Kispiox.

"Tum - L - Hama" — The Pleasant Place; The Level Place; The Clear Place ... The Good Place for Man.

There stood the homes of many thousands of the Native People.

For in those days the People were many. All through Ksan they had their towns and cities.

So many were they that a man could not know all the towns, nor begin to be acquainted with all the people.

Those ancient times were ones of unfailing prosperity; of harmonious living and unbroken peace.

Laws they had; but these were few; laws framed by Wise Men who watched the face of nature; who pondered long on the workings of *Gyamk*, the Sun God who lived in the Sky City of Lahah; laws that [5] were made as they watched cause and effect work out their ends in the lives of men.

Some happening came to the people. The result was good and fortunate. "This is right," said the Wise Men. "This shall be embodied in a new law so that good fortune may be still more assured to our People."

And when misfortune came these Wise Men delved deeply to find its cause.

At last, satisfied they had learned that which they had sought for, they said, "The action that lies at the root of this difficulty is wrong. Our People must be protected in the future that the same error may not be committed again. We make a new law forbidding that action."

So grew the Code. So were the children instructed in the ways of Right and Wrong.

So generation followed generation, each one more vigorous; more prosperous.

3. The Little Goat

THROUGHOUT the land of Ksan a rhythmic procession of duties came with the cycle of the seasons.

Hunting, fishing, berry picking; the gathering of roots: all had their places in the well ordered life of the People.

But in the Fall, when September came, there was a lull: a breathing space between duties. A time of holiday-making, of visiting and of feasting.

In such a time a group of young hunters set forth to climb the heights of Stekyawden. Armed with bows and arrows; with spears and clubs, they climbed to the rocky heights seeking goats for meat and raiment.

Success came their way. A herd was found. Some they killed and carried down to the city. Others escaped.

In that foray one small kid became separated from its fellows [6] and a young hunter, seeing it deserted, caught it and brought it to the town.

Here, close by his house, he tied it to a stake.

Children of the city gathered to see the small, wild animal.

They stood and watched its efforts to win back liberty.

But watching did not satisfy them. Childhood urges brought them closer, and still closer to the kid. At last they touched it.

A small step; and they were playing with it.

Its reactions to their motions amused them. They tried one thing after another, the bolder spirits becoming rough in their play.

There came the time when they untied the rope that held it to the stake. Then, in sport, they frolicked through the city streets taking the little creature with them.

That day other children had toiled on the river's bank, gathering driftwood against the evening hours when they planned a bonfire and a picnic.

As children and goat danced through that street they came to the blazing pile.

Fear seized the kid.

To all creatures of the wild, fire is terrifying.

It struggled to win clear. Its efforts served only to amuse the children more.

They urged it closer, and still closer. Their excitement mounted as its struggles became more frantic.

Sparks flew from the burning embers. These, as they came close to the kid, still further increased its terror.

In the mind of one lad an idea was born.

From the fire's edge he picked up small pieces of blazing jack-pine bark, holding them over the kid's back; then dropped them.

The searing touch of burning wood drove the kid wild with terror.

The children laughed, and older people, drawn by the commotion, lent their smiles to the general merriment.

So one thing led to another. Inventive youth brought fat jack-pine splinters, tied them to the horns and tail of the kid and lighted them. The rope was loosed and the crowd exulted at the wild racings of the kid.

Seeking to flee, unseeing of direction, the little animal came close to the fire.

One youth stood close to its path. As it leaped between the lad and the fire a push sent the kid into the blaze.

So the sport continued. Soon the kid became exhausted; its coat was seared from head to tail; blisters had risen on its skin; death was not far away.

It was then that a man chanced that way. [7]

He was not of the lineage of the Chieftain Blood; a poor man of the common people — but Wise.

He saw what went forward — and intervened.

"Shame on your children," he said, "To so ill treat an animal."

"Shame on you people," he added, "Who stand and laugh as children practice cruelty."

"This must stop," was his command. "The kid is almost dead. Left alone it will perish. I will take it and care for it."

As he finished he stooped and gathered the little animal in his arms.

Lifting his blanket he gave it sanctuary next to his body. He turned and made his way to his home.

Poor was that man; but wise. In his years he had learned much of healing. Many years had been spent compounding salves that soothed and cured.

Once in his home he took a vessel in which lay a mixture of grease from the inside of a bear, compounded with the fat of ground hogs.

Tenderly he rubbed the healing ointment on the blistered skin. Gently his fingers worked in their mission of healing.

Soon the soreness began to depart. The angry heat was drawn from the kid's skin.

Hour after hour passed as strength ebbed and flowed in that tiny life.

At last, when midnight had passed, the kid grew better.

Once more the wise man lifted it and gave it shelter close to his body.

Then he set forth.

Across the river he made his way. Through the forest he followed the trail until, at last, he came to the slopes of Stekyawden.

There he set the kid on its feet.

There he left it, knowing that the ancient instinct of the wild would guide it on its upward course until, at last, it won to the rocky crags and joined its fellows. [8]

4. L-La-Matte

To Tum - L - Hama there came a messenger, clad in the regalia of one who bore good tidings.

His was the privilege of carrying an invitation from the people in another town to have the Chiefs, the Elders and the Wise Men of the riverside city pay them a visit.

His message told of a great feast that was planned. It told that the invited guests were chosen to be the honored personages at the festival.

Such messages were common occurrences; especially in the month when there was respite from the labors of the year.

True, the Chiefs of Tum - L - Hama did not know this man nor did they know of the city of which he spoke. But that, too, was a common thing in a land where there were many towns.

Invitations such as this often came. It was the custom to accept them without question.

A messenger served also as a guide. He led his guests over the trails he knew; brought them safely to his town.

Peace and goodwill reigned in the land of Ksan; no thought of danger entered the minds of the People when such offers came.

So it was, on the day that followed, the Chiefs and the Elders and the Wise Men of Tum - L - Hama set forth on their journey. In their company were other "men, burden bearers, for the robes of ceremony were heavy and bulky. Each chief had a helper to carry the regalia he would wear at the feast that was to come.

Thus it came about that the poor man — who was wise chosen to help his ruler with the burden.

Confidently, joyously, the party set out. Much talk echoed through the forest as they trod the trails. Speculation was rife concerning the entertainment that was to come.

What new thing would their hosts show them in the great new [9] guest house? What was the size of the city they were to visit? and Where, and how, was the city situated?

Their guide was skilled in his craft. He knew the easy trails, and in due time he brought them to the foot of Stekyawden.

Through the dense forest of the mountain's lower slope the trail wound, following an easy gradient.

Gradually it climbed, and came to where the altitude and fogs had dwarfed the trunks of trees; still higher, to where trees stunted, twisted and gnarled told that the timber line was near.

Finally it rounded a great granite buttress and a town, built on a rocky ledge, stood before them.

Down the road from that city came the Chief Ruler of that place. Garbed in splendor, he carried the ceremonial rattles of welcome in his hands. On his shoulders was draped a cape of weasel skins, snow white as the fur bearers had worn them in the cold days of winter. The black tipped tails made a graceful, dignified pattern against the silver background.

On the Chief's head there rested a crown fashioned from the skin of a sea lion, beautiful feathers were waving on its rim, swaying to the cadence of the dance, keeping time with the rhythm of the rattles as they sent forth their message of greeting.

Thus did the Chief of the Mountain Town bid welcome to his guests.

Then, turning, he danced his welcome again as he led them up the road to the great guest house that stood within the town. Close to the cliff's edge the guest house perched. Mighty timbers had gone into its construction. Ninety 90 feet it measured in length, 60 in breadth.

Great timbers, hewn from the lower forests, formed the corner posts. The ridge pole was a huge cedar trunk. Smaller timbers, cunningly fitted together, made the walls.

Cedar bark, in great strips, roofed the whole, making it secure against the elements.

So to this house the guests were led. Each one entered; in turn, according to his rank. [10]

5. The Feast

FROM within a drum sent forth its booming notes.

A choir of women, keeping time to the throbbing sound, sang the song of welcome.

The Guest House had been well prepared.

Seats had been placed in readiness for the expected guests.

Behind each seat a man stood, a servant whose duty it would be to serve and honor the one who sat before him.

First entered the ranking Chief of Tum - L - Hama. As he crossed the threshold a serving man spoke the traditional welcome, and bade him be seated in the place of honor.

Behind this Chief came the second one in rank. He, too, was welcomed, and seated with due respect to his rank.

So, one by one, the guests entered and were cared for. Last of all came the burden bearers.

Great as that Guest House was still there was not room for all these lower men to find seats. They ranged themselves around the wall, stood close to the great supporting pillars, made themselves comfortable in places that suited their fancy.

And so it came to pass that the poor wise man chose to stand beside a pillar. Close at hand another doorway led to the outside. And by his side stood a stripling youth of the mountain town.

The sun was sinking in the west as the guests came to the town, It had dropped behind the mountains before all were seated.

That night, by the light of a great central fire, the mountain people entertained their guests.

Slow and stately had been the songs as the guests had entered. When all were seated the tempo quickened and a livelier air burst forth from the choir of women.

Times such as this were filled with expectancy. Each town that [11] gave a feast vied with its neighbours to provide entertainment that was unusual; different and better than any that had been before.

So, with the quickening pulse of the drum, a hush fell over the guests.

Then, through the doorway, a great goat entered.

A goat unlike any goat that had been seen before.

Instead of two horns adorning the head, one only was there, and that springing from the centre of the forehead. Down his face a red streak of paint slashed his right cheek.

Slowly, deliberately, the animal advanced. In perfect time with the throbbing drum it paced to the nearest corner of the house.

Then, as the music paused, it raised a hoof and stamped.

With the clash of that horned hoof the building trembled and swayed: tilted and came to rest with one side lower than the other.

Again the drum took up the beat. The goat moved on, pacing its way to the second corner.

Again the music ceased. Again a clashing hoof shook the great building, causing it to rock and settle still lower on its side.

A third time the goat made its measured way to the corner that lay ahead as drum and choir kept time with beat and music.

Again the music halted and once more the great guest house quivered in response to the hoof's command. When quiet came the building listed perilously towards the canyons brink.

One corner still remained unvisited. To this the magic goat made his way, hoof beat in time with the boom of the drum.

Here, in the last corner, the building rocked and swung as the goat stamped.

Guests clung to their seats; those who stood clutched the supporting timbers lest the floor's steep angle bring them down.

Once more the music started and the goat turned, retracing his steps to the third corner.

Answering the command of stamping hoof the building rocked again, this time coming to rest more upright than before the shock.

To the second corner the goat journeyed: once more the clash, and with it a tumult of creaking, groaning timbers.

The noise subsided, and the building stood once more erect.

So, in the next corner the sequence was repeated, and when all had stilled the guest house stood almost level,

One more journey lay ahead of the beast. Seven corners he had visited, one remained to complete the double circle.

Here, in the last corner, the hoof crashed with added might and when peace came at last the trembling house stood square and erect as before.

Far into the night the entertainment lasted. [12]

Colorful was that house with robes of rank and faces painted with the historical symbols of the people. Dignity and pomp balanced diversion. Finally the end came and a man stood forth.

An Announcer: A Master of Ceremonies.

His was the duty to allot the guests to homes where still more entertainment awaited; to give each honored one an entrance into some home where a mountain dweller would regale them with the choicest of food and conversation.

Two by two — host and guest — the men left the Guest House.

First to leave was the ranking Chief of Tum - L - Hama; with him went his host for the remainder of the night.

Chief followed Chief; Elder followed Elder; the Wise Men according to their precedence. Each accompanied by some man whose rank assured all the regard due to it.

Still by the great pillar the poor wise man stood. His was a lowly place, his turn to leave would come near the end. As he stood there a voice spoke in his ear.

"Do not go with the others," were the words of the stripling. "Stay with me. I will take care of you."

So, side by side they stood, wise man and youth. Past them flowed the stream of happy men, proceeding to fresh treats and food.

Dawn was streaking the mountain peaks when the last pair left, leaving the lad and his guest alone in the empty house.

With their going the great roof vanished, fading stars looked down on this man who had tended the injured kid.

The timbered walls melted into thin air.

Giant pillars, massive ridge pole — all disappeared, and the wise man found himself standing on the brink of an abyss.

Behind him cliffs towered to the heights. Before him the rock wall dropped sheer to the mountain's foot.

Trapped on a narrow ledge, the man looked for some way of escape. He looked in vain and fear gripped him with a cold, deathly clutch.

Again that youthful voice whispered in his ear. Turning, he saw a kid beside him. A kid with a red streak down the white hair of the right cheek.

"Be not afraid," came the comforting words, "I will look after you. I will bring you safely down."

"Damach" — my friend" — continued the young goat, "Place your hand on my shoulder, come with me. Step by step I will lead you from this ledge."

Obedient to the command the wise man rested his hand on the hairy back of the animal. The kid stepped, and, keeping time, the man advanced his foot — to find space and emptiness beneath him. [13]

Quickly he drew back, fearful of what would come with his slightest move. Tears streamed from his eyes. Death stood at his elbow.

Feeling the pause the little goat halted in his stride and saw what was amiss.

"Damach," he said, "I will lend you my cloak."

From across his breast the kid untied the thongs that held the goat skin to him. The cloak came free and was handed to the man.

As it passed from hand to hand the kid spoke comfortingly. "I give you my Wais — my blanket. Wear it, it will help you."

With trembling hands the man draped it round his shoulders, brought it to place and tied the thongs; making all secure.

"Say 'Yahallo hous' — "sand slope," came the command.

And with these words a gentle slope of sand extended from the feet of the man.

Far down it ran, its foot resting in the valley, and down this slope man and goat Journeyed until the level ground was reached.

So the wise man came to safety. There, on the valley's floor, he untied the Wais and handed it to its owner.

"Um goos waal" — "I thank you," he said in words warm with gratitude.

As he spoke the sand slope disappeared. Instead, a wild gulch rose high on the mountain's flank, a rock filled gorge, and on the rocks blotches of red were scattered.

"Come closer," suggested the kid, "Come to the rocks and see what these strange marks mean."

Step by step, filled with foreboding, the man advanced.

His worst fears were realized. For there, before his eyes, lay men — what had been men — broken, crumpled, distorted as they had struck the jagged edges after falling from the height.

"You see?" remarked the kid, "You see? These are your people. Last night they saw The Magic Goat stamp in the Guest House. You saw your people leave to become the guests of the people of the Mountain Town.

"They never reached the homes. Each of your men as he stepped through the doorway fell down the cliff's side; each was dashed to pieces on these rocks.

"They died. They all died. Only you are left.

"They died because of the vengeance of the Goats.

"They died because they failed to teach their children kindness;

because they stood and laughed while a kid was tortured and burned in your town. They had become indolent and careless.

"They had ignored the Law of *Gyamk* the Sun God.

"Knowing what was right they turned their backs and permitted evil. [14]

"So they have died.

"But you were kind. You had pity on the little kid as he suffered. You took him and cared for him, and healed him. When his strength had returned you carried him to Stekyawden and gave him liberty again.

"So you have lived.

"For this reason I have taken care of you and brought you to safety.

"I am the kid you cared for.

"Go back to your town," the kid continued, "Tell the remnant of your people what has come to pass. Tell them to remember the Law of *Gyamk*; to have compassion and not kill heedlessly."

To the city of Tum - L - Hama the lone survivor made his way.

There, on the banks of the Skeena, grief swept over the people as they learned of the great disaster.

Back to the fatal gorge the wise man led his people.

With their own eyes they saw what remained of their proud Chiefs, their Elders, and their Wise Men.

"L - La - Matte" they called that place. "L - La - Matte" — The place where the Goats feasted men' — has been its name since that day.

And since that day the Men of Medeek have taken their right to wear the head-dress of the One Horned Goat,

That head-dress is the insignia of the scion of the Royal House; the emblem that denoted the youth who would, in due time, be raised to the seat of rulership.

For so it is decreed.

So the law runs: When a man dies in another land "The Power" of that land goes to his descendants. When a man dies in a strange land it is the right of his successors to use the emblem of the place in which he died.

So says the Law.

So, in obedience, the Men of Medeek have taken and used that strange crown — the Goat head with a single horn rising from the centre of the forehead; while down the right check a vivid streak of red stands out against the silver whiteness of the hair. [15]

6. The Law

YEARS passed after the feast of L - La - Matte, the Feast of the Goats.

Children grew to manhood, young chiefs took the places of those who had died on the rocky slope.

Throughout the Land of Ksan a new Law ran. "Men must respect the creatures of the wild," its dictate ran. "*Gyamk* has said that birds, and fish, and animals may be killed when food and raiment are needed; when their sinews are to be used in making utensils — when all their parts are of service to the men who take them.

"To take in sport the life that *Gyamk* gave is forbidden. "So, too, the blood, and hair, and any parts of animals that are left on the hunting grounds must be buried, or hidden. For *Gyamk* is grieved and angry when he sees carelessness and waste with the creatures of His Land.

"Teasing, tormenting, and ill-treating is forbidden. For *Gyamk*, who gave you life, gave life to these creatures as well.

"Mark well," it ends. "*Gyamk* has his messengers of vengeance, his {*naxnox*} Narnaks — the Spirit Life of the wild creatures can help the humans; they can also wreak revenge.

"Ill treat a bird and its Narnak will exact retribution. Torment the Beavers and the King of the Beavers will claim your lives in return." [16]

7. The Vengeance of Medeek

MANY years passed over Tum - L - Hama.

New chiefs had been raised up to take the place of those who had died on Stekyawden when the Goats took their terrible revenge.

The children of the city had grown up, matured, and in turn their places as elders had been taken by others.

With the passing of the years had come forgetfulness.

"Do not abuse the wild things," the Wise Men had taught. "Beware lest you spoil the work of *Gyamk*, the Sun God. Do not destroy His work for sport, nor make jest of His creatures."

But as the years had passed these teachings had become less and less heeded.

Tum - L - Hama, once more, was a place of peace and of plenty; of wholesome work to provide for the needs of the people; of ample time for recreation and the intimacies of social contact.

The years were filled with activities.

In the springtime came the work of preparing the traps with which the salmon were taken. Throughout the summer months the silvery horde passed up the river and the people took their toll, curing the fish and storing it against the winter's need. Wild roots, in their season, were gathered from the forest to provide food and medicine. A succession of berries, raspberries, huckleberries, saskatoons, soapberries, and others were harvested and dried as they matured.

With the shortening days preparations were made for the winter's hunt that provided meat and raiment.

But in September — The Dry Month — when the salmon was safely stored, when the harvest of roots had been completed and the cake of berries had been dried and preserved, there came a lull, a time of holiday making.

It was a time of intertribal visiting, an opportunity to relax on the sunlit shores of the nearby lakes. [17]

So it became the custom for the maidens of the city to spend this time by a lake that nestled near the foot of Stekyawden.

Half a mile it stretched east and west, narrow across. Its sparkling waters came fresh from the mountain's slopes. Salmon spawned on its sandy bars. Trout followed in shoals to raid the new laid eggs.

On the banks of this sylvan retreat the maidens built brush houses, frail shelters from the infrequent rains.

Their days passed pleasantly. Much time was spent in catching trout. Before long each house had its stack of fish backbones piled neatly beside the doorway.

Fishing, resting, playing, this was the order of the day. And one thing more!

The period of camping was also the time of learning the Dances of The People.

Girls, then as now, delighted in rhythm, in the cadences of songs and chants, in the lithesome movements of the body to the time of music.

Healthy and well-nourished, muscles in fine fettle with the summer's work, the learning of the formal dances added another joy to the time of holiday making.

So, under the bright warmth of the September sun, the maidens learned the dances; The Dance of Greeting; The Dance of Welcome; The Dance of the Chief.

As some practiced the graceful postures others perfected themselves in the songs and the chants that made the music. Massed choirs rendered the traditional songs of Tum - L - Hama.

At times they sang as one great choir; at others divided into two parts, the choir sang strophes and anti-strophes, carrying their theme in questions and answers as they sang back and forth across the space in which the dancers moved.

Back in the city the girls had seen the elaborate capes and head-dresses of ceremony that were worn by the Chiefs at times of festival. To add grace to their dances the maidens mimicked the dress of their elders. Improvised robes took the places of the capes of ceremony; lithe withes, cut from the berry bushes, were fashioned into crowns.

Rivalry was constant as they sought to make their displays more perfect.

Thus it happened that one day a maiden paused before a cooking place where many trout had been toasted over the wood coals. At her hand lay a pile of bones.

With a questioning smile that told of the birth of a new idea she reached out and took up one of the bones. Then, holding it by the side of the coronet, she danced.

The bone was complete; the backbone was finely forked, tail still attached. [18]

In the crystal mirror of the lake she saw, as she bent over, the backbone quiver in time with her movements; the tail waving to the tempo of her steps.

Still holding the bone she ran to the others of her class; danced with the waving tail, and showed the new beauty she had discovered.

Eagerly the maidens seized the idea. Fresh coronets were woven by the lake shore that day; coronets so devised that they held a circlet of trout bones erect, tails uppermost.

So, with this newly fashioned headgear, the maidens danced. Often, in those days of leisure, the older folks crossed from Tum - L - Hama and spent pleasant hours by the lakeshore, watching their children.

So it came to pass that many of the Chiefs and Elders, the Wise Men and the people of more common rank saw this new dance.

Yet so far into the past had faded the precepts of the days of the Goat Feast that none reproved or warned the maidens of their violation of "The Law of The Wild Creatures".

Thus, for the second time the Narnaks — The Spirits of Nature — were challenged as the bones of wild things were tossed in playful sport,

So, for many years, matters proceeded.

Tum - L - Hama, in those days, was a prosperous town. Ranging for many miles along the banks of the Skeena River, the town had successive streets that ran parallel with the stream.

The place of honor was the river front. Here dwelt the Chiefs.

Here, in a place called An - Gud - Oon — "The steep place on the river bank where a man is pulled up with the right hand of a friend" — dwelt Neas Hiwas, titular Ruler of the City.

Close by his house dwelt his five brothers, also Chiefs, whose ranks were only lesser than his own.

Their houses faced south, across the river.

On the far shore a creek emptied into the river — the creek that ran from the Lake of the Summer Pavilions.

On the south bank the giant cottonwoods made a fringe of brilliant green; behind them the primeval forest of conifers of a more sober hue stood rank on rank.

Into this peaceful scene, one day, came fear.

Unseemly events were taking place far back in the forest.

It soon attracted the attention of the people, and as they watched, they saw great trees thrown high above the forest top.

The disturbance came nearer. Some gigantic force was coming down the valley of the creek. [19]

As it came the forest was torn apart, trees uprooted, trampled down. A wide gash in the greenery told of its passing.

Closer, and still closer to the river came the turmoil, and at last a bear came out on the river's margin.

A bear. But unlike any bear the People had ever seen. A giant grizzly bear; one capable of uprooting trees, of snapping giant trunks as though they were grasses.

The bear paused; and glared at Tum - L - Hama.

Then he moved down the bank and entered the water.

"Speed the alarm," called a Chief who stood and watched the strange sight. "Call the warriors. Have them prepare themselves that they may kill this creature that dares to approach our city."

Far and wide through Tum - L - Hama went the message. Warriors seized their weapons. Hunters picked up their spears. Bows and arrows in the hands of skilled men sped to the fray. Strong weapons were they.

Spears 20 feet long, shaped from slender, straight grained cedar and tipped with sharpened bones.

Bows of hard red wood that had been brought from the coast. Bows reinforced with the sinews from the backs of caribou and goats, strung with the dried intestines of bears twisted into cords.

Arrows fashioned from the wood of saskatoon bushes, tipped with bones that were lashed with thongs and cemented with the gum of the pines.

Clubs of hard woods; of birch and mountain maple. Clubs made of the antlers of caribou.

Stone hammers, hour glass shaped, and fastened to the hand of the fighting man with a sinew thong.

So, with weapons tested and proven, the men of Tum - L - Hama advanced to meet the invader.

That day the Street of Chiefs became a place of battle. Scorning danger, the warriors joined battle with the monster of the forest and lakes.

Brave warriors! But they went forward to defeat, A Narnak, no less, confronted them.

From that Spirit animal the arrows bounced, sped into the air and fell to kill and wound the defenders. The sharp spear points were useless; the cedar shafts broke in the hands of the warriors. Caribou antlers that would crush the skull of a man crumbled as they hit the bear. And through that confusion the giant grizzly moved like the wind. On haunches he walked, with forepaws swinging. Each time he hit the head of a man that head was smashed from the body. [20]

Speedily the Street became a shambles. Warriors lay where they had fallen.

That battle ground was three miles long. The bear moved from house to house, killing all who opposed him. Only when he came to the westerly edge of the town did he turn and re-enter the liver. Then he crossed the swirling waters and disappeared into the forest.

In the days that followed brave men crossed the river and viewed the devastation he had wrought in that timbered land. They followed back over that trail from whence he had come.

The trail led up the valley of the creek. It came to where the creek flowed out of the lake — and there it disappeared.

Quite evidently this creature — this Narnak — had come out of the Lake of Pavilions.

8. The Grizzly Bears

GREAT disasters are the landmarks of a people who are wise.

They mark the ending of a time of error.

They set a starting point for a better mode of life.

So in the days that followed the visitation of Medeek, the giant grizzly bear, Wise Men pondered long over what had come to pass. To them the situation became clear. Once again *Gyamk*, the Sun God, had been offended. The dancing maidens, decked with trout bones, had violated the Law; they had desecrated His beings.

And the Spirit of the Trout People, taking the form of Medeek, had been sent to exact recompense; an awful retribution from the men who had failed to train their children in the ways of wisdom. In due courses Neas Hiwas called a Council. Many things had to be done. New Chiefs had to be raised up in the place of those who had been slain.

New laws, governing the proper training of children, had to be made. [21]

In that Council Neas Hiwas brought to memory the gift of The Goat Crown.

Here was a like instance.

"From this day," he announced, "I take as my head-dress the head of Medeek, the Grizzly Bear. It is the Law that when men die in a great disaster those who follow after them have the right to take unto themselves the name of the destroyer. Thus, from this day on, I take the name of Medeek. It shall be the crest of my Totem."

Months passed and spun themselves into years. Years waxed and waned.

After many years the Spirit of Neas Hiwas passed from his body.

In the funeral rites that followed a new chant was sung. A funeral chant that has come down through the ages, and is still sung when a Chief of The Grizzly Bear Totem dies:

> Leig yu hou — dis caan caana yu haw law aw hee hee
> The trees fall all ways when the grizzly comes on.
> ee-ya haw law ya haw law ah hee hee.
> Will guik koi dex me dee-k yu haw law aw hee hee.
> Here comes the Grizzly Bear out of the lake.
> ee-ya haw law ya haw law ah hee hee.
> Gis see ya guehth me dee-k yu haw law aw hee hee Tum - L - Hama.
> The Grizzly Bear comes down through the town of Tum - L - Hama.
> Will wahl-da yu haw law as hee hee.
> Ee-ya haw law ya haw law ah hee hee. [22]

9. Famine

SPRING in the land of Ksan was a time of hopefulness.

As the rigors of freezing weather moderated there came the month of Hawakt — the Mild Time when the Sun's rays drink up the snow.

Close behind came Lasiyans — "Springtime" — and then in quick succession came Lasiwheehawn — The Moon of the Salmon Hordes".

As the winter snows faded before the rays of *Gyamk*, the Sun God, the creeks and ravines once more gave forth the joyous sounds of running water.

Then the people of Tum - L - Hama busied themselves with the great salmon weir.

From side to side of the Skeena River they stretched it. Stout poles were driven in the river^s bed, and placed so close together that no salmon could pass through.

On the south side it was strongly braced to the river bank. On the north side a great pile of rocks held it against the rush of waters.

Just upstream from the north side a giant tree rested on a gravel bar. The weir came close to its roots and its top rested on the river bank.

In front of the tree an opening was left in the weir; closed by a gate until all was in readiness.

Days of watching followed the preparations.

At last there came a day when the first spring salmon came up the river. It swam strongly as it sought the spawning grounds.

Downstream it had gloried in the tumult of fast waters, had lazed in the slow moving back eddies.

Now at Tum - L - Hama a strange obstacle confronted it. A fence spanned the river, closing the passage from the gravel of the bottom to the sunlit waters of the surface.

Along this fence the salmon swam; came finally to where a gate had been moved from an opening. Here, then, was the way. The salmon [23] passed through, only to find a great tree trunk shutting off all further progress.

Salmon as they surge upstream to spawn move upwards. Never do they go back towards salt water. Age-long instinct urges them to press onwards until, at last, the fine gravels of the ancestral spawning grounds are reached.

Here, then, the leader of the salmon weaved back and forth, ever seeking an opening that was not there.

Here the watchful people took him as their prize; the first fruits of the coming harvest.

The first salmon was feted, honored, and treated with all due ceremony. Honour had to be given to the Narnaks — The Spirits of the Salmon — to ensure a plentiful supply for the needs of the People. It must needs be made plain that such fish as were taken would be used for food and not wasted.

This was the custom. For many years after the vengeance of Medeek the People of Tum - L - Hama had been zealous in the performance of the rites.

But, as always, time dulled memories; prosperity, long continued, brought a relaxation of vigilance. Time spent on such ceremonies, to some, seemed wasted.

Thus, as the years passed, due reverence was neglected, and there came a time when a man — reported to have been dull witted — made jest of the backbone of the great fish.

Forgotten was the warning of the first precept; "Offend not the Narnaks of the wild creatures lest they have their land with their kind and bring barrenness and want to your people." No notice was taken of the jest. And no more fish came.

Throughout the season the fishermen watched the pool below the log. Not a fin moved. No fish were there to be caught, and cleaned, and cured.

Days stretched into weeks. Weeks ran into months. The Dry Month — September — now known as Lasimedeek, came and the food racks were still empty.

Nor in the land was there the accustomed amount of game.

Caribou, deer, rabbits, grouse and goats all seemed to have vanished.

As the days shortened, want and privation confronted the people. Famine was approaching — and winter was drawing near.

That fall, Neas Hiwas called a Council of the Chiefs and Elders. He brought in his Wise

Men. Long discussions were held. Ancient wisdom was recovered from the failing memories of the old men. [24]

It was clear that the Narnaks had been offended. That they had retaliated for the lack of respect on the part of the people.

Only one way out of the peril remained; they must be won to view the People of Tum - L - Hama with favour again — and new hunting grounds in which game abounded must be located.

10. Purification

THE eldest nephew of Neas Hiwas sat quietly in the great Council that sought to solve the problem of famine.

To sit in this manner was his right.

Always the eldest nephew accompanied his uncle. For in due time the duties and responsibilities of the uncle would pass on to the eldest son of the Chief's eldest sister. It was only proper and expedient that the youth should become familiar with what lay ahead. Only so could he be prepared to take up his task when the time came.

So he listened to the discussions. He followed the reasoning. Reheard the decision.

The task was one for a young man. Who better than he, the future titular ruler, could perform the task?

So in the Dry Month, in Lasimedeek, the young man began the Rites of Purification.

For only to one who had cleansed himself by fasting, by purging, and by self-sacrifice, could success in such an undertaking come.

His first duty was to cleanse his House. Then in succession, cleanse many other houses, so the sin might be purged from the People.

Thus it came about that in Lasimedeek, the chief-to-be went to the corner of his house and there he washed himself.

He stayed in that corner for that day, and there he stayed for the second and third days.

On the fourth day he moved to the second corner of the house, and again he washed. Two other days were spent in this corner. In those days he did not lave his body. Again he moved to the third corner [25] and washed. Again he remained unwashed for two other days, and in the fourth corner the three day rite was repeated.

Twelve days had passed. Days of rigor of his body. Days of fasting, of drinking sparingly, of chewing the green, inner bark of the devil club which purged him and brought out impurities through the pores in beads of sweat.

Twelve days of privation that the sins of his House might be removed.

As the twelfth day ended the rite came to a close. But those days did not complete his task.

He moved to another House, and there, repeating the ritual of the twelve days, acted as Propitiator for the people who lived within.

So, through the shortening days, on to the turn of the year, still on through the days that grew longer as the cold became more intense;

on until the warming rays of *Gyamk* once more began to lower the deep snow levels.

When March came — the month of Oolichans — the young man completed his task. Fifteen houses had been cleansed. He had been purified. He had acquired "Spirit Power" — success on his coming quest might be expected.

11. *Guell Haast*

OUT of her meagre stores the wife of Neas Hiwas brought small quantities of food.

These she gave to her nephew as he set forth in search for new hunting grounds for his people.

He travelled down the river bank until he came to where Kitzeukla now stands.

Here he turned south, following the shoulder of the mountain that flanked the creek.

As he journeyed he had crossed virgin snow, snow unmarked by tracks of animals or birds. [26]

As he climbed the mountain slope he came, at last, to a track that ran ahead of him. Further he came to other signs. Each track told the same story: the animals had journeyed south, each step taking them further from the land of Ksan.

Climbing and still climbing he came at last to a place where he crossed the summit and looked down into a valley that stretched away to the south.

From where he stood he saw many creeks coming down the mountain sides. Timber lay below him in unbroken ranks. Glaciered peaks shut in the distant horizon.

Here, he believed, was the land he sought.

Snow still lay deeply on the mountain tops. In the valley below the massed forest had held the sun's rays from breaking the crust.

Down the mountain side the young man made his way. As he came to the lower levels he saw signs that told him here was game in the valley.

Southwards the young man pressed and came to a land where there were many beaver, a land of marshes and dams and aspen stumps. Further off he saw bands of caribou. Ranging the mountain flanks he found cliff-walled stables where many goats had spent the winter.

So he journeyed in the valley we now call the Zymoetz — The Copper River.

He came to where the Kitneakwa flows into that stream from the south; to a height of land from where the Telkwa River flows to the north and east. Still later, he looked down the valley of the Morice to the eastern plain.

Southwards still, until he came to where the mountains rose steeply to bar his progress.

Here he halted.

Here he set his mark and claimed the land.

"This country," he said, "I take for the hunting grounds of my people, the Men of Medeek. I take it that it may be used, not wastefully, nor with wanton destruction of the animals and the birds and the fish that dwell therein. But that my people may have such food as they require. That the skins of the caribou, the marten and the mink; the fisher and the ground hog may give my people clothing and blankets to keep them warm.

"That we may take of the increase and leave the broods, and thus following the dictates of *Gyamk*, the Sun God, we may refrain from provoking the Spirits of the Wild."

Here, for the night he stayed.

His long ordeal was over. The time of self-denial was past.

Taking such wood as came to his hand he prepared to light a fire and cook a little food. [27]

From under his blanket coat he drew a little pouch. In it he had finely shredded cedar bark mixed with powdered resin of the pine. Taking his firesticks of cottonwood roots he twirled until a spark appeared, and with this spark he lit the mixture; fire sprang up.

Fed and warmed, he made his bed beneath a close limbed spruce and slept until the break of day.

Again, he lit a fire. As he ate he looked around. Close by stood a giant tree.

Strange!

The night before it had not been there.

And at the foot of that tree there grew a single *Haast* — a fireweed.

Tall and slender, leaves trembling in the breeze.

A *haast* growing out of the snow? Surely some magic. Such a plant was far ahead of the season of its kind.

His curiosity was aroused. He left his food and moved closer to the plant.

It was fresh and green. It still stirred with the breeze.

Still closer, and closer he came to it.

His hand, at last, reached out to touch the foliage — and as his hand came close the *haast* vanished.

"*Guell Haast*" — the single fireweed, — he called that place. To this day "Guell Haast" is the southern boundary of the hunting grounds of the Bear People.

And from that day Guell Haast, the single fireweed, has had its place on the totems to tell of the time of famine and how the salvation of the people was wrought.

12. Success and Hardship

NEAS HIWAS called a Feast.

Mild spring days had come in the year that followed the famine. And from over the southern mountain range his nephew had returned with joyous news of a land of plenty. [28]

That all might know, the Ruler called a Feast and there the young man gave an account of his travels.

He told of the beaver meadows, the moose and caribou; the goats and all the other game.

He held his hearers spellbound with the story of Guell Haast.

It was a time of happiness. Food in abundance was assured. Starvation soon would be nothing but a bitter memory.

In that formal conclave Neas Hiwas set forth his claim to the land of Guell Haast. With stately phrases he gave its bounds and took it as the hunting ground of his people for all time.

Joy reigned at that feast.

But as months and years sped by it became evident that rich as the new land was, the taking of those riches was difficult.

The hunters found that all the young chief had said was true. Game abounded. They took of the increase of the meat animals; of the fur bearers, and still the supply was undiminished.

But a lofty range of mountains lay between that source of supply and the population of Tum - L - Hama, a range that entailed toil to traverse with heavy packs of food and fur.

It slowed down the hunters. Work as they would they could not keep pace with the demands made on them.

Supplies ran low, clothing and blankets wore out faster than they could be replaced.

True, the Narnaks had accepted the propitiation of the young chief. They had granted a new land — but to the Land of Ksan no animals returned, nor did the fish come.

Striving under the handicaps of distance and toil the men of Ksan saw their families becoming more impoverished with each passing month.

13. Migration

NEAS HIWAS watched and meditated.

His was the responsibility for the well being of his people. On his shoulders rested the task of finding a remedy for the growing distress He spent much time in the inner councils of his spirit. He spoke [29] but little. The problem was his chief concern, and he explored all possible solutions.

Dimly at first, more clearly as the matter took shape, crystal clear at last with a rounded scheme, came the outcome of his long hours of thought.

"It is clear," he told his assembled councillors, "No more will the game come close to the houses of Tum - L - Hama. A great range divides us from the valley where game abounds. We need that game. If we wish to enjoy a fuller and more prosperous life it remains for us to move."

"Go forth and tell the people," he commanded — for rarely did a chief speak to the people himself, but through the mouths of his council his decisions were made known — "That they prepare. That they gather such goods as they can carry; that those things that are most needed, things that will be of the greatest use in a new land, be prepared for moving. The rest, prized as they are, won by hard toil, must be left. This is a time of sacrifice.

"This is a time when we discipline our bodies; only by so doing can we hope to enjoy good fortune as we set forth for a country that as yet we know not."

Days passed. Winter crept slowly along; then the warming rays of *Gyamk* ate away the snow.

Days there were of heart searchings, of reluctant surrender of cherished possessions. Days of discussion. What would be of greatest use? Which of the choicest goods could be carried along the trail?

Then in Lasiyans, the Month of Leaves, the birches, the alders, the cottonwoods and willows put forth their tender shoots of greenery. From the brown earth and leaf mold of the forest floor eager plants pushed up their shoots. Soon the bare limbs of trees were bright with the coming season's foliage.

In Lasyans, the Month of Leaves, there came a stirring in Turn -L - Hama, a stirring as the Men of Medeek moved slowly from their ancestral homes, and surged forth on the trail.

Men, young and old, women in their prime, and old women who tottered, children keen for a new adventure, babes in arms, a motley multitude.

Thus Neas Hiwas led his people forth. A multitude burdene-ri with the last ounce they could carry, a concourse of people leaving all that was familiar and dear, hoping that in some distant land a measure of the glories of their forefathers would return to them.

Neas Hiwas led the way. The first *night* he brought his people to camp a scant mile from their deserted city. Such a horde could move but slowly. The pace of the fastest must be brought down to that of the slowest, the feeble needed help.

A mile they moved that day, and many days thereafter saw no [30] longer trek. Often the people stayed at one place for days as the hunters ranged for food.

Ten miles, and the long flatlands of Tum - L - Hama came to an end. Ahead, mountain shoulders jutted out, and over these spurs the laden people scrambled. "For 20 miles their route was varied. Sometimes flatlands offered pleasant travel. Again at times, the steep flanks of the mountains made toil doubly hard.

So, camping, resting, toiling on the trail; hunting for food, fishing with spears in such shallow creeks as they came to, they made their way. When midsummer came they drew near where another people lived.

Four brothers helped Neas Hiwas on that journey. Blood brothers, second only in rank to the Ruler, these Chiefs marshalled the people, gave guidance, settled disputes, and sought, always, to keep strong the hearts of the Bears,

Now, with this new town in sight, Neas Hiwas called his brothers to sit with him in Council.

"We have travelled far," said Tumknoon, "Let us stay in this valley until we can search the land."

"Winter will be here before many moons have passed," pointed out Che-ve-Sar — 'He who catches the grouse by the leg before it drums on a log in the spring time' — "Our people must be prepared, or they will perish for lack of shelter in the cold days."

"I agree that what has been said is right," added Saaks, whose name ranked him as 'Grandfather of the Sun and Moon'. "We must prepare for the days to come. Let us ask permission of this people that we be allowed to stay close by. Then we can find shelter and food against the hard days of frost and snow."

And Neas Cloccs, the fourth agreed with the plan. [31]

14. The Land of Coor

IT was a good land, a land of plenty, where Coor the Eagle Chief lived with his people.

This ruler did not repulse the advances of Neas Hiwas. After some thought he granted the request that the trail-wearied people might settle near him for the time.

That summer was a busy one for the Men of Medeek. Berries were there in abundance, and women and children worked long hours gathering them and drying them in readiness for the winter when food was hard to find.

Across the river Seven Sister peaks thrust towering pinnacles, ice clad, far into the sky. Here, and on the flanking mountains, the wild goat ranged. Deer and caribou roamed the lower levels and in the willow-brakes and young jackpine flats countless rabbits fed.

From the river the Bear men took their toll of cohoe salmon, of humpbacks and steelhead trout.

Food was assured, and toiling men wrought with stone axes as they made sure that shelter would be ready when the ice began to form on the waters of the pools.

Yet through those months there was time for some measure of social intercourse, and before the leaves fell many friendships had sprung up between the peoples.

So, for that winter, the Eagles and the Bears lived in amity. Side by side, hunting the same grounds, gathering in the same forest the roots and materials they needed.

Spring came, and with it the busy interests of re-awakening life. Lured by the goodness of the land, with the abundance of food, with the constant novelty of new trails to explore and new scenes to view, the Bears lingered.

That summer they fished, they gathered berries, and under the [32] guidance of the nephew of Neas Hiwas the young men took heavy toll of the game.

Again winter came, and with shelters that had been improved as the days had sped, with food in plenty to assure comfort until Lasiyan came once more, the Bears went into winter quarters as neighbours of the Eagles.

But beneath the surface trouble brewed.

The age-long story began to re-assert itself. A land that is sufficient for one man will often fail to give satisfaction to two.

The young chief-to-be of the Bears had spurred on his hunters. Throughout the winter he was zealous in keeping them busy to provide fresh rabbit meat, new furs and skins for his people.

His zeal reacted on the wild life. The balance of Nature was being disturbed; depletion was beginning.

Thus, as the months passed, the Eagle people of Coor found hunting becoming more difficult. Longer journeys were necessary to secure the food they needed for their families. The work grew harder.

Murmurings started.

At first a small sense of uneasiness, a lurking feeling that all was not as it once had been. Then a slow realization that there was a definite decrease in the game supply — and that the wild creatures, through much hunting, had been disturbed and made more wary.

These things were spoken of one to another. Soon the reason was plain. The Bear people, under the leader of their hunt, had moved affairs from their smooth channels, had broken the even tenor of the ways of life of the Eagle People.

Discussions swelled, rose to grumblings in the hunters' ranks. It spread through the houses when supplies of food fell short.

The time came when, on the trails, the Eagle men as they met Men of Medeek with fresh killed game, looked askance at the newcomers.

Bickerings arose. Infringements of rights were alleged.

The situation developed into individual quarrels and lone fights.

So, with the developing strain in the relationship between the peoples, there came to their Chiefs tales of the troubles.

Kawawyem — Springtime — saw discontent flare into violent
passion.

Coor, for months, had listened to complaints, had brooded over the change in his people. He had grieved that where once peace and harmony had reigned now there was unrest and bitterness.

At last he came to the breaking point. The cause, he saw clearly, lay at the doors of the Bears.

"Move these new people," he reasoned, "And we return to our former way of life." [33]

So there came a day, as new life was bursting from all the growing things, when Coor led forth his men and made war on the Men of Medeek.

The battle was short, but decisive. The Eagles were too many for the followers of Neas Hiwas. They had the element of surprise in their favor.

The fight, from the first, went in favor of Coor.

When it ended Neas Hiwas gathered his people, and loaded as they had been in the year they moved from Turn " L - Hama, they started out on the trail again.

They moved westward, still plodding along the north bank of the Skeena. They followed the waters of the river as it raced to the great salt sea.

They moved mile by mile ... and behind them, lying dead, and whom they had been forced to leave, was the young man, who, when the time had come, would have been raised and exalted as a new Neas Hiwas.

15. Hard Journey

DEFEATED and humiliated, Neas Hiwas led his people westward. He had been surprised, overwhelmed, compelled to move on again. But, while some of his men had been killed, he had saved his people from a major disaster. He still had the main body of the people he had led from Tum - L - Hama.

Westward he led his people. Slowly, mile by mile, the Medeek men travelled. Slowly the glistening spires of the silver peaks fell behind them.

As they went forward the river valley narrowed. The flanking mountains stood closer to the water's edge. These were more massive, more rugged. The rolling flatlands they had known so well in their ancestral home were becoming memories; no such places were found here. [34]

Creeks and rivers became more numerous. They were shallow. turbulent waters, tumbling down steep channels. Except when the rains swelled them to torrents the salmon found meagre refuge between, their banks.

Moving short distances, resting while the hunters sought food, camping at places that offered opportunities of town building while mature men explored the resources of the surrounding land. So, throughout the spring and summer the people of Neas Hiwas slowly and steadily came down the valley.

Summer was far advanced when, at the end of forty miles, Neas Hiwas led his people across a creek that flowed on the east side of a buttress. Round the rock shoulder the people journeyed as best they could — and came to where they looked on a well-established town in which dwelt many people.

16. Klew Nu

HE wearied people looked down from the mountain's shoulder.

Before them, lay Klew - Nu — "The Place where the Moon hides behind the mountain."

Again there was the time of formal greetings, of the age-old courtesies extended from one people to another.

There were entertainments and feasts, the giving of presents, the cautious advancing of ideas, and the probing of the intentions of the other man.

In the end Neas Hiwas gained his end.

In Klew - Nu there was ample room, for the time at least.

Here was sanctuary for the Men of Medeek until a new land could be taken.

Chief Stee How, titular head of the "Wolf People, granted the desired boon. Neas Hiwas and his people might enter and stay until he could find a land suited to his needs.

"Stee How" — "A Man who was Haughty and Grudging in his [35] Gifts" — was not alone at Klew - Nu. As his partner he had a Chief of the Crows: L - Veill - Lahah — "The Half Heaven" — and his people shared the townsite that stretched over two miles of pleasant flat lands.

Here the Men of Medeek found a land unlike any they had seen.

In their upriver home they had been familiar with small lakes and fast running streams.

Here they lived beside a river that moved slowly; that spread out and formed a great lake.

Two miles below the town the river raged through a rock walled canyon. At the upper end of the chasm an island stood in midstream-Between the rocky points great dams of clay held back the waters, dams of clay interwoven with poles and brush.

This was the work of the beavers.

The dams piled up the river's water until it stood as a lake close to the top of the bank. It surged over the dam and spilled in foam down the canyon's bed.

In that lake lived many beaver.

Here, then, the Bear People saw, was a land of plenty. A lake close to town in which was rich meat, and fur for robes and garments!

North from the town ran a well beaten trail, the goat trail down which many carcasses came for the feeding of the people.

Creeks abounded, and fish were taken with ease.

A paradise, no less!

Perhaps this was the end of the quest. The fulfilment of the highest hopes!

OK months life ran smoothly.

The new contacts of Bears and Wolves and Crows gave novelty to intercourse. Delightful hours were spent hearing and telling of other lands. Friendships sprang up.

But here, too, there seemed to have been established a delicate balance of nature. [36]

The Wolves and Crows took of the increase of the beavers; enough were left to ensure a continual supply. It seemed to be a partnership between man and animal in accord with the dictates of *Gyamk*, the Sun God.

And the coming of a new people upset the balance.

Before many moons had passed Stee How spoke to Neas Hiwas. "The beaver are mine," he complained, "And your people kill too many of them."

But the Medeek men, of necessity, had to take them for food and clothing. They continued to hunt the flat-tailed tribes.

From moon to moon the dispute grew.

As in the town of Coor, harmony faded into bickering. That led to individual disputes. Men began to quarrel.

In the end Stee How came to Neas Hiwas again.

"These beaver are mine," he insisted, "The Bear people kill too many. The water lodges are being emptied. Before long we shall all come to want for food.

"Such a thing," he continued, "Shall never come to pass. This is my lake, these are my beavers. You have no rights here. Take your people and depart."

Once again a great responsibility bore down on Neas Hiwas. His plans were not yet completed. His final choice of a land had not been made. Until that time came he must needs provide for them.

Time was needed and with Stee How he pleaded for a respite.

"Wait awhile," he asked, "We will take only those animals we actually need. I have sent my young men out. They are viewing the country further down the river. When they return I shall be able to decide. Till then, I ask you, let us have peace. Then the Men of Medeek will leave. Let us remain friends."

But the dispute continued.

Each day Stee How became more insistent. Daily, Neas Hiwas sought to stave off the task of leading his people out on an unknown quest.

And with the rising of each sun the Wolves and Crows became more incensed as they saw the Bear People killing the beavers.

There could be only one outcome.

Individual fights became more frequent. They developed into factional brawls.

They ended in a battle that lasted for days.

Once more the Men of Medeek were outnumbered. Again some of the finest of the young men were slain.

Forced to draw away with a remnant of his people, Neas Hiwas led the Bears down the river bank.

They passed the clay dam of the beavers. [37]

Three miles below Klew Nu they came to a level place rimmed with steep mountains.

Here Neas Hiwas made his camp.

Here dwelt the Men of Medeek.

Anger was in their hearts. Anger because of the indignities heaped on them by the people of Klew Nu, but worst of all those bitter memories was that of the body of a man.

It was the body of one of the bravest of the Bear People.

As they had left Klew Nu they had seen that body spitted with a stake, as a man spits a fish for roasting.

That stake was driven in the ground near the lake's edge — a thing of derision, of jest, of contempt.

It was the supreme insult offered to Neas Hiwas and his Men of Medeek.

For that body was all that remained of Turn Noon, blood brother, and fellow Chief of Neas Hiwas.

18. Fsem-Y-How

IN the flat place on the west bank of the big canyon Neas Hiwas chose his camp site.

Below them the waters of the Skeena raced through the rocky gorge. Upstream, it spilled over the great clay dams of the beavers. Downstream the river widened out in quieter waters.

Here the Men of Medeek, battle worn and weary, awaited the return of the young chiefs who had gone out to view the land.

At last they came.

They brought news, good news, wonderful news!

Those who had travelled down the west bank came with tales of shallow mountain creeks, of salmon in their hordes lying en the gravelled bottoms. Of a wide valley a few miles down stream. That [38] valley reached away to the north and to the south. It gave promise of abundant game.[17]

Those who had crossed the beaver dam and ranged the eastern bank came with good tidings. Across the Lake they had found the Creek Guetz.[18] It, too, had appeared a good place to take salmon with spear and gaff.

Across the rocky point that made the canyon, and downstream from it, the Kleanza, another creek, offered good fishing. Its channel ran miles back into the mountain's heart. In the valley game abounded.

Best of all was the word of the men who had gone still further south on that side of the river.

A few miles below Kleanza they had come to a swift river that flowed down a great gorge. Fish swarmed in its waters. Here they had sensed something that would change the

---

[17] The Kalum and Lakelse Valleys: Terrace district.

[18] Singlehurst Creek.

fortunes of the Bear People.

They had followed that river upstream for a few miles — they had found camps that they recognized, camps that a few years ago they had used!

They had found some of the resting places they had stopped at as they hunted their new territory of *Guell Haast.*

The thing was clear.

From Tum - L - Hama they had crossed a great mountain range to come to the river Zymoetz. Now they had found where it poured its waters into the Skeena.

No longer were they faced with the fierce toil of packing food up steep slopes and over crests. From this time on they could travel the valley bottom, and on good trails bring much food to the people.

So, at last, the reward had been granted.

The care, the diligence, and slow maturing decisions of Neas Hiwas had reached a rich fruition.

Many places had he looked over. Pleasant valleys had offered haven. But, always, something had been lacking.

Now he had those things he had longed for. Here, his people would have good fishing that would be unhampered by the varying levels of the river. There was no need for building great weirs to hold the fish until they could be taken. Instead, with gaff and spear, the river's harvest was assured.

Good hunting, too, in the flanking mountains behind the camp. And especially, across the river, up the valley of the Zymoetz, his hunters could range as far as Guell Haast. All could be done in safety and comparative ease.

The die was cast. [39]

Fsem - Y - How, the city on the banks of the Canyon, began to take its form.

From that day the Men of Medeek came to be known as "Kit-Se-Las" — "The Dwellers on the Canyon".

The flat ground on which they built their city was roughly half moon in shape.

Along the river front, as was the custom of the People, the Chiefs built their houses. Here was established the centre of Government — The Street of Chiefs.

Behind this two other streets ran, each parallel with the one in front.

Facing the streets, the people of lesser ranks established their homes.

Down the steep mountain side they brought their timbers. Temporary shelters were erected at first. These, as the moons passed, were replaced by more solid structures.

The long trek was over. The people had come Home.

19. Revenge

YEARS came and passed. Winter snows followed on the heels of busy summers. Children grew to lusty manhood, ran their courses, grew old and passed on.

At Fsem ~ Y - How great changes were wrought. Buildings of substance stood where the Men of Medeek had placed their first shelters. Buildings sound, and strong, showing the weathering of many years.

Newer buildings, also, told of the way the Bear People had prospered, spoke of the steady increase in numbers.

Prosperity had returned: life was easier.

And with that growing ease the "New Men" — the generations that had succeeded each other — had provided experimenters. [40]

Gradually new ways of life had been devised; new implements had been fashioned.

Life was easier — more efficient.

But always, in the Councils of the Chiefs, as the people sat in their houses, on the hunting trails, fishing, trapping, building — it mattered not what was afoot — the thoughts of the Men of Medeek ran back to Turn - Noon.

From generation to generation there had been passed down the vivid tale of the harshness of the Stee How, of the degradation with which lie had treated the body of the Bear Chief.

Years swept on, centuries passed. Yet the dead was not forgotten.

Klew Nu still stood. There, succeeding Stee Hows had ruled.

And through those years no recompense had been made for the Blood of the Chief. No payment had been made by Stee How to settle the debt.

Always in the minds of the Men of Medeek there echoed the Law of the People; "When the Blood is unpaid retribution must follow".

As the Bear People increased in numbers that day of settlement drew closer.

At last there came a time when Neas Hiwas called his council together.

Once more he recounted the indignity that had been meted out to his forefather — the desecration of the body of Turn Noon.

"Now," he went on, "Our people have come to a great power. We are many. No longer can we be slighted. No more shall Stee How and the people of Klew Nu regard us with indifference. They could have paid for the blood of Turn Noon. Then all would have been well. But they have treated us with contempt. They have regarded us as weaklings, as a people unable to exact the just dues, as a race of women who cannot fight and uphold the Native Law.

"That time has ended.

"Now, we have come to the time for action. Our honor demands that we mete out the punishment for the ancient crime.

"Chiefs of the Totem of Medeek, Councillors of the People, go lorlh. Prepare all things in readiness. When all is done Klew Nu shall be utterly destroyed." [41]

20. Preparation

THE scene changed.

Ease and leisure disappeared.

Instead, the Kitselas People passed through two years of intense activity.

Tum Noon, the holder of the title of his ancient ancestor, was charged with the training of the warriors. On his shoulder rested the responsibility of preparing the men who, when the time came, should wipe out the score.

Hunters ranged the hills incessantly. Meat came to the city in a steady stream. Others cleaned it and hung it in the smoke houses to cure. Meat of the bear, the caribou, the deer, the goats from the peaks;

the ground hogs and the rabbits — all added to the growing store.

Men skilled in working wood ranged the nearby forests. They chose straight grained trees, felled them, and with stone tools split the logs into thin, wide boards. These they took to the river pools and for weeks left them lying in the water, well weighted lest they float away.

Soaked and pliable, the boards were taken one by one, a great log placed on the middle of each. With infinite care the ends were brought up. Day by day the bending continued until, at last, the ends met and the sides of a box were formed.

Cords of cedar bark lashed the bent wood in position until it dried.

Careful craftsmen, working with chisels made of the teeth of beavers, cut mortices in which the tops and bottoms fitted. Other boards were fashioned to fit the slots.

As the meats cured they were taken from the smoke houses and left for a night on nearby berry bushes so that they might dry.

Each finished box was picked with the meat. Each box, as it was filled, was fitted with its top and all seams were sealed with smooth

So meats were cured and stored. [42]

War was coming! Then there would be no time to hunt.

Such meats would keep for 10 years.

Each June, increased numbers of women gathered the inner bark of the hemlock, pounded it to a paste with water, cooked it in a bed of clay and heated rocks. So they laid up stores of sweetness.

Each summer the women and children toiled long hours gathering wild berries, crushing the fruit and drying it over the slow fires. Just before it had set into a solid cake each strip was rolled up, and hung in the storehouse for winter's use.

Salmon in quantities far larger than usual were caught and cured.

So, with the day of battle drawing closer, the people made sure of ample food to carry them through the days of stress.

Antlers of caribou came in from the hunt. These were fashioned into clubs that, at one blow, would crush a man's skull.

Men busied themselves splitting thin boards from jackpine logs, from chosen logs that ran rich in resin. Three, four feet long they made them, twelve to fifteen inches wide, shaped at one end to make a hand grip.

Others spent their days preparing Hag - Wa - T - Za — The Fire Maker. Cedar bark came to the town in great slabs, there to be dried before the fire, and teasled out into fine strands that still held their oils. Still others ranged the forest and gathered the resin that hung to the trunks of the jackpines. In the town the sound of stone pestles striking the mortars echoed all day long as this concentrated flame was ground to a powder. Then cedar bark and resin were mixed.

In those ancient factories a jackpine paddle was covered with a layer of the resin-bark compound. Another paddle was laid on top, then a second layer of compound, and still another paddle covered it. Lamination completed, the whole was bound with cedar cord.

So Hag - Wa - T - Za — the Fire Maker — was fashioned.

A year passed and the stores stacked high. Stores of spears, of bows, of bone tipped arrows, clubs of wood, of stone, clubs fashioned from the horn of animals. Food boxes were there in piles.

But not enough.

Another year sped, and as the turn of the summer came, Neas Hiwas decided there could be no lack.

From then on until Lasimedeek — The Dry Month — the final training of the warriors was carried on.

Tests of weapons were daily happenings. Detailed plans for the coming battle were made and practiced.

The plan of campaign had been decided on long before. It would be a surprise attack. A raid in the early hours of the morning when men slept their deepest. [43]

21. Blood's Price

LASIMEDEEK: the Month of the Grizzly Bear's revenge!

That year the "Dry Month" brought grim vengeance to the foes of the Totem of Medeek.

Late one afternoon the warriors sallied forth from Fsem - Y - How.

They were heavily laden. Hag - Wa - T - Za, spears, bows and clubs were many and weighed down the men as they stole along the forest trails.

Theirs was a leisurely progress- Many hours must pass before the action started.

Before darkness had fully fallen the men of Neas Hiwas were settled in the forest's edge.

In front of them Klew Nu lay all unsuspecting of what was to come,

Smoke curled lazily from the holes in the ridges of the houses. The thatches of cedar bark were tinder dry after weeks of hot weather.

Gradually, the fires died down in the houses as the Wolves and Crows dropped into slumber. The barking dogs quietened. At last all was still.

Yet the Bear men waited.

It was not their plan to attack men newly asleep.

Attack must be held until the early hours when man's vitality is at its lowest.

So midnight passed, and nothing stirred.

Three hours more, and the Bear men stole quietly into the town.

Each man had his allotted station. Ample time was given for all to reach their posts.

In the hands of each man was a Firemaker. Two men were stationed at each house, one on either side.

Stealthily they raised the cedar thatches and placed the fire sticks under the tinder-dry material. [44]

A signal and every man applied a spark to his stick. Hag - Wa - T - Za burns like a powder fuse. In an instant each stick was a mass of flames. In a few seconds each roof was a roaring furnace.

And throughout that town resounded the cry of the Owl — "Oooooh, Eeeeeh, Ooooh, Oo, Oo, Oo!" — rang through the town as the Men of Medeek gave deep throated voice to their war cry.

Sleep-numbed, Stee How and his followers staggered through their doorways. They were met by Kitselas men alert and keen to make short work of their task of revenge.

It was a fierce fight, but the issue was never in doubt. Everything was in favour of the invaders, and that night most of the men of Klew Nu passed to the Spirit World.

Stee How escaped with wounds. L - Veill - Lahah was equally fortunate.

Before dawn they gathered the scattered remnants of their people and escaped over the ancient goat hunting trail.

Behind they left a shambles of dead and dying, a town reduced to a smoldering heap of ruins.

For them, life had taken a violent, disastrous turn. There was no hope of coming back. Klew Nu was left to grow up in forest once more, and became a hunting ground until centuries later the Willow Men — men with white skins — built Usk on the ancient site.

As the morning sun lifted over the eastern mountains they made what speed they could up the mountain slopes. Wound-weakened, at times they had to rest.

They were in the grip of the most primitive emotion — the -will to escape, and survive.

So throughout that day, and other days, they followed their chiefs as they led through the high passes between the peaks-There came a time when their stumbling footsteps brought them to the crest. Before them lay the wide, western valley.

Here the partner chiefs took their separate ways.

Stee How turned northwards. Many miles of travel brought him to Git - Lac - Damix on the banks of the Naas River. Here he joined forces with another people and established new homes for his people.

L - Veill - Lahah and his Crows held on to the west. Down the mountain side they journeyed, until they came to a river. A silver lake lay to their right.[19] From this lake the river flowed.

A few miles below the lake the river narrowed as it flowed between sheer canyon walls. [45]

Here, on the lofty benches above the boiling waters, they made their homes.

But back on the Skeena the Men of Medeek held revel as they gloried in their triumph.

At last, after long centuries, the insult had been wiped out.

Many years passed before their trails crossed those of their ancient enemies, the people who perched on the overhanging cliffs had been named Kit Aalum — The Dwellers on the Cliff Brink.

New life entered the Kitselas. The ignomy of the defeat of Klew Nu had been wiped out. They had gone into battle; they had emerged victorious.

No longer could scornful people narrow their movements.

In the years that followed they took such land as they desired.

There was no thought of moving to a new location. Canyon dwellers they were; so they remained. Masters of the bottle neck that controlled the river above and below them.

Twenty- two miles upstream at the Creek Ksegank — white men call it Fiddler — they set their mark. Eight miles below their abode they set another mark where the great steel bridge now spans the Skeena River. This became their western boundary.

Already they had the land of Zymoetz. Now they took possession of thirty miles of the Skeena valley with its rich creeks, its flanking mountains teeming with game, and valleys in which food abounded.

22. Down to the sea

YEARS of prosperity followed the taking of Klew Nu.

Freed from the narrowing confines to which their enemies had held them the Bear people met their needs with greater ease.

More time was left for planning new ways of life: fresh appliances were invented to make work lighter.

It was in these days that young men found how a log could be fashioned into a canoe. From the first primitive crafts they developed [46] graceful vessels of cedar like those used by the Peoples on. the coast of the great salt water.

A mighty tree went into the shaping of each canoe. Fine smooth lines made them easy to

---

[19] Kalum Lake.

navigate, and bows and stems, carved in high, sweeping curves, lent beauty to their shapes.

With this development there came a new mobility of the people. Practical horizons widened and laborious journeys on foot became easy passages on the waters of the river.

In turn came fresh ambitions.

Klew Nu had been a prize worth taking why should not more distant towns prove equally worth the task of capture?

First came the vague idea: discussions followed.

Young men who had tasted victory longed for new adventure.

Finally the schemes began to crystallize.

"Now we have twenty big canoes," said the Warriors. "Each canoe will hold a 'Man' of warriors.[20] Four hundred fighting men can do much."

So they planned, and after many councils a great raid lay ahead.

"Down on the sea coast," said the warriors, "There are many towns. There the people have great riches. We will go and raid them. At each place we shall take *aiyesks*, and buckskins and slaves: more slaves than we need for Kitselas. Those we do not need shall be sold; in return we shall receive more *aiyesks* and buckskins. We shall come back with much wealth."

So months passed while war stores were gone over. The bows and arrows, the spears and clubs, and the Firemakers were brought to full repair and efficiency. New weapons were made to increase the store.

August came to a close and the fishing season had ended. Food for the winter was stacked in the storehouses. There was more than enough.

With the last days of the month and as Lasimedeek — The Dry Month — approached, the fleet set out.

Down the swift waters of the Skeena the canoes sped. Neas Hiwas was in command; his nephews and brother chiefs were in charge of the other canoes.

Tidewater, and the fleet hung to the south bank of the estuary. Below Spokeshute the course curved to the south.

At last, the river left behind, the war party sped to the south east along the Inside Passage.

Kitamaat Arm dropped astern as they held their course. [47]

23. Kitlop

AT last a town was in sight, Kitlop, nestling close to the sea shore.

Some miles from the objective the fleet hove to. They waited for darkness before venturing a closer approach.

Long after the sun had set they swung back to their course again.

When the early hours of morning had come, and the dwellers of the coast town slept soundly, the river warriors landed and took their stations.

Then came the signal. Again the Cry of the Owl echoed back from the rimming forest as Hag - Wa - T - Za roared into flame beneath the thatches of the roofs.

---

[20] 'Man' was the unit of counting. 'Ten fingers and ten toes' was the mode; so a 'Man' was the total — 20.

That night the horrors and killings of Klew Nu were repeated.

Taken by surprise the people of Kitlop were no match for the invaders. Many of the coastal warriors were killed. Some, seeing the battle lost, escaped to the forest. Women and children were captured and made secure. Slavery would be their lot as long as life lasted.

Rich booty fell to the Bear Men that night. Aiyesks {coppers}, buckskins, silky sea otter robes.

When all was over the river canoes were far more heavily laden than when they had put ashore.

But there was one, a nephew of Neas Hiwas, who was not satisfied. The sight of new riches only added to his longing for more. He returned to the town again to find some goods that had been missed in the first search.

Sharp, vindictive eyes watched him from the forest's edge. Well inside town he found himself surrounded. Before aid could come he had paid for his greed with his life.

From the beach the river men saw the killing. From their throats rang the lament that had come down through the ages.

Ni te ge gad Kitlop.
"Kitlop is holding."

So, [48] too, the ranking lady of Kitselas sings as she holds a new born babe. So, too, the people mourn at the grave of a child.

A future chief had died. Revenge must be had if honor was to be vindicated.

From the beach there surged a war party to make short shrift of the men who had done the killing.

But the men of Kitlop were equally swift. They had the advantage — they knew the country.

Along forest trails they led the invaders. High into the mountains they lured the pursuers.

When morning came the Kitselas stood at the foot of a great cliff. Above them, on the brink, stood the defenders. From the height came a jeering song that taunted the enemy with their inability to catch them.

The danger was too great. An attempt to climb was out of the question: great rocks might be rolled down on those who ventured — and the trail that led to the higher level was unknown.

The course of wisdom prevailed. The chase was abandoned. The river men returned to the beach.

After all, why risk life for revenge? That coast held many other towns that were equally rich.

The early morning saw the Men of Medeek launch out and turn the prows of their canoes to the south east.

24. Bella Bella

SOUTHWARDS, and the fleet came to open water where the waves of the great ocean rolled in without hindrance.

Still southwards, and one day, they saw a small mountain on their left.

It rose up on an island, and some distance up its slope smoke curled between the trees.

Curiosity aroused, the Bear men put ashore.

No signs of life greeted^ them on the beach. A cautious stalk brought [49] them to where they saw a brush house, a frail shelter against the summer rains.

One of the nephews of Neas Hiwas — there were many nephews — moved stealthily, and came to where he had a view inside. A woman sat there. In her arms lay a baby boy.

With a quick spring the young chief was inside, and the woman captured.

Looking around, the young chief saw many smokes coming from the ground.

"What are these smokes?" queried the warrior.

"The girls," came the reply.

Here was a prize worth capturing.

In those early days great care was taken of the girls as they came to the borderline of womanhood.

It was not considered right or fortunate for maidens, with approaching puberty, to remain in a town with the rest of the people.

So, according to custom, a camp was maintained some distance from the town. Here in a house, a matron — a woman of high rank — stayed on guard.

Around her house cubicles were excavated in the ground. Each compartment was roofed. In each a fire burned to keep the occupants warm.

To these cubicles came the girls as womanhood dawned. Here they stayed until they were ready to take their places in the life of town.

Many smokes rose before the eyes of the Bear warrior; many girls were hidden under the roofs of the pits.

Such a number bespoke a town of size, one that might be expected to hold great booty.

Calling the rest of his party the warrior made a tour of the area. Every girl was captured, and the party including the chief's sister and her son, set off for the beach.

"Where is your town?" asked the nephew of Neas Hiwas.

The woman pointed for them to paddle around the point of the island.

"What is the name of your son?" asked the young chief as they sped on their way.

Silence greeted him.

Again he asked the question. Once more a stare of contempt was the answer.

Angered, he asked the question a third time.

Much hung on the answer. Here was a lad, who, in due course, would be a chief. His capt.or, if he could learn his name, would be entitled by the laws of the People to take that name as his own; to have added power that would come with the name. [50]

So, angered by the woman's refusal, the Bear warrior raised his spear. Pointing it at the chief's sister, he exclaimed "Tell me the lad's name. Refuse and I will kill you."

The threat had its result. "Oiaks - Gwin - Nat - Nootk - Car - Ast -Waar - Kunt - Lask", said the woman. — "He who hears the cries of crows as he hunts in the early morning."

So passed that name and its power to the Men of Medeek.

The canoes swept onwards. Round a point they came to the town of Bella Bella.

As they neared the town Neas Hiwas commanded the fleet to heave to. With paddles poised for instant action the Bear men sat in their craft as they swung in the waves just offshore from the beach.

From Bella Bella men rushed down, armed and ready for the fray.

But the woman called to her brother, the Head Chief, "Hold the warriors. I, with my son, and the girls have been captured. If our men fight we die. "Unless a ransom is paid we all go as slaves."

The Crow Chieftain saw the danger. It was too great. A false move would bring the loss of the babe who, when the time came, would be raised to his place. It would mean loss of many maidens from the life of his people.

Negotiations followed. Bartering for the sum of ransom went on for hours.

At last a price was set. From the storehouses of Bella Bella came *aiyesks*, and buckskins, and robes and blankets of fine sea otter skins.

The ransom was piled on the beach. The terms of peace were agreed upon.

Then, the prisoners restored to their people, the Bear men with canoes loaded to the limits of safety, the Men of Medeek turned their prows to the north.

The highest hopes of the Kitselas had been realized. Booty beyond their fondest dreams was theirs.

No further need of fighting.

Homewards they sped with their wealth. [51]

25. Um-I-Am

VICTORIOUS!

And homeward bound!

The Kitselas fleet went northward and the hearts of the warriors were light and joyous.

They made the trip in easy stages. Each night they camped in some secluded bay. Each day they swung their paddles to the rhythms of their songs and chants.

Just before they came to the mouth of the Skeena they sighted another fleet coming to meet them.

Twenty canoes were in the strange fleet. The forces were equal.

Had Neas Hiwas desired conflict he would have held his course.

But, desiring peace, he followed the Law and swung his fleet in the path of the advancing strangers. He slowed his paddlers that he might be overtaken. Such was the sign of Peace upon the waters.

The canoes coming from the north drew near; they came abreast; they stopped.

Tsimpseans, Coast men, warriors who used the salt waters as their highways.

The men of this fleet did not recognize the Men of Medeek. Strangers evidently, certainly River Men.

Up in his canoe rose the Chief of the Tsimpseans. "Um - I - Am," he shouted in jest to Neas Hiwas. "Um - I - Am" — "What do you wish to do."

So he sought to deride the boatmanship of the Kitselas.

And as he spoke the words stung the younger warriors to the quick.

Like a flash the young chief who had captured the Bella Bella woman came to his feet. Angry words rushed to his lips. Tension hung in the air. Had he spoken a battle would have started.

A quick gesture from Neas Hiwas held the young man in check.

"Wait," came the command, "Do not be angry. This is good. From [52] this day I will have a new name — 'Um - I - Am' will be my name because of this happening."

So peace prevailed.

Then, accepting the invitation of the Tsimpseans, the upriver flotilla paddled in time with the strokes of the coast men.

Once again they travelled to the south.

A few miles sped by and they turned to the west, swung around a jutting promontory they turned north into a sheltered inlet. An hour passed, and rounding a bend, there opened up before them the view of a town that stood on the banks of this sheltered cove.

It was still daylight when they came to this town.

On peace intent, they stood in boldly. They beached their canoes as the townsfolk gathered to greet their visitors.

26. Kitkatla

EXCITEMENT swept the men who stood on the shore.

Was all well, or was this a ruse?

But from the canoes came the assurance. "It is well. We come as friends. As friends we wish to stay and be your guests."

Dressed in his Cape of Ceremony, shaking his rattles, dancing his greeting, Loot - Quitz - Ampty - Wich — "Lightning" — Head Chief of the Eagle Totem, came to meet his guests.

And here, as his honored friends the Kitselas and Tsimpseans stayed for ten days.

Feasts, ceremonies, and dancing filled the days as the Eagles and the Crows lavished entertainment on their guests.

As the days sped a great friendship sprang up between the Eagle Chief and Neas Hiwas.

Then, as the time drew near for the visitors to depart, the Kitkatla Chief made a proposal.

"I like you and your people," he told Neas Hiwas. "I should like [53] to have you as my partner and neighbour. Stay with me, make your home here."

Then Neas Hiwas called a Council of his brothers, the Chiefs of Medeek. He placed the offer before them.

"I cannot stay," he pointed out. "My home and my 'Power' are on the banks of the Big Canyon. But our people are many. We have increased in numbers. It may be well that some part of our Men of Medeek travel down the river and here, with this friendly people, establish new homes."

In those days of feasting Che - Ve - Sar and Saaks had seen much of the town. Their hosts had shown how the people secured their food.

In the creeks salmon abounded. Fisherman caught halibut and codfish, clams were there on the beaches for the digging.

As they had talked with each other they had said, "Here is a land of plenty. Here there is no danger of famine such as came to our forefathers in the days of Tum - L - Hama."

And now this offer!

It could not be lost.

Che - Ve - Sar and Saaks, each in his turn, stood forth. "We will stay here," they announced. "From now on Kitkatla will be our home. Here we will bring our wives, and our families."

The outcome delighted Loot - Quintz - Ampty - Wich.

A great feast was called. There the Eagle Chief spoke to his people.

"This day I am very happy," he began. "This day these two chiefs of Medeek have promised to come and make their homes with us.

"I am pleased. I am honored.

"They are mighty chiefs. They are of ancient lineage.

"Their promise demands the highest honor I can give them.

"I can do no less.

"To these two chiefs, to Che - Ve - Sar and to Saaks, I give the right to rule over you, the people of Kitkatla."

And Che - Ve - Sar became the Head Chief.

Even to this day many Chiefs of the Totem of Medeek rule over and care for the people of Kitkatia.

It was the parting of the ways. A splitting up of the fellowship of the brothers of the Bear Chieftainship.

But the matter pleased Neas Hiwas.

To the Eagle Chief he said: "Um gosh waal" — I thank you for your kindness and for what you have done for my brothers.

Then Neas Hiwas and his warriors sang the Funeral song of Medeek over Che - Ve - Sar and over Saaks. For they were become Chiefs of Kitkatla and no longer Chiefs of Kitselas.

And when the dirge had ended he led his men in the Song of War, and throughout the town there rang Ooooh, Eeeeeh, Ooooooh, Oo, Oo, [54] Oo, that is the Song of the Owl, and the shout of Victory of the Men of Medeek.

The War song echoed and re-echoed. So the Bear men heard it thrown back to them from the forest walls. And their hearts became strong and they did not grieve over the loss of their Chiefs.

So the great feast ended. The time of parting had come and Neas Hiwas led his fleet out of the harbour, and turned their bows to the Skeena and home.

27. Neas Waias

KITKATLA and the time of feasting were memories.

Neas Hiwas led his war fleet northwards once more and came to the mouth of the Skeena.

Light hearts kept the warriors cheerful. They had faced north, tested their strength and skill against the sturdy men of the coast; they were returning laden with the spoils of conquest.

With Neas Hiwas travelled Che - Ve - Sar and Saaks.

At Kitkatla the formal ceremonies of separation had been performed. But, still, there remained certain things to be done before they gathered their families and took up their new abode on the shores of the salt water.

Up the wide estuary the war canoes sped, the steady dip of paddles driving them, and the incoming tide adding to their speed.

Near Kwinitza they came to where tide and river met. From there progress was slower.

War canoes laden with the spoils of Huus - Ki - Get — "The War of Raid and .Ransom" — needed much effort to carry them upstream against the swift waters of the river. Often paddles had to be laid aside, and poles and tow-lines of cedar-bark rope were brought to play.

By dint of much pushing against the gravelled bottoms, stout hauling on lines by men who walked along the river's bank, the canoes won mile after mile of the homeward way. [55]

When evening fell the fleet hauled into the mouth of some creek. There, in a secure back-eddy, camp was made until another sun called them to renewed labours.

One nightfall found them at the mouth of the Gitnidox River.

Here, in the cool of the evening, Chief Neas Waias — a scion of a junior branch of the House of Chiefs — viewed the land.

Salmon surged in the water of the river. Upstream a wide valley held out invitation of good hunting and plentiful fur.

A goodly land. unoccupied, it appealed to the Bear Chieftain.

To Neas Hiwas he went with his thoughts. Long into the night they discussed the matter. Before they slept a conclusion had been reached.

The next day saw no travel for the warriors.

An impromptu feast was held and Neas Waias made known his plan.

Gitnidox and the land around should be his. Another offshoot of the Men of Medeek would be established. In due course he would journey from Kitselas with his family and this rich valley would be added to the land of the Grizzly Bears.

Again the ancient funeral dirge rang through the forest as Neas Hiwas and his men bade formal farewell to the chief who would head the new project.

Then again, the forest resounded with the heartening war cry — The Call of the Owl — and the Medeek Men proclaimed their strong and steadfast hearts.

Before they left to resume their up-river journey Neas Waias took the native paint, powdered red rock compounded with the oil from the salmon roe.[21] With this paint the Chief marked rocks on the shore that all who saw might know that here was a land claimed and possessed; a land that would, in due time, become the site of a new town and its activities.

When all was completed the toil of ascending the river started again. Back-eddies in which canoes sped upriver with easy paddling alternated with swift waters and riffles that made progress difficult.

The swift riffle of the mouth of the Aalum River was passed at last. The boiling waters round the mid-stream rock, Sask - Ka - Neaskt, at the entrance to Hell-Gate slough dropped astern. A few miles and they came to the little Canyon.

Onwards, and a few miles saw the end of the journey.

The victorious warriors were home on the cliff banks of Kitselas. [56]

28. Reunion

JOY swept through Kitselas with the return of the warriors, joy for the safe return of husbands and sons.

Gladness because the time of privation was past. The People, women and children as well as men, could once more live without the rigors or restraint of war days; for on the women fell a heavy duty when their men were away.

Whether the absence was due to hunting or to war the wives of those who were away must practice a stiff, unfaltering self-denial.

Feasting in the absence of a husband was taboo, carefree visiting was forbidden.

On the women rested the task of spiritually upholding their men.

So, as the warrior ate sparingly on a campaign, his wife, who stayed at home must be equally abstemious in her feeding.

Only by rigorous self-denial of the appetites of the body, of mental self-discipline on the part of the wife, could that spirit force go forth to ensure success and safety for the man-Any relaxing of the code placed their men in danger; wilful disregard of the rule was sure to bring disaster.

So ran the Law.

And so, through the weeks the warriors had travelled on the salt water, Kitselas had been deathly quiet, lacking the normal activities of life. It had been a place where those who had remained at home had observed with minuteness the rites and ceremonies of such a time. Great things were at stake. The lives, of many men depended on the projection of that guardian Power of Spirit.

But with the safe return of Neas Hiwas and his warriors the time of rigor ended.

Rejoicings marked the reunion of families. There was much to tell and talk about. [57]

---

[21] The base of the red paint was a clay that came from a creek bottom two miles south of Aalum Lake. This clay was burned and pulverized, the finest being taken as coloring matter.

Neas Hiwas called a great feast so that the triumphant conclusion of the venture might be fittingly celebrated.

All due formality marked that festival.

At it the Men of Medeek were told of the momentous decisions that had been made.

Neas Hiwas told how Che - Ve - Sar and Saahs would take their families and start life anew as the rulers of Kitkatia; how Neas Waias and his people would establish a cadet clan at Gitnidox, this in turn to revert to the Totem of the Wolves as his wife was of that crest.

He told of the taking of a new name and how, from that time Neas Hiwas would also be known as Um - I - Am.

And he told of the capture of the Bella Bella Prince and how his name and power had been taken to add lustre to the distinguished list of Bear titles.

So the people feasted, and rejoiced, and looked forward, some with wonder, some with expectancy, others with a lurking fear of the unknown, to what would come to them in the months that lay ahead.

But before that time there still remained great things to be accomplished.

Two major victories had brought added confidence. Out of that spirit of achievement came the determination to wipe off the other ancient score.

Still in the hearts of the Men of Medeek a bitterness gnawed, a memory of the death of a young chief who, through self-denial and strength, had won for them the rich hunting lands of Zymoetz.

Coor, of the Eagles, had never made recompense.

29. Whaap-Kum Raanskt

NEAS HIWAS called another feast

He laid before his people the full plan for the restoration of the pride of Medeek, for the exacting of the penalty that Coor had incurred in failing to pay for the Blood of a Prince. [58]

Much labour was entailed in the execution of the plan. A building such as had never been seen on the Canyon banks had to be erected. The people, refreshed, inspired, set forth on the new task. On a selected site men began to dig. A great oblong pit was opened up. When it was completed it stretched sixty-six feet from end to end; it was thirty-six feet wide. The floor was eight feet below the level of the ground.

Around this pit a shelf was leveled; twelve feet wide, and smooth of surface.

As men dug others went into the forest with their tools of stone. Giant cedars were cut down, trimmed and dragged to the site.

Here great sills were placed — the outline of a building that should be sixty feet across and ninety feet in length.

On these sills great cedar trunks were set as uprights; corner posts, wall supports, and pillars to carry the ridge pole that spanned the centre of the structure.

Each upright was grooved on two sides, morticed to take hewn cedars that were squared and shaped to fit the slots.

Thus fitted together, the securely interlocked sills, and posts, and massive cedar caps, with wall timbers neatly joined in slots, the building rose like a solid piece of timber. No chance of entrance or exit other than the one provided.

Over all, other cedars reached from eaves to ridge pole; smaller poles were placed crosswise on these. The lighter sticks, in turn, carried the thatch of cedar bark.

Whaarp - Kum - Raanskt, he called that house, for at one end he had skilled men fit Mee - Haa - Shan — "The great door that locks".

Jackpines made the timbers of that door.

Ten timbers, each ten inches square. They were fitted together and made solid with braces. Fifteen feet the door reached to the lintel, and hung from that beam with many thongs of moose skin.

Cedars hewn to squares of twelve inches, set solidly into the ground, made the door posts.

The door did not hang straight down. Instead an entrance was built on the outside of the house, angling from the ground, its foot seven feet from the building's wall.

Thus, when the door was lowered its weight pressed it against this approach. So heavy was the task of moving it that one man, alone, was powerless.

Outside the great door the skin of a giant grizzly bear hung. Finely tanned, it was arranged that those who were outside could not see what went on within.

And inside the doorway there hung another bear's skin, its lower edge four feet from the ground. [59]

So, as a man entered, he must stoop and bend, and thus pay his respects to Neas Hiwas and the Men of Medeek. Men of great skill fashioned great drums.

Wide boards, over sixteen feet long, were riven from straight grained cedars. Finely dressed, these boards were bent and moulded in the manner of the making of meat boxes. One end was tightly closed with fitted boards; the other end was open.

Two drums were made, one to hang on one side of the pit, the other to be swung opposite to the first.

Completed, the drums had great resonance: beaten in measured rhythm their booming could be heard a mile away.

Other craftsmen made great horns with which the voices of men were magnified. With such an instrument all other sound could be drowned.

So the Men of Medeek laboured. For months the toil continued that all might be completed against the day of a great feast that was to come.

As the men toiled, on the women fell tasks well suited to their skills.

Ceremonial robes, new and elaborate, more gorgeous than any seen in the past, had to be planned and made.

Robes for Neas Hiwas, and for the other Chiefs, robes for the Elders, for the Musicians, and for the women who would have so large a share of the task of entertaining the guests.

Long hours were spent making "Scheoon" from the hides of caribou. This buckskin was worked until it had the softness of fine cloth.

Aprons for the Chiefs were made from the skins and on them were sewn the beaks of many birds, and hooves of mountain goats.

Leggings of buckskin were made and on them patterns embroidered with small white shells that had come from the sea's shore.

Moccasins, decorated with symbolic designs, were fashioned from the same materials.

Head-dresses like crowns were designed. Fine, silky furs were the fabric.

Weasel skins, taken in the depth of winter, were chosen, and with them capes of ceremony were fashioned.

Other women, specially skilled, prepared the wool from the mountain goats. This they cleansed, and carded, and with deft movements of the hand on the upper leg, twisted it into strands.

Different weights they spun, some lighter in thread, others heavier.

With dyes from roots and the juice of the wild berries they gave bright, contrasting colors to the skeins. Then taking the material they wove the Capes of Ceremony, capes to be worn by the Chiefs as they danced the steps of ritual. The lighter twists went into the weaving of [60] the cape itself, heavier threads were fashioned to make the collars, while the edges of the capes were draped with long tassels.

One year, it took, for a woman to make a cape.

Fine workmanship, an appreciation of colour values, and a careful following of symbolic design, were woven into the capes as the coloured wools took shape under a woman's deft fingers. The brightly contrasted patterns told the stories of the history of the wearer, and the long lineage that ran behind him. They spoke of the traditions of his race, and the 'Power' of his Chieftainship.

For the women dresses of symbolism and beauty were made. Their footwear was fashioned from the finely tanned skins of groundhogs; skins that were finished with a velvet softness.

So were the costumes for the coming feast prepared.

Those months were filled with busy days.

Yet in spite of the labors there were times of singing.

Many hours a day the voices of the women were raised in song.

Not in chance song, but in the chants of tradition as the great choir was trained for the coming feast.

Four hundred women were in that choir. It was arranged in two parts.

On one side of the Guest house two hundred women ranged on a sloping platform: across from them, on the other side, another two hundred women had like positions.

"When you come into Heaven — Into the House of Many Chiefs — Do not hide your face and be Ashamed," was the theme of one group.

From across the house the others told the tale of "The Sun and the Moon that Fall down from Heaven".

So strophe and antistrophe passed back and forth across the pit, each phrase developing the theme, each filling its place in telling of the deeds of the mighty men and of the Supernatural Beings who had had a place in their earlier history.

Thus, throughout the months, the varied works went on. Through the winter and through the days of early spring. The waxing summer saw the task almost finished. When Lasimedeek drew near, the month of holidaying and visiting, all was in readiness. [61]

30. Kitwanga (Land Of Coor)

AS Lasimedeek drew near Neas Hiwas set forth on a Journey. The high waters of the spring freshets were past, the slower waters of the fall run-off made progress easy.

So the Bear Chief came to Kitwanga — in those days lying on the south bank of the Skeena.

Here he landed, and with the blowing of great horns his men signalled his approach.

Singing the ancient funeral song of Medeek, Neas Hiwas entered the town. Such was the Law of the People when a Chief came to visit others of high rank in distant towns.

Coor, the Head Chief of the Eagles, came to meet him. He met Neas Hiwas with dancing, with the shaking of rattles, and led him to his house on The Street of Chiefs.

There Coor gave a great feast in honor of his guest; there Neas Hiwas gave to Coor presents of buckskin.

The next day the second ranking Chief of Kitwanga claimed the honor of host to the visitor. Another feast was held, other presents of buckskin were given.

So, on each succeeding day the Kitwanga Chiefs, in order of precedence, feasted the great Chief of Medeek: each in turn received gifts of largesse from their guest.

At last the feasting was over. The time of departure was close at hand.

To Coor came Neas Hiwas "Urn gosh wall — I thank you," said the Canyon Chief. "You have dealt royally with me; you have honored me. Now I return to Fsem - Y - How. There it is planned that a great feast be held. I bid you welcome to that feast. You, and your brother Chiefs, your Elders, and your Wise Men. Come down the river. Take part with us at our feast. Let us entertain you."

The invitation pleased Coor. "I thank you," he said. "In ten days our canoes leave here. In ten days we launch out and journey down to Fsem - Y - How that we may share the feast with you." [62]

31. Coor's Downfall

NEAS HIWAS, back from Kitwanga, put final preparations in hand for the coming feast.

To every man a duty was allotted, each knew exactly what had to be done.

Ten days passed after his return.

On the eleventh day a fleet of canoes appeared upriver during the morning.

They came down stream and made their way to Loor - As - Shaw — "The place of the tying up of canoes".

Here they were met by men of Medeek, who sped back with news to Neas Hiwas that Coor and his party had arrived.

Guides went forth to bring them to Fsem - Y - How, where they would receive their formal welcome.

And as they walked along the trail from the great beaver dams they found a serving man with a fire burning. Food had been prepared, and the guests were invited to eat before proceeding to the ceremony.

As they ate and refreshed themselves Neas Hiwas completed his final preparations.

That morning the choirs of women had taken their places early. They had fasted, and even when their guests feasted on the canyon's bank they refrained from food. So they did honor to Coor.

Inside the guest house seats had been arranged for the guests. Behind each seat stood a man who was to serve the one who sat in front of him. His would be the duty to see that all needs were satisfied as the ritual proceeded.

Other men stood ready to greet the guests as they approached the great door that now stood open and supported by stout timber props.

By each prop, erect like a sentry, a young man stood in readiness.

Still others were in readiness to lift the grizzly bear skin of the [63] outer portal. Men stood inside the inner portal, ready to meet Coor and his party as they stooped under the second skin.

The great cedar drums hung in their places; behind each stood a drummer, his hand bound with rawhide thongs. Already they sent booming notes to where the feast was being held.

The guests had eaten, and now they approached the city.

Neas Hiwas, clad in his regalia, advanced to meet them.

On his head rested the head-dress of the One Horned Goat. In his hands were the ceremonial rattles of welcome. As he danced the beaks of birds and hooves of goats brushed together, making smaller rattling sounds. The sea shells on his buckskin leggings rustled with a pleasant sound.

So Neas Hiwas met Coor, the chief of the Eagles.

As the procession approached the outer portal the announcers spoke in deep, measured tones, and told those within what was taking place.

The party came near the doorway, and Chief Coor was the first to enter.

The men at the outer portal lifted the bear skin, dropping it behind him as he passed within.

"Coor, Chief of the Eagles, enters," called the announcer.

Inside the chanting of the women increased in volume, the drums took a deeper note as they received heavier blows, the great horns magnified the voices of men, adding their volume to the storm of sound. It was the traditional welcome to a Great Chief.

Coor came to the inner portal. Great Chief as he was, he needs must stoop to pass under the inner skin.

Inside two men waited to greet him.

As the head of the Kitwanga Chief appeared the Kitselas man who stood behind his chair called the formal greeting: "Kaa - sa -Moonkt" he called — "Here, Chief, is your chair."

And as the serving man spoke the arms of the inner wardens flashed down in sweeping strokes. In each hand reposed a war club. The clubs struck the stooping chief on the head. He fell forward, dead, and tumbled eight feet to the bottom of the pit.

Chief after Chief each according to his rank, followed the leader. Each fell beneath the blows of the war clubs.

After the Chiefs came the Elders. The Wise Men followed in their turn. Man after man met the same fate. The guardians of the props stood alert, ready to knock out the supports from under the door should a man, by chance, sense the danger and seek to flee.

There remained the last to enter. He came closer behind his predecessor than usual, and as he stooped to pass beneath the skin he had a view of a pair of heels swinging backwards and upwards. [64]

Quick wits told him something was amiss. Not in such a manner did a man enter a feast hall. That man ahead must have fallen. That, in turn, suggested danger.

His homage to Medeek was never finished. Like a flash he wheeled, and dashed for the outer door.

So quickly did he move that the sentries had no time to drop the door, but as he sped to the open, one man slashed at him with a knife.

That did not stop him. The blow was not fatal. In spite of a gaping wound he escaped to the forest.

There he evaded pursuit and secured some respite and rest.

Many days later, wounded and weak, he reached his upriver home and told his tale.

That night Kitwanga resounded with the grief of a leaderless people.

32. A Mission Of Peace.

A NEW Coor ruled Kitwanga.

Twice had the salmon come, and throughout these years the young Chief had pondered the problem of Peace or War.

The final feast had been held and now, in the full estate of his Chieftainship, he had to make the decision that would govern the years to come.

A third season passed, and with an impressive escort of warriors he made his way down the river.

Again the fleet of Kitwanga came to rest at the place of the tying up of canoes.

Coor and his party approached the Canyon town with signs of peace and friendship.

Neas Hiwas met him.

Evidently this Coor had recognized the justice of the belated retribution, and had seen that, as his predecessor had not paid the Blood [65] of a Chief, Neas Hiwas, in honor bound had been compelled to take revenge.

So Neas Hiwas welcomed him and called a feast.

Here was the end of the quarrel of centuries. Now peace was established through the Land of Ksan.

Coor, in his speech, was equally anxious that the old feud be dropped.

To Neas Hiwas he said, "For many generations there has been war between your people and my people. In the ancient days my ancestor killed the nephew of Neas Hiwas. Only three years ago, my uncle was killed by you.

"So runs the law of Ksan. The price of the ancient blood has been taken — the score is settled.

"Why continue the trouble? Why waste ourselves and our people with further fighting? Let us have peace."

Here then, was the achievement of the dream of peace that had so often had a place in the Bear Chief's mind. Here was the settlement of the old dispute. Fsem - Y - How, at last, could settle down to a future of peace, contentment, and prosperity.

Intimacy grew with the passing days. Each, to the other, discussed the pleasures of the pleasant years that lay ahead.

And as the visit drew near its close, Coor made his request.

"Peace runs in Ksan," he began. "Our troubles are over. Let us bind our houses more closely together. Your daughter is beautiful, she is comely. It is pleasant to be in her company, I am a young man. It needs must be that I marry a maiden of the Royal Blood. The Law dictates that she be of a different Totem from mine. You are a Bear — I am an Eagle.

"I ask that you give your daughter that she may be my wife. That she may go with me to Kitwanga, and there preside over my house."

Joy ran riot in Fsem - Y - How.

The Blood Tie would cement the compact. Peace, lasting peace, would result.

From the storehouses Neas Hiwas brought royal gifts to shower on the Bride. Hers was a dowry worthy of one who was playing such a momentous part in the life of Medeek.

Coor's canoes were laden with treasure, and with raiment for the damsel, with choice foods.

The Eagle fleet sped upriver with the Chief and his Bride.

The journey would be made in easy stages. It would be a time of stately progress. It would be a regal trip, this bringing the Bear damsel to Kitwanga as Queen.

That first afternoon, as shadows lengthened, the fleet hauled inshore to near where Pacific stands today. [66]

There camp was made for the night. Food was prepared and eaten.

Th cooking fire was piled high with fuel to ward off the chills of the autumn evening.

In the early hours of darkness that camp fire was ringed with happiness and rejoicing, But in the blackness of that night tragedy lurked in the shadows. As the flames leapt to their highest Coor turned to his bride. Before she was aware of what was to come to pass she had been bound and the Eagle chief had hurled her into the heart of the fire. So died the maiden. So Coor, the young Chief of the Eagles, exacted grim recompense for the death of his uncle.

33. A Family Visit.

WINTER passed. Came Lasiyans and the passing of the snows, Lasiweehawn and the busy days of the salmon harvest.

Then, once again, the days grew shorter.

Throughout the busy months Neas Hiwas spent many hours thinking of his daughter in the house of Coor.

With the coming of Lasimedeek he gathered a chosen band of warriors, loaded his canoe with gifts, and made his way upriver.

As the canoes came near the landing at Kitwanga, Chief Coor had a young babe taken to the river bank. As Neas Hiwas drew near, the child was held out to him. The Bear Chief took it in his arms, nursed it for awhile, and returned it to safe keeping on the shore.

Often in this manner did the Ancient People make known that a guest was received in peace.

And thus, as Neas Hiwas nursed it in his arms, he gave the sign that the hospitality of Coor was welcomed by the visitors.

So Neas Hiwas landed, and came near the centre of the town — close to the house where Coor and his family lived.

As he approached the Street of Chiefs Coor met him, dancing, and singing and shaking his rattles. [67]

And that day Coor gave a feast in honor of his guest.

True, Neas Hiwas, as yet, had not been granted permission to see his daughter.

He made a request that he might see her.

But Coor had pointed to the rear of the house. There, as the custom of High Rank was, a partition divided the house into two sections. On the upper floor, above the rear half, quarters were provided for the Queen and her children.

Here the young princes and princesses lived. Here they were trained. Their rank made it necessary that they be not allowed to mingle with the children of the lower people. Such contacts might spoil them for the duties that awaited them in maturity.

At times they were allowed to come to the lower floor, to partake of a little food with their elders,

Silence and dignity marked these visits. When they were over the children returned to their higher quarters.

So, when Neas Hiwas asked to see his daughter, Coor had replied "It is good. I love my wife. But at present she is behind the partition. Later you shall see her."

The request was not repeated. Between chiefs no second petition was made. That would have been degrading to the dignity of a Chief.

Neas Hiwas, following the decorum of his rank, waited until the time should come.

That day Coor had his dancers display their skill for the entertainment of the visitors.

In the open space in front of the Chief's house lissom women performed the traditional steps.

But one woman, as she danced, acted differently from the other members of the troupe. As she danced she bent her body forward until her hands touched the ground, then, slowly rising, swept her hands upward in front of her, continuing with them fully extended, until they were high above her head.

Time and again the movement was repeated; evidently some signal, considered the Bear warriors.

To Neas Hiwas it conveyed no meaning. "She is a woman who jokes" was his conclusion. "She seeks to make fun of us."

Then came the time of gambling.

The next morning the contests started in front of the House of Coor.

Gambling with sticks was a favorite pastime. Rarely did a Chief or a warrior leave his home without his pencil shaped instruments of chance.

So they gambled, Kitwanga men seeking to outwit the men of Kitselas. [68]

And close by, in a house that stood next to Coor's, lived the woman who had danced the strange dance.

A woman who had been born to the Totem of the Bears, who had regard for the well-being of Neas Hiwas and his men.

So, as the Chief gambled, the woman drew her small son to her and charged him with a message to whisper in the ear of the Chief.

Childlike, gripped with the excitement of the news he was carrying, and the importance of his being entrusted with such a message.

"Um - I - Am," he shouted, "They are going to kill you." And all the players heard.

Throughout the morning the game continued. Long into the afternoon the gamblers played.

Again the woman drew the child to her side. This time she gave grave warning to speak slowly, to whisper the message so that the Bear Chief, only, could hear.

And again the lad could not control his voice and shouted, "Um -I - Am, they are going to kill you."

So the afternoon sped. As the hours passed the crowd of onlookers increased. As the shadows lengthened the Street of Chiefs was filled with the men of Kitwanga.

A tenseness seemed to hang in the air.

Suddenly the storm broke. Weapons flashed, in a few seconds the Men of Medeek lay dead, and Neas Hiwas had been made a prisoner and securely lashed with cedar ropes.

Round and round the Chief they twined the strands. At last, like some bundle, he was unable to move, and could do no other than stand erect.

Outside the House of Coor lay the Great Seat.

Three fathoms long, two feet across, and six inches thick. Hewn from a single tree, made as one plank, it was used for some of the rituals of rulership.

Massive, heavy, more than a man could lift.

That day Kitwanga men seized the Seat of Coor, lifted it, and carried it to where Neas Hiwas stood a prisoner.

High over his head they held it. Then slowly, lowering it, allowed the weight to come on his head.

Slowly it pressed him down, bent his body forward.

Helpless, but bearing the strain with dignity, he was subjected to the scoffings and revilings of his enemies.

"Now, Great Chief," they jeered, "Show your skill. Here is the time for you to become a great man. You! You! You who can do such great things. Show us how you kill our Chiefs."

"Speak softly," answered the suffering Chief. "Speak softly and do not boast. [69]

"You have me in your power. You may kill me. But heed my words. Your time will come."

As the weight was allowed to come more fully on the Chief, Neas Hiwas was bent to the ground.

So died the avenger of the ancient wrong.

Then the men of Kitwanga took the body of Neas Hiwas and cast it in the river, in the Skeena, near the great rock it fell.

"Un ge ees" — The Place where the bound man was thrown in" they called the place.

"Um ge ees", even to this day, is the name of the great rock.

But one escaped. A lad, the nephew of Neas Hiwas.

Unable to help when the attack had come he mingled in the crowd. Overlooked in the excitement, he had watched until the final calamity had fallen.

Then he had stolen away, and escaped from the town.

Days passed, and a lad, footsore and weary, came to the Canyon Banks.

A lad bearing a tale of treachery, of disaster and sudden death.

34. Kwin-Watza

UM - I - AM was dead.

Um - I - Am, who had led his people to victory and riches in the
coastal raid, who had avenged the ancient wrong by the House of Coor.

A new treachery had laid him low.

In due time a new Neas Hiwas rose in his place.

A young man, the nephew of the dead chieftain, came to the place of supreme authority, and on his shoulders rested the momentous decisions for the days to come.

At the final feast, when he was fully installed in the Chair of his Grandfathers, it became his responsibility to declare the policy.

In that solemn conclave sat his uncles, Che-Ve-Sar and Saaks, who still stayed until the final word had been said. [70]

Until Neas Hiwas had been satisfied that the future should be peace — or a full payment of the score of Coor, they could not leave
for their new homes in Kitkatla.

Neas Waias, anxious to establish his new town at Gitnidox, also remained at Fsem - Y - How. His responsibility to his ancestors was like to that of his brothers.

For them the feast held much of importance.

When the new Chief rose to state his mind they hung on his words with bated breath.

"We know our history," he began. "To us the story is a familiar one. How our ancient ancestor sought a new land for our people and how the Coor of that day slew his nephew and drove the people forth in confusion,

"Centuries have passed. With arrogance Coor has refused to pay for the blood of the slain prince.

"So it came to pass a few years ago my uncle Neas Hiwas, who took to himself the new name of Um-I-Am, built the great House. There Coor, and his Chiefs, and his Elders, and his Wise Men died.

"The debt was wiped out. The score was even.

"Three years passed, and he who had been raised up to become Coor came to Fsem-Y-How with words of peace on his lips.

"Words of Peace, false words.

"He was received as an honored guest. He was feasted. He left with the daughter of Neas Hiwas as his Bride.

"Now we know what happened that night he left our city. We have learned how he slew the damsel, cruelly gave her to the bridal of the roaring flames of the camp fire.

"Two years ago when Um-I-Am went to Kitwanga to see his daughter he, too, was taken, and with his warriors, cruelly slain.

"The score had been evened. Now it is out of balance.

"One thing, only, remains to be done. There is no other course for Neas Hiwas and the men of the Totem of Medeek.

"I prepare for war. When all is ready I go to Kitwanga and there Coor shall die and the matter be settled."

Anger, bitter and lasting, had eaten at the hearts of the Medeek men sirice Neas Hiwas had died.

So this decision brought to them satisfaction and a determination that this time there should be a definite conclusion of the matter.

Once again the men of Medeek turned their energies to preparing for the day when retribution should sweep on the upriver town.

As in the days before Klew Nu was burned the hunters ranged the forests and brought to the city an unending supply of game.

New food boxes were fashioned as of old, and as they were completed they were filled and sealed. [71]

Weapons, bows, arrows, spears and clubs were readied; many new ones were made. Canoes were repaired and a new fleet built against the day of the war party setting forth.

Five years passed before Neas Hiwas was satisfied.

Stores at Fsem-Y-How were useless to warriors who fought seventy miles upriver.

Advance bases had to be established, stocked, and much freighting had to be done before the war material had been brought within striking distance of the enemy.

One year that work consumed. One year of back breaking toil as laden canoes were poled and paddled — at times hauled with lines — against the fast running river.

"Kwin - Watza", — The Place of the Otter, was chosen. Here, some fifteen miles below the town of Coor, steep rocky shores bounded the river.

In these fastnesses the Men of Medeek stored their foods, and their weapons, and their Hag-Wa-T-Za against the day when they would attack,

So that year passed.

35. Tum Barkt.

AS SUMMER waned activity on the Canyon Banks increased.

Then there came the most trying time. Preparations were completed, a time of waiting lay ahead.

Upriver, at Kitwanga, each succeeding September had been a time of anxious care.

The Dry Month — The Month of Wars — had come with the last warm days of summer, and Coor and his warriors had kept vigil lest the men from the Canyon come to exact recompense for the wrong that had been done.

Years had passed, but with each one the watch had been renewed. [72]

So, in this decisive year, the Eagle people of Kitwanga had stood guard as autumn had closed in.

The Month of Wars waned; and tension lessened.

October and the rains came — "Danger is passed" said Coor, and his men resumed their normal lives once more.

But with the gathering clouds of the wet season the Medeeks launched their canoes. The great fleet surged upstream and came to Kwin - Watza where their stores awaited them.

Night travel on a swiftly running river is dangerous.

But when darkness fell the war canoes and those that carried the food and weapons drew out from Kwin - Watza and breasted the current once more.

Miles slipped astern, and they came to where the high lands of the river ended.

Here. marking the boundary between the rocky ridges and the flat lands that lay ahead, a creek flowed to meet the river.

Turn Barkt they called it. "The creek that flows out of the thigh of the high bank." '

On its bank rested the western edge of the Eagle town.

Here the Men of Medeek put ashore. In the forest that flanked its banks they ranged themselves with weapons, with Mag - Wa - T - Za;

with instruments of death and destruction, and others to secure the many prisoners they planned to take,

Quietly, stealthily, the battle line formed.

No hint of impending doom reached Kitwanga.

The town gradually settled to the slumbers of the night as angry eyes watched fading fires from the forest rim. [73]

36. The Price Of Peace.

MIDNIGHT came. Three more hours passed, and shadowy forms stole, through the length and breadth of the town.

The war cry, the Cry of the Owl "Ooooh, Eeeeh, Oooh, Oo, Oo, Oo," rang through the stillness of the night as the Medeek men answered the signal for attack.

Hag-Wa-T-Za flared at the touch of fire. The bark roofs caught, and in a minute the town was a roaring furnace.

Some houses escaped that night. So large was the town that there were not enough warriors of Medeek men to fire them all.

And death rode on the roaring flames.

Lulled to security by the passing of the Month of War, Coor and his men were totally unprepared. They stumbled from their houses to be slaughtered as they came into the glare of the fires.

Spears stabbed, bows twanged, and arrows sped to their marks. Clubs, deftly swung, crushed skulls with single blows.

Confusion reigned, and in the turmoil, Coor, himself wounded, made his way to the river bank.

With a scattering of warriors he crossed to the other side. Up the valley of the Kit-wan-cool they followed the trails, until three miles to the north they rallied on a small round hill to make their final stand against the foe.

Many prisoners were taken that night.

The ancient law still ran in Ksan. Women and children were safe from harm. Theirs, in the years to come, would be the lot of slaves.

Many women and children were gathered in by the Medeek men that night. So many that their safe-keeping was a problem.

This had been foreseen in the councils of Neas Hiwas. Preparations had been made.

As each prisoner was taken a small hole was pierced in the lip; a small cedar cord was passed through and made fast. [74]

Near at hand a long cedar rope stretched. To this rope the small cords were made fast. It became a weaving line of people going into life long servitude.

Deadly as the battle was, it soon waned.

Before it ended news came to Neas Hiwas of the escape of Coor.

Much had been accomplished, but while the Eagle chief remained alive and defiant the end was not in sight.

So, in the waning hours of the night, the avenging Chiefs gathered warriors and set out in pursuit.

The trail was easy to follow. It led to a small round hill.

As the Medeek men drew near lights were seen in the four houses that sat on the summit.

Here lived four families of the Totem of the Crow.

Activity at this hour betokened something unusual afoot.

Cautiously Neas Hiwas deployed his men, swinging a cordon until the place was surrounded.

The hill was small, but steep.

On the crest lay great logs. A push would start them rolling. A few men could bring great havoc to an attacking force.

The Men of Medeek, filled with the lust of blood prepared to face the death dealing timbers, but Neas Hiwas held them in check.

"Wait," he told them, "Coor is trapped. He knows it. He must do something soon; or he must propose some plan for the settlement of the matter. Wait! He cannot escape. Let the next move come from him."

So they waited, while, above, Coor and his few men stood at bay, desperate in their plight, ready to sell their lives for the blood of their enemies when the attack came.

Dawn came. With it came clearer vision.

Round the hill Coor saw the ring of his enemies.

The situation was desperate, hopeless. He might kill some of these warriors who waited below, but in a fight he and his men would go to their graves.

Then, in the growing light. Neas Hiwas stood forth and spoke to Coor,

"Coor, Chief of the Eagles," he began, "Let your mind go back to the ancient days. Think well of the time when my ancestor Neas Hiwas led his people to a new land. Disaster had fallen on my people. Death and privation had marched through our city of Tum - L - Hama. So it came to pass as the people of Medeek journeyed they came to a town. Your ancestor, the Coor of that day, was the ruler.

"At first Coor was friendly. Later he made the lot of my people hard. Finally he drove them out, and in the fighting he killed a Prince of the House of Neas Hiwas. [75]

"Many years have gone since then. Many men have sat on the Chair of Coor. But none of your Chiefs has followed the Law of Ksan and paid for the blood of that prince.

"So it has come to pass that when all hope of a settlement by peace had gone Um - I - Am, my uncle, killed your uncle and the score was evened.

"That was right. That was proper. That was the fulfillment of the Law: the Law that rules over your House and over my House.

"But to you this was not enough. Treachery was in your blood. You came to Fsem - Y - How talking peace. With you, as you returned, went a Princess as your Bride. She you slew in the blaze of the camp fire on the bridal night.

"The next year, when my uncle came to you to see his daughter you took him by stealth and slew him.

"Now the score is balanced.

"This night I have burned your town. This night your women and children have started on a journey to captivity. They will be the slaves of Medeek.

"Now, like a wounded animal, you stand at bay before the hunters.

"Still there is hope.

"Blood is not what I seek.

"To you I offer an honourable settlement.

"Pay for the blood that lies on the hands of Coor and all shall be well.

"Refuse to pay and I come up the hill and slay you."

The decision had to be made. Coor, Chief of a House where arrogance had reigned, saw fate confronting him.

No escape was possible.

Surrender — and honourable settlement was the only way out.

As the sun rose in the east he capitulated.

"As you say," he replied, "I settle, we pay the score of Blood, and peace shall be between your people and my people."

Behind that hill, in the morning hours, the long standing accounts were settled.

From the People of the Crows, Coor borrowed buckskins. With these he paid the ransom of the blood.

With buckskins he paid for the ancient killing of the Prince; and for the killing of Um - I - Am at Kitwanga.

Neas Hiwas, on his part, made settlement for the slaying of Coor at Fsem - Y - How-

And Coor paid for the killing of the Princess on her bridal night.

Finally, as was the Law of Ksan, he gave Neas Hiwas a woman of high rank to be his wife, this in payment for the life of a Chief who had been killed. [76]

37. The Feast Of Peace.

LASTING peace was sealed between the Eagle people of Kitwanga, and the Men of Medeek who lived on the Canyon's rim.

A great feast was held that night.

From such resources as had escaped the destruction of battle, stores were drawn to give lavish entertainment to the victors.

That night Neas Hiwas and Coor' swore lasting peace between their peoples. Old scores were settled, better that they be forgotten. So it was agreed.

But in that settlement an added price was taken from the vanquished.

From that long line of prisoners some older women were chosen. These Neas Hiwas released.

But, fearing treachery, he took with him the younger women and children.

Their fate was a grim reminder of the vengeance of the Men of Medeek, an assurance that the rising generation would not dwell on that night of terror and with coming manhood seek war and retaliation. [77]

38. Partings

THE DAYS had shortened before Neas Hiwas returned to Fsem - Y -How.

Once more he called a feast.

It was a feast of triumph, of rejoicing that the days of war with the men of the upper river were ended.

And it was a feast of parting from the families pledged to move to new homes in distant parts.

Che-Ve-Sar and Saaks still awaited permission to move to Kit-katla. Neas Waias longed to make a start at Gitnidox.

At that feast Neas Hiwas recounted the History once more.

"I remember how Stee How slew my ancient uncle," he began.

"When another Stee How was killed that account was settled-

"I remember the story of the Prince of our House who was killed by Coor. To settle that matter my Uncle killed Coor, and that account was settled.

"Then my Uncle, Um-I-Am, gave his daughter to be the wife of the new Coor. Coor burned her, and later killed Um-I-Am.

"Now we have fought with Coor. We have triumphed. He has paid the Blood.

"I am satisfied. I plan no other wars.

"My Uncles! For years you have awaited this end. You have stayed here while other homes called you. You have helped me. You have upheld the honor of Medeek.

"No longer is there need of your'aid in warfare.

"Go, then, in peace. Go to the place you have chosen as your homes. Go in peace, and the brotherhood of Medeek will stretch far beyond the bounds of the Land of Ksan."

Winter, that quiet time, saw unusual activity in Fsem-Y-How that year. [78]

Much work was done as long cherished family possessions were prepared for the journey. Many feasts were held as friends and relatives entertained the families that would leave the town.

Spring came, and winter's ice broke up. Once more the Skeena flowed clear and free past the Canyon walls.

Before the waters rose with the freshets of spring the Chiefs loaded their goods, and their families, and set out on their journeys.

Early summer saw Che-Ve-Sar and Saaks settling their families at the head of the lagoon where Kitkatla stands.

Before fall came Neas Waias had built the beginnings of his town at Gitnidox, and with his people had taken possession of the rich lands that lay along the river's course.

Down through the ages Chiefs of Medeek have held sway at Kitkatia, have cared for the people, and ruled as they were given the power by Loot-Quintz-Ampy-Wich.

To Gitnidox Neas Waias took with him his wife of the Wolf Totem.

Since then, from descendents of that wife, the Totem of the Wolf has been supreme in that town.

39. Quiet Years.

YEAR followed year in the Land of Ksan.

Each year saw contentment and peace reign along the banks of the Skeena.

Old hatreds and grievances faded into the past. New generations rose. matured and aged in a land where food was plentiful, raiment easily come by and ample hours remained for social contacts and leisure.

Throughout, the years when suspicion was rife the people had travelled but little.

Life had been semi-nomadic; moves had been made with the recurring seasons. In the springtime families moved to the fishing stations that had been allotted to them by their chiefs. Berrying grounds were visited when the bushes drooped with luscious fruit. In the waning [79] year hunters fared forth to the valleys that had been part of the family heritage, and from which, for long generations, meat and clothing had come.

Semi-nomadic, but within strictly confined areas.

But with the growing peace there came a greater desire to visit other towns in the Ksan, to become acquainted with other people, and to establish friendships that would continue throughout the years.

So it was with the Men of Medeek — the men who dwelt on the Canyon rim.

For them there were reasons for trips of friendship.

Che-Ve-Sar and Saaks welcomed friendship. At Kitkatla they delighted in visits with their relatives, made them welcome.

Neas Waias, whose home at Gitnidox was on the main route of river travel, saw much of the people who journeyed on the Skeena. Here was a convenient place to stop for the night. Here his relatives rested on their trips.

So the bonds of blood and friendship were held taut. The federation of the scattered peoples of Medeek grew stronger with each succeeding generation.

Other towns lay along the river's bank. Towns to which Coast dwellers came when the salmon swarmed in the creeks, towns whose navigators held commerce with the haughty Haidas on the islands across the bitter water.

Suspicion was dead, friendship flowered. It was only natural that travellers should linger at these points and come to know the dwellers who made their homes at the mouths of the rivers and creeks.

So, thirty miles downstream from the Canyon, Neas Ham Geiss ruled over the town of Git-luet-zar, close by where the waters of the southern lake[22] joined those of the Skeena.

From the town a rich valley reached to the south and east. Up the river millions of salmon swam each year to spawn in the lake and its feeder creeks.

Here the Eagle people lived well, waxed rich.

In time they became the friends of the Medeek people.

There came a time when a sister of Neas Hiwas became the bride of the Eagle Chieftain.

A great wedding feast was held at Fsem-Y-How, and the Chief and his bride went downstream, canoes laden deeply with gifts from the maiden's people,

Less than two years later a son was born to the Royal pair, "born to the Eagle, his Mother a Bear" as the lineage reads. Neas Nawah they called him. [80]

Eight years passed, and the lad waxed strong. Wisdom had its beginnings in his countenance; strength and dignity were in his bearing.

Day after day the Chief watched his son. Here was a fitting successor for his post as Ruler.

Normally succession followed different lines. Unless a special Law was invoked the son of the eldest sister of a Chief inherited the "Power" when his uncle died.

Neas Ham Geiss pondered the matter for many months.

At last he made a decision and called a feast.

A great feast, one to which came all the lesser chiefs, the Elders, the Wise Men — and all

---

[22] Lakelse Lake, twelve miles south of Terrace.

the people of the town.

From his storehouse Neas Ham Geiss took gifts for all, gifts that varied according to the ranks of those who received them.

From his storehouse he chose buckskins — "A Man" of the finest, and piling one on the other, constructed a platform of the velvety skins.

To the top of this pile he lifted his son, Neas Nawah.

Then, turning to the watching throng, "This day," he proclaimed, "My son goes to my Chair. To-day he becomes Ruler in my stead. Until he is of age I shall watch over the people, act in his stead. But when he is grown to manhood he will be your .Ruler. From this day on. Neas Nawah is ruler of Git-Luet-Zar."

Thus. in the self-sacrificial manner of the special Law the father abdicated, the son was raised up in his stead.

Born to the Eagle, his Mother a Bear, descent ran through the distaff side of the family.

And so it came to pass that the Eagle Totem moved to the place of second rank.

Medeek, the Grizzly Bear, the Totem of the Canyon folk, became supreme.

So was another link forged in the lengthening chain of the federation of Medeek. A chain that stretched along the river banks into the Land of Ksan. [81]

40. Nagwalik

THE mountain top is the place of vision, of vision and self searching.

There man feels puny. There, viewing the immensity of the works of *Gyamk* the Sun God, he comes to see something of his smallness.

So it was with the Men of Medeek.

Often as they hunted the heights they chose a resting place.

Usually an eminence from where they could see the distant horizons.

At these times speculation was often rife.

True, in their journeyings they had seen much land, Yet before their eyes lay lands of which they had no knowledge.

Often from the flanking mountains that walled the valley of the Zymoetz these hunters viewed the country to the south.

A close matted mass of dark green lay beneath their feet. It stretched away to distant mountains. It bespoke the dense conifers of the forest in which game abounded.

South, a few miles, a glistening lake broke the somber mass. North and south it ran, at each corner a short, stubby arm. Its contours made the picture of a bear skin stretched for drying.

Another silver sheet lay beneath the far off mountains. Another lake, the hunters supposed. In their rangings the hunters had never reached it. The need had never arisen.

They knew of it: but to them the nature of that water remained unknown.

Out of the southern forest, one year, when Lasimedeek came round and men spent leisure in visiting and exploring, a strange man came northwards.

Seized with a keen curiosity for what lay in the mountains ahead he moved by easy stages day after day.

He came to the shores of the bearskin lake, ranged the mountain slopes that flanked its eastern side. [82]

From the heights he saw the waters of a mighty river.

Still northward he came, and picking up the trails of hunters, he followed one.

A few miles and he came to the bank of the river.

Close at hand lay Fsem-Y-How.

He came in peace. He was received with gladness.

To Neas Hiwas he told of his journeys. His home, he said, was at Kitamaat. It lay on the shores of the northern end of the distant water.

That water was salt, he explained. It was not a lake, but an arm of the great salt sea in which many islands were found.

"Eagle is my Totem," he told the Chief. "We are of the People who live in the great land across the stormy sea."

Taller, more lithe in build, he differed greatly from the Medeek men, typical of the Haidas who lived in the land that white men call the Queen Charlotte Islands.

Feast after feast was given in his honour. House followed house as the leaders of the Canyon dwellers vied with each other to entertain their guest.

To his new friends he told a tale of migration.

Of a peaceful life on the great island to the west, of abundance and ease — and growing carelessness.

The Laws of *Gyamk* were forgotten. A spirit of malicious sport entered the hearts of some.

There came a time, when at a great feast, a living frog was thrust into the heart of the fire.

Disaster swooped as the Narnaks wrought retribution.

Dispersal followed. The young man's ancestors crossed the wind-swept straits, found a new home on the mountain-rimmed coast.

Later, seeking a more sheltered abode, they moved again. So they came to Kitamaat.

Warm, bright days sped by. The season of the rains drew near and the young man turned his face to the south, and retraced his steps to his seashore home.

Before he left he promised that when Lasimedeek came again he would return, promised that with him would come others of his people who would visit with the Men of Medeek.

The year passed.

With the Dry Month the young man returned. With him came some of his friends.

Again a time of feasting celebrated the presence of the guests.

Many times Neas Hiwas let his eyes dwell on the young men. Well built, presentable, intelligence and initiative were written on their countenances.

"Here," he mused, "are men after my own heart. As yet Fsem-Y- How [83] has but one Totem. Better far that another stands by the side of it. What Totem is to be preferred to that of the Eagle?"

In many talks he sought information.

From the young man he learned that three Houses of the Eagles stood on the shores of Kitamaat. Three great families had sought refuge and home there.

"It would please me to meet more of your people," the Chief told his guests. "Happy should I be if they would come here. Your 'Neas' as my partner, so would we be strong, two Totems side by side, one helping the other. The land is great. If they will come there is enough for all."

"Last year, when I returned," the young man replied, "I told my people of your land, and of the welcome I had received. The story pleased them. Often they spoke of seeing it for themselves."

So Neas Hiwas pressed the invitation. So the young men left, promising to make the welcome known.

Snow blanketed the land that year as winter came. But with the returning warmth, as *Gyamk* turned the snow to running waters, preparations for a journey were completed on the shores of Kitamaat Arm.

As the green mosses under their feet dried, and became springy once more, the Eagle families set out on their northern trip.

The Wedeene Rivers, running with the spring freshets, were crossed. A few miles brought them to a small lake that nestled in the forest. The creek that ran from it led them northwards to one of the paws of the bear-shaped lake.

Mile after mile, journeying easily, they made their way until, at last, they came to where the waters boiled through the rock walled canyon.

Here, with due ceremonial, with dancing and the pleasant sound of rattles, Neas Hiwas met them and bade them welcome,

So to Fsem-Y-How came Neas Na-Gwalik, Head Chief of the Eagles. With him came his brother chiefs, Ghard Har, and Skhilas Ghilas.

Busy months followed, warm months of summer in which the Eagle people established their homes.

Close by the Men of Medeek they built. As the years sped their Totems stood side by side with those of Medeek.

Power, added power, came with them to Fsem-Y-How. As the years sped by prosperity and contentment grew.

The alliance was ideal. The Eagle people excelled the highest hopes of the Bear Chief.

One sister of Ghard Har, especially, won his favor. Before many moons had passed she had entered his house as his wife.

True, several wives already were there, that was the custom of the native Chiefs. [84]

But this maiden brought with her the sealing of a new compact, a new alliance. Her presence cemented the federation of the Totems with a closer tie — the tie of blood.

Years passed and a son of that union grew from faltering steps to sturdy boyhood. Of all the children of Neas Hiwas he was the chosen one. "Here, in the fusing of bloods of two great Peoples" thought the Bear Chief, "is the fitting one to carry on the task of Rulership."

The idea became fixed, unshaken by the passing years it settled into a resolve.

Dignity and strength was in this lad.

There came a time when Neas Hiwas called a feast.

Like that of his Eagle brother of Git-Luet-Zar, it was a feast for the transfer of power.

From the stores of Medeek came the skins that were given to the guests. Others, the finest of all, were made into a mound, and on this pedestal Neas Hiwas raised his son.

Proudly he faced his people, and the Eagles who stood with them.

"This day," he said, "I raise up my son. He takes my Chair."

"To him goes the Chair of the Headship of Medeek.

"His will be the duty to rule over all.

"His will be the Power to be first in the Councils.

"To the Bear Chiefs there remains the power over the land: theirs will be the right to rule the Canyon; to say who shall pass and journey to the upper country."

So passed the supreme power from the Men of Medeek. Down through the ages that power has been held by the leader of the people of the Sitting Eagle.

But in the hands of the Men of Medeek has stayed the rulership of the river route. In their hands has remained the power to control the commerce of the great river.

Only with the consent of Medeek have the Sea Shore dwellers travelled to the upper country, and traded there.

Only with their consent have the men of the upper reaches of the Skeena been allowed to pass through the Canyon and have commerce with the men who have their homes by the sea.

At times Medeek has barred the Canyon. At those times commerce has ceased until the ban has been removed. [85]

41. Kitselas

PLEASANT years sped by.

Each year brought the accustomed duties. Each held a goodly measure of relaxation.

Medeek and the Eagle lived peacefully side by side.

Peace reigned, food abounded.

There came a time when Fsem-Y-How became cramped and too small to hold the peoples of the Totems.

Across the Canyon the land was more open. The Kleanza Mountain had its foot two miles back from the river's rim. In the intervening space lay ample room for wide expansion.

So, after many councils, it was decided a move should be made.

On the flat topped hill, east of the Canyon's bank, a new town rose.

Each totem had its area; room was left for the growth of population.

In front of his House Neas Hiwas erected a new Totem. The symbolic Bear topped it, the *Guell Haast* decorated its base.

Neas Nagwalik had skilled men carve a great cedar trunk. His House was marked by the Totem of the Eagle.

So the years sped.

From the coast came a new People, families of the Totem of the Crow.

Koorm was their chief.

To them was extended a welcome. To them was given a site for their town.

Three Totems. The might of three strong Peoples, ruled the Canyon country.

Prosperity grew with the passing years. [86]

42. The Arrow

AN ARROW broke the sylvan peace of Kitselas.

An arrow sped out of the night and found its mark in the breast of Neas Nagwalik, Chief of the Eagles.

Straight to his heart it made its way. The Chief died before morning broke.

Whose arrow had thus wrought havoc in the serenity of life of the Canyon folk?

The question was a perplexing one.

Arrows bore marks of individual craftsmanship. Their owners were known to all.

From hand to hand this shaft passed.

It was unlike any arrow seen in the country!

Smooth, glasslike, was the shaft. Delicate work had gone into the making of the missile.

Some enemy, evidently, someone unknown to the people had drawn near.

So were the people troubled and disturbed.

If one arrow, then others of its kind might be near at hand.

Neas Nagwalik had died, who would be the next victim?

The matter brooked no delay. The mystery must be solved — measures taken to protect the people from the unknown danger.

Here was something for all to consider.

The proper thing was done, a feast was called.

In the great guest house the people gathered. To each man came the opportunity to hold and examine the weapon; to offer some idea for the solution.

From hand to hand the shaft passed. Each man studied it. Each, in turn, admitted he did not know its maker.

Close by the door, that day, two men sat. [87]

Unlike their fellows they held their blankets high. The edges of the robes came under their noses. Their mouths and chins were hidden.

In due time the arrow came to one of these men. He examined it, and a light of comprehension dawned in his eyes.

Turning to his fellow he whispered, "Oh. Yes. There is no doubt. This arrow belongs to Bellum Owa."

Feigning puzzlement, he passed it to his neighbour.

The second man, also seemed bewildered. Long he held it, so long that the talk in the house drifted to other subjects.

Fresh interests held the gathered people. They did not see the two men steal quietly from the house.

Some minutes later a man remembered the whispered words. "Bellum Owa". Who was that? He looked towards the doorway.

Too late, the men had gone!

Quick suspicion seized him. Swiftly he rose and went to the doorway. Up the trail, leading to the great beaver dam, two figures moved.

The men! The ones who had some idea of the answer of the arrow.

Along the trail he sped, intent on catching the men and putting his question.

The sound of his steps came to the men ahead. Looking back they saw their pursuer — and they began to run.

Fleet of foot, the Bear man gave chase. Quickly he closed the space between himself and the men he sought.

At the dam he was almost within touching distance. Their escape seemed impossible.

But there was no hesitation.

Straight to the brink they ran. They scarcely paused.

They dived into the waters of the lake.

Close by two beavers rose.

Grasped between his teeth, one animal held a glasslike arrow.

Beaver men!

That was the answer.

That, too, was the answer of the high held robes.

Only so had these beings been able to hide the chisel teeth of their kind. [88]

43. Twin Towns

FOR CENTURIES the Beaver Lake had been a prized possession of the people of Kitselas.

In its marshes generations of beavers had lived. There they hadbuilt their houses. There they had raised their young.

Beaver, so many that they could not be counted, had had theirhomes in the still waters.

From their numbers the Kitselas had taken a steady toll. Never depleting the numbers of animals in the colony they had taken of the increase.

Rich skins, skins for robes, and garments.

Good meat for eating, sinews for making their goods.

Thus, year after year, men and beavers had lived side by side.

But in these latter years the balance had been disturbed.

Perhaps it was because of the coming of people from far distant parts, people who had not been accustomed to such plenty.

Or, it may be, that the regard for the Law of *Gyamk* had been dulled with increasing prosperity.

Whatever the reason, there was no doubt that the beaver had been killed ruthlessly.

They had been hunted for sport. Many times their bodies had been left to rot on the margin of the lake.

Now, with disaster striking suddenly at the leading Chief, people began to fear.

Once again the Narnaks had reached out and punishment had fallen on an offending people.

Here was the fulfilment of that ancient prophesy: "Torment the Beavers, and the King of the Beavers will claim your life in return". [89]

If one had died in that retribution who could tell how many more would fall before the score was evened?

Some measure was needed to protect the people.

Long hours were spent in Council. Many suggestions were put forth.

At last a plan was agreed upon. A self imposed punishment was chosen.

Better to lose the beavers than that lives might be wasted. As long as the beavers remained in the lake the people would be afraid; other deaths might come.

Only one way was open by which the beavers would leave, seeking new homes.

With this decision came new problems.

Throughout the centuries the Men of Medeek had ruled the Canyon.

Theirs had been the power to permit or deny to others the privilege of passing through the gorge. With the dam in place river traffic had been controlled with ease.

But with running water, and no barrier, the task would become more difficult.

Their city lay on the east bank of the Canyon. Travellers could keep close to the west shore and pass in defiance to Medeek, who had the "Power".

That west bank must be guarded.

Two towns must rest on, and dominate, the canyon banks.

Kitselas must be divided, and from the twin towns the rule must be maintained.

Once again Fsem-Y-How was a scene of building as half the people prepared to move there and re-establish their homes.

In Council the plan was carefully worked out.

All must have their share in the duties.

To ensure this three Totems would dominate each side of the river. Lesser chiefs were allotted new responsibilities. They became the Heads of Houses as the plan demanded.

To Neas Hiwas remained the titular headship of the town. With him, on the west bank, Gard Har, his brother-in-law, would rule the Eagle people. Oon, the Crow Chief would make the third on the left side of the Canyon.

Across from them, on the hill-top town of Kitselas, Liget-Was-Arskt, nephew of Neas Hiwas was to take up his Chieftainship. Neas Nagwalik, head of the Eagles stayed with him, while Gubber Skhun would be the ruler of the Crows. [90]

So it was decided. So the plan was worked out.

Building was pushed apace. Possessions were moved across the dam. On the west side Fsem-Y-How again became the home of the People.

When all had been completed preparations were made for the great task of tearing out the thick wall of trees, and poles, and brush and clay of the dam of the Beaver people.

Close at hand lay a new rope of cedar bark, a rope that the Men of Medeek planned to stretch across the Canyon, a rope that would be the symbol of their Power, and a sign that the Law of the River travel still ran between the rock walls.

44. Wreckage

THE RIVER was at the low stage.

Little water ran over the top of the dam as the work began. Down to the canyon's floor went a wise man. A man skilled in the knowledge of building. One, therefore who could measure the stresses that played through the masses of the dam when it began to weaken.

Carefully he chose his starting point.

Slowly he took away the first tangles of brush and cakes of clay. The beginnings of a tunnel showed. In its mouth he brought timbers and fitted them to brace the sides and roof.

Foot by foot he won his way into the heart of the wall. With each step he took fresh bracings and set them to hold all secure till the task was near completion.

Foot by foot, slowly the work progressed.

Finally there came a time when oozing moisture began to show.

Now all was ready. There remained only the final weakening.

Then inrushing waters — and collapse.

That day, when water began to show, work stopped.

Early the next morning the hunters gathered on the canyon's banks. Each man carried a long spear, sharp pointed, barb tipped. [91]

When they had assembled, the wise man entered the tunnel for the last time.

At its inner face he knocked out the last props he had set in place. Retreating, he removed each support as he came to it.

As the strain grew there came groanings as the hidden trees took up new stresses.

Fresh trickles of water broke through the weaker spots. Before he had retreated to the entrance a growing stream told that the end was near.

In the entrance he pulled out the last timbers, and sprang for safety.

As he leaped to higher ground a rumbling and crashing sounded at his heels as the water's pressure overcame all resistance.

Mud, tree trunks, poles, water soaked brush, a mass of debris began to sweep down the canyon as the rushing waters tore the gap wider.

In a matter of minutes the lake's water, in full spate, swept all before it as it surged down the canyon in a tumult.

On the shores, the watchers saw the lake's level begin to drop.

Inch by inch the water receded from the margin; low spots close to the shore began to bare. The domes of beaver houses rose higher and still higher above the waters.

Inside those houses the beavers began to be disturbed. Something unusual was happening — something that threatened their homes and their mode of life.

45. Bellum Owa.

STILL the waters dropped. Finally into the minds of the animals there entered a certainty of disaster.

Each minute increased the number of animals that swam on the surface seeking to find what had come to pass.

Then, downstream, came a beaver. No dam confronted him. Caught in the quickening waters near the canyon's lip he sped for the gap. [92]

As he entered, spears flashed. Sharp points pierced his vitals. Barbs held fast and he was drawn ashore.

The exodus of the beaver increased.

Soon the hunters were working at top speed.

Many beavers died that day, but some escaped.

Last of all came a giant. Gubbers Skhun, on the right side, set his spear. On the left bank an Eagle of the House of Ghard Har struck at the same instant.

They pulled, striving to bring to the shore the Beaver King — and the spear of the Crow Chieftain slipped.

Held fast by the barb of the Eagle's spear the beaver came ashore.

Truly a giant beaver, unlike other beavers.

For on his back there was the figure of a man. Legs, arms, body and face, all were complete.

A man riding, face upturned, on the beaver's back.

So died Bellum Owa, the Beaver King.

So, falling to the spear of the Eagle, his history has been recorded on the Totem of that People.

46. Fear.

FEAR of the future spurred the Kitselas to the killing of the beaver. A dread that overcame their sense of justice.

They had planned a self-inflicted punishment. They had turned to a deed of revenge.

Their Council had decided to drive the beaver people from the lake. Instead, they had sought to utterly destroy the tribe. The deed was done.

And fear of the Narnaks gripped them as their excitement died. Fear, icy, heart-gripping and breath-taking, surged into their souls. The slaying had been great. The retribution might be equally severe.

To that terrified people life close to the canyon's bank was unthinkable; at any moment a messenger from *Gyamk* might strike. [93]

High above the canyon, just downstream from Fsem-Y-How, a great rock spur jutted out to form a cliff wall.

Here, on its crest, they sought refuge.

Here, for years they lived. Large pits were dug. New houses built for comfort and protection.

On the east side of the Canyon the Kitselas left their town. For many moons they camped at Kit-Asish — "The edge of the Lake" — until they felt all danger had passed.

Still later the men of Fsem-Y-How moved to a flat land a mile below the canyon.

Here the Narnaks of the beaver found them. Here, beneath the ground, in from the river banks, the beavers drove their tunnels.

So it came about that as men went about their affairs they came to places where a booming sound came from beneath their feet.

Still later, as the surface soil was undermined, men fell into the pits and were drowned in the water that flowed in from the river.

Many men died, and there seemed no end to the matter.

At last, seeking more solid ground, they returned to Fsem-Y-How.

But not for centuries did the Medeek men return to the tunnelled land.

"Doon-Doon" — they called the place.

Doon-Doon — "The place where the Beavers drowned the men".

METLAKAHTLA

A TRUE NARRATIVE OF THE RED MAN

By GEORGE T.B. DAVIS

Chicago
THE RAM'S HORN COMPANY 1904
Facsimile Reproduction 1964

METLAKAHTLA
By JULIA A. WILLIAMS

Metlakahtla! beauteous isle,
On the broad Pacific's breast;
What hath God wrought? an holy calm
Where once was fierce unrest.
In the dense light of human hearts
A glorious Light hath shined —
A dazzling shaft from Calvary's cross
With love and mercy twined.
Slumber, to wake no more,
Within that city's sea-girt wall,
The passions once untamed
That held our brethren there in thrall.
Metlakahtla! precious jewel
On the bosom of the sea,
God hath made thee what thou art,
Unto Him the glory be.

Chapter I
The Visit of the Warship

THE British warship H.M.S. *Virago* was steaming northward through the Pacific Ocean near the southern boundary of Alaska. The steady throb of the ship's engines was the only sound that broke the stillness of the beautiful mountainous islands among which the vessel was wending its way.

It was the year 1853, and several days had passed since the ship had left Victoria, five hundred miles southward. The warship had kept close to the Canadian coast throughout the journey and was now nearing Queen Charlotte Islands, where an American schooner had recently been plundered and destroyed by the savage Indian inhabitants. The warship had come to punish the offenders.

The commander of the vessel, Captain [10] J.C. Prevost, was a robust Englishman of middle age, who was as thorough a Christian as he was valiant a commander. After anchoring in the bay a searching investigation of several days was made, but Captain Prevost was unable to fix the guilt upon any particular tribe. Hence, he assembled the various chiefs and gave them stern warning of the power of the white man, telling them how easily his guns could thunder forth shot and shell and destroy every vestige of the village. In his own mind, Captain Prevost believed that Edensaw, the head chief of the Hydah tribes, was the guilty person, but certain proof being lacking, he could take no steps for his punishment.   Before leaving, however, he took one step, very unusual, alas, among the commanders of warships. Calling Edensaw to one side he presented him with a copy of the New Testament, on the fly-leaf of which was written: "From Captain Prevost, H.M.S. 'Satellite,' trusting that the bread thus cast upon the waters may be found after many days."

As the Captain handed the Indian chief the volume, little did be dream of the beautiful sequel to the action which would occur a quarter of a century later.

After leaving Queen Charlotte Islands, the ship kept her course northward for nearly a hundred miles further until Fort Simpson, a station of the Hudson Bay [11] Company, was reached. This trading-post was a heavily barricaded fort, surrounded by a large body of fierce Tsimshean Indians. So savage were these tribes that the inhabitants of the fort had on certain occasions kept sentinels on guard day and night for weeks at a time for fear of an attack and wholesale massacre. Captain Provost's visit to the fort was for the double purpose of ascertaining whether all was well with the garrison, and of making some needed repairs to his vessel.

"When the ship had dropped anchor the Commander ordered a number of small boats lowered and, surrounded by a heavy guard of armed marines, lie was rowed ashore and the company marched to Fort Simpson, several hundred yards distant. As lie passed through the long lines of fierce-looking and painted Indians, Captain Provost was struck at once by their fine physique, but equally impressed by the degraded, savage, murderous appearance of their faces. He was filled with compassion for these ignorant children of the forest, who knew naught of love or peace, or true joy, but whose lives from the cradle to the grave were filled with fear and cruelty, and hate, and murder. At this time no protestant missionary had ever come into the Northland to tell the red men of the, message from God contained in the Bible, and the only religion they knew was the Devil Worship taught by the cruel medicine men. [12]

Arriving at the Fort, Captain Prevost received a hearty welcome from the garrison, for they thought the presence of .the warship would have a salutary effect upon the red men. For a number of days the ship remained there undergoing repairs, the Captain meanwhile improving the time id studying the wild, untamed children of the forest. The more he saw of their nature, bold and defiant even in the face of immianent destruction, the more deeply was the conviction borne in upon his soul that what was needed to permanently restrain the Indians from murder and pillage, was not the presence of a warship, but of a missionary of the Gospel. He believed that the glad tidings of salvation could transform even these sad, warlike savages into happy, peaceful Christians and citizens, and a great desire sprang up in his heart to be himself the means of giving them the light.

The repairs completed, Captain Provost ordered the vessel southward to Victoria, and during the following weeks and months, he went here and there in the North Pacific waters, quelling an Indian uprising in one place, settling an international dispute in another, and in general preserving the status quo in that far-off region.

But during all that time he did not forget the sad, dusky faces of the Tsimshean Indians at Fort Simpson. His desire to uplift them and enlighten their eyes that they [13] might see the true glory of life, grew rather than lessened with the passing months.

'At length, in 1856, Captain Prevost was summoned to England for a conference with the officials of the English navy. While in London awaiting assignment to a new command the Captain attended an anniversary meeting of a leading missionary organization. Here he met Rev. Joseph Ridgeway, an official of the Church Missionary Society, and to him he poured out the desire of his heart concerning the Indians at Fort Simpson. Mr Ridgeway was impressed by the graphic picture of the needs of the red men of the Northland, but declared there was no money in the treasury of the society to equip a missionary and send him out to that far distant region. However, he invited Captain Prevost to write an article on the land and the people of the North Pacific coast of America for their periodical. The Church Missionary Intelligencer. The Captain gladly accepted the offer and wrote an able article giving the history of the country, describing its soil, climate and products, and showing what promising field was open to the missionary. He said in part:

"It is difficult to ascertain, with any degree of accuracy, the total number of the native population; a mean, however, between the highest and lowest estimates, gives 60,000, a result probably not far from the truth. It is a fact, well calculated to [14] arrest the attention, and to enlist in behalf of the proposed Mission the active sympathies of every sincere Christian, that this vast number of our fellow-subjects have remained in a state of heathen darkness and complete barbarism ever since the discovery and partial surveys of their coast by Vancouver in 1792-1794; and that no effort has yet been made for their moral or spiritual improvement, although, during the last forty years a most lucrative trade has been carried on with them by our fellow countrymen. We would most earnestly call upon all who have themselves learned to value the blessings of the Gospel, to assist in rolling away this reproach. The field is a most promising one. Some naval officers, who, in the discharge of their professional duties, have lately visited these regions, have been most favorably impressed with the highly intelligent character of the natives; and, struck by their manly bearing, and a physical appearance fully equal to that of the English, whom they also resemble in the fairness of their complexion; and having their compassion excited by their total destitution of Christian and moral instruction, they feel it to be their duty to endeavor to introduce among them the knowledge of the Gospel of Christ, under the conviction that it would prove the surest and most fruitful source of social improvement and civilization, as well as of spiritual blessings, infinitely more valuable, [15] and would be found the only effectual antidote to the contaminating vices which a rapidly increasing trade, especially with California and Oregon, is bringing in its train."

The plea of the Christian Captain met with a quick response. Among the gifts received by the missionary society soon afterward was one of $2,500, given by "Two Friends" for the work among the red men described by Captain Prevost.

In spite, however, of this gift the society hesitated to act They had the money, but where was a suitable man to send. Thus, two or three months passed, when Captain Prevost came to them with the announcement that he had been re-appointed to his former naval station on the North Pacific coast, and was to leave almost immediately in command of the warship Satellite. Further, by the sanction of the Admiralty, he was enabled to offer a free passage in his ship to whatever, missionary they might choose to send to the Fort Simpson Indians.

Eleven days before the Satellite was to, sail on her journey to the other side of the globe this was the situation: Thousands of Indians at Fort Simpson needing the Gospel; $2,500.00 in the bank to send put a missionary; a warship ready to transport the messenger of peace; and yet the committee unable to find the right man for this,. important missionary undertaking. [16]

Could they find a man and could he get ready to embark in the short time remaining, was the problem that confronted the society. On the tenth, day before the warship was ready to leave England, a young wan then attending a missionary training school was suggested and his name approved by the committee.

Who he was, how he boarded the warship a few hours before its departure, and his strange and perilous experiences among the red men of America, m bis efforts to win them to Christ, will be related as our story proceeds. [17]

Chapter II
The Arrival Among Red Men

THE young man chosen by the committee for the hazardous mission to the American Indians was a student in the Highbury Training College in London named William Duncan. On the eighth day before the ship was to sail, Dr Alford, the principal, called young Duncan into to his study and, pointing to the north coast of America, asked whether he would volunteer to go there as a missionary to the Indians. The young man declared he had no objections whatever; that he was glad to go to whatever place the Society should assign him. Dr. Alford then informed him that he had been selected for the undertaking, that a free

passage on the warship *Satellite* had been offered, and that he had only eight days in which to prepare his outfit, bid farewell to his relatives, and reach the ship at Plymouth. [18]

The young man at once set about in haste making the needed preparations for his journey to the other side of the globe, from which it was quite possible he would never return. Just here, as he is earnestly striving to take advantage of the generous offer of Captain Prevost, let us glance at his previous life and see how he came to offer himself as a missionary to the heathen.

William Duncan was born in 1831, his early life being spent in Beverly, Yorkshire. While in his teens he entered the employ of a wholesale house, and showed such proficiency that in a few years he became clerk and traveling salesman. He was a member of the Church of England, and one evening, in company with another young man, his chum, attended a quarterly missionary meeting. It was a rainy night and there were only a few people present. Nevertheless, the speaker delivered an earnest address upon the condition of the missionary world at that time. He declared there were regions that sorely needed missionaries; that there were funds in hand to send out workers, but the men and women to go were lacking. These words made a deep impression upon the mind of young Duncan. He asked himself why he should not go, and decided that he would if an opportunity offered. The first person to whom he spoke on the subject was the bosom friend

with whom he had attended the meeting. He suggested that they both [19]   WM DUNCAN

offer themselves for the work, and the friend consented. But, upon the young man's suggesting the plan to his mother, she declared his going would be her death-blow, and he reluctantly relinquished the idea.

Young Duncan, however, was not daunted by his friend's turning back, and told his pastor, Rev. Mr. Carr, of his newly formed desire. What was his surprise when Mr. Carr turned to him and said: "William, while we were listening to that address I thought of you and prayed in my heart that God would lead you to take up that work."

The minister wrote at once to the Church Missionary Society recommending William, and the result was that he was accepted as a missionary candidate and nominated to attend the Highbury Training School.

When William went to announce his resignation to the two men at the head of the wholesale firm he encountered strong up-position to his going. He was a valuable young man and they wished to keep him in their employ. One of the firm said that not only did he regret it. The other partner said he thought the missionary would be better served by better served by bringing natives from heathen lands to England and then sending out missionaries to be killed. Their opposition did not alter young [20] Duncan's resolution in the least, but to do the fair thing he offered to remain for six months longer, until they could secure a suitable man as his successor.

At the expiration of the allotted time he resigned his business duties, and entered Highbury College with what result we have noted above.

The *Satellite* was to leave Plymouth on Tuesday. On Monday evening the young man had succeeded in visiting his nearest relatives to bid them a hasty good-by, had bade farewell to the officials ot the Church Missionary Society and had secured the needed outfit for the long journey. At 8 p.m. he left Paddington Station, London, accompanied by Dr. Alford, and reached Plymouth at 6 a.m. Tuesday morning. Together they went aboard the man-of-war, *Satellite*, where the doctor remained some hours giving final advice and encouragement to the young man, twenty-six years of age, who was about to depart on such an important mission. At 2 p.m, on the 22d of December, 1856, the ship steamed out of the harbor, and put to sea for a voyage of nearly twenty thousand' miles around Cape Horn to the naval station at Victoria.

As he stands on the deck of the warship, taking a last look at the receding shore of England, let us inspect more closely the appearance and character of this brave young man who is starting on a heroic yet extremely hazardous enterprise to the other [21] side of the globe. He ii of medium height. but firmly and strongly built, with every muscle instinct with life and energy. His face is beardless; his eyes large, blue, honest and fearless. His whole countenance and posture indicate a young man of strong [22] resolution and iron will. He is an idealist, but he has the force of character necessary to transmute his dreams into realities in the face of obstacles however difficult.

Clah, from whom Mr Duncan learned the Indian Language

the Like Paul, greatest missionary, he is not a man to shun dangers and perils by land or sea, but rather to exult in them, if thereby he can win men from darkness to light; and many are the perilous experiences through which young Duncan is destined to pass ere he again sees the shores of his native land.

In rounding the Cape terrific storms were encountered by the *Satellite* and on more than one occasion it was feared the ship would sink. But finally the dangerous regions were passed and on the 27th of June, 1857, after a voyage of over six months, Victoria was safely reached.

On landing, the officials of the powerful Hudson Bay Company informed Mr. Duncan that the Society had made an error in appointing him to Fort Simpson; over five hundred miles north of Victoria, as the Indians in that country were in a most barbarous condition, and the' officials, of the-company could not be responsible for his safety. They advised him to work among the Indians around Victoria, where he could be afforded ample protection. Sir James Douglass was then governor both of Vancouver Island and of the Hudson Bay Company in that vicinity. Shortly after the arrival he and Captain Prevost walked [23] with Mr Duncan to the home of Rev. E Cridge of Victoria, discussing the matter. Sir James plainly gave the Captain to understand that he and others objected to Mr Duncan's proceeding northward. But the Captain scouted the idea of his not going forward and declared that if the company refused to let Mr. Duncan proceed to Fort Simpson that he would carry him back to England on his ship.

At this point the governor turned to Mr Duncan and said; "As you are the most interested party I would like to see you in private on the subject. Please come and take dinner with me this evening." After dinner the Governor appeared in a more conciliatory frame of mind and after stating his fears that his life would be taken, said: "Do you still persist in wishing to go northward ?"

Mr Duncan replied: "I cannot possibly entertain any change in my plans. I have been assigned to Fort Simpson. and cannot work elsewhere without first consulting with the Society in London which would take a year's time. If you will permit me to go all I will ask of you and the Hudson Bay Company is that I be given the protection of the Fort until I can speak the native language. Then I will take the risk of going out among the Indians without involving the Company in any further responsibility."

Sir James then very kindly said:, "You [24] shall go and I will give instructions to the Fort to treat you as one of the officers. The only condition being that you do not call the Indians within the Fort for any meeting."

Mr Duncan was now ready to proceed at once to the northland. But for the following three months he was compelled to remain in Victoria, as a steamer only went to the Fort twice yearly; once in the Spring and again in the Autumn.

In the latter part of September he embarked for the final journey of five hundred miles. One of the ports where the ship called was *Fort Rupert*, where there was a settlement of one thousand Indians, and there Mr Duncan caught his first glimpse of the savage, ferocious character of the northern tribes. It was a sight dreadful enough to make the heart of any save the most heroic missionary quake with fear. Scattered about on the beach lay the dead and mangled bodies of a band of Hydah Indians who had stopped there on a journey homeward a few days previous, and had been attacked and the bodies hacked to pieces by the resident tribes. All but two of the party had been killed and those were held as prisoners. The arrival at Fort Simpson occurred at night when it was so dark one could not see his hand before him. Soon their coming was heralded throughout the Indian camp, and in a few moments the beach was [25] alive with excited figures running hither and thither waving fire-brands of welcome.

The following day Mr. Duncan examined the Fort and found it consisted of dwellings, and warehouses, trading stores and workshops enclosed within a stockade one hundred yards square. The palisade was very solid, being built of heavy tree trunks sunk into the ground and projecting about twenty feet upward. At the corners were wooden bastions, mounted with cannon. On the inside of the stockade near the top a platform or gallery had been constructed from which one could view the surrounding country, or fire at an enemy, and on which the garrison was accustomed to take daily exercise. The entire garrison numbered scarcely more than twenty persons, while two or three thousand Tsimshean Indians lived nearby. Hence the greatest caution had to be constantly exercised for fear of a wholesale massacre. For this reason more than two or three Indians were never admitted into the Fort at one time.

Immediately, Mr Duncan set about to find an Indian from whom he could learn the Tsimshean language. He selected Clah, who had access to the Fort, but who was unable to speak English, and began without delay.

The evening following his arrival at the Fort Mr Duncan beheld with his own eyes the awful fact that the Indians he had come so many thousand miles to win to Christ [26] were not only savages, but in a sense cannibals! In the twilight he was walking on the gallery of the Fort when he saw a slave woman murdered on the beach at the command of a chief and the body thrown into the water. Presently two parties of Indians approached the spot, each headed by a naked medicine man, who performed wild and weird motions and gave forth horrible gutteral sounds, and in every way endeavored to work the minds of their followers into an hysterical, devilish condition. On reaching the body it was torn to pieces by the teeth of the beastly, demoniacal red men.

Within a week another significant event occurred, calculated to inspire fear and discouragement in the soul of any save a missionary whose heart was aflame with love and who did not count his life dear, provided he could follow in the footsteps of his Master. In the near vicinity of Fort Simpson there were located nine tribes of Tsimshean Indians. Each tribe had its own chief, but a famous medicine man named Legaic was the head chief of all the tribes of the Tsimshean nation. Legaic was several times a murderer and one of the most desperate and wicked Indians on the North Pacific Coast. A few days after Mr Duncan's arrival he had, while partly intoxicated, been holding a conference with some subordinate chiefs. Their words had angered him, and he departed from the [27] meeting in an irritable mood. Meeting a strange Indian from a neighboring tribe within a few hundred feet of the Fort, he shot him down in cold blood, simply because he was feeling disgruntled. Then with Satanic indifference, he ordered two of his men to go and fire two more shots into the helpless, wounded Indian. An officer of the Fort, walking on the gallery; had witnessed the chief's devilish deed, and Mr. Duncan himself saw the last shots fired by the subordinates.

Paul Legeic

Was Mr Duncan discouraged by this appalling outburst of savagery? Not at all. But it was well that he did know what the future held in store for him not many months distant in connection with his same Legaic. [28]

Chapter III
Rescued, by Providence

WITH the assistance of Clah, who became warmly attached to him, Mr Duncan made rapid progress in learning the Tsimshean language. His method was as follows: Selecting fifteen hundred of the commonest English words from the dictionary "he sought to discover from Clah the Tsimshean equivalents for them. Many were the difficult and often amusing experiences which occurred in this attempt to formulate and put down in order for the first time the native tongue of the Indians. By patient and oft-repeated signs he finally wrote phonetically in English 1,500 words and 1,100 short sentences.

Early in the year 1858, not long after Mr Duncan's arrival at the Fort, he received a [29] significant visit from one of the Tsimshean Indians.

The native said to him: "What do you mean by 1858?"
Mr Duncan informed him that 1858 represented the number of years that had passed since Christ came to earth with the message of salvation.

The Indian then said; "Why didn't you tell us of this before? Why were not our fore-fathers "told this?"

To this pertinent arid accusing query Mr Duncan could make no reply, for he realized anew the guilt of the church in taking its ease for so many centuries while thousands and millions of men and women and children, red and yellow and black, were perishing without the Gospel.

The Indian then asked: "Have you got the Word of God?"
Translated into English the Indian's query meant: "Have you got a letter from God?" Hence Mr. Duncan answered:

"Yes, I have God's letter."

"I want to see it," said the native.

Mr. Duncan went to get his Bible, glad of an opportunity to impress upon the Indian mind the fact that he had brought a message, not from any human being, but from the King of Kings, the God of Heaven. It had been rumored throughout the Indian camp that the white missionary had a message from God and this man was eager to see it and confirm the report. [30]

When Mr Duncan brought the Bible to him he asked: "Is this the Word?" "Yes," said Mr. Duncan, "it is."
"The Word from God?"
"It is."
"Has He sent it to us?"
"He has, just as much as He has to me," replied Mr. Duncan. "Are you going to tell the Indians that?"
he asked,
"I am." "Good, that is very good," he said, and departed to spread the good news throughout the camp.

It was not until the summer of 1858, after a period of eight months of diligent study of the language, that Mr. Duncan ventured to formally address the Indians in their native tongue-During the winter, however, he frequently visited among them, endeavoring to prepare the way for the presentation of his formal message in Tsimshean. To the Church Missionary Society in London Mr. Duncan wrote a vivid letter, describing his first general visit among the natives. Part of it read as follows:

"It would be impossible for me to give a full description of this, my first general visit, for the scenes were too exciting and too crowded to admit of it. I confess that cluster after cluster of these half-naked savages round their camp-fires was, to my unaccustomed eyes, very alarming. But the reception I met with was truly wonderful [31] and encouraging. On entering a house I was saluted by one, two or three of the principal persons with 'Clah-how-yah,' which is the complimentary term used in the trading jargon. This would be repeated several times. Then a general movement and a squatting ensued, followed by a breathless silence, during which every eye was fixed upon me. After a time several would begin nodding and smiling, at the same time reiterating in a low tone, 'Ahm, ahm, ah ket, ahm, *Shimauget*' (good, kind person, good chief.)

"In some houses they would not be content until I took the chief place near the fire, and they always placed a mat upon a box for me to sit upon. My inquiries after the sick were always followed by anxious looks and deep sighs. A kind of solemn awe would spread itself at once."
In the course .of his visits among the people Mr Duncan carefully noted the religious ideas which the Indians had held in their savage condition. As the result of his observations he found the following peculiar beliefs held sway over their minds and hearts, and doubtless had done so for ages past:

"The idea they entertain of God is that He is a great Chief. They call Him by the same term as they do their chiefs, only adding the word for above: thus, 'shimauget' is chief and 'lakkah' above; and hence the name of God with them is Shimauget Lak-Kah. [32] They believe that the Supreme Being never dies; that He takes great notice of what is going on amongst men, and is frequently angry and punishes offenders. They do not know who is the author of the universe, nor do they expect that God is the author of their own being. They have no fixed ideas about these things, I fully believe; still they frequently appeal to God in trouble; they ask for pity and deliverance. In great extremities of sickness they address God, saying it is not good for them to die."

With these hazy feelings of a divine Ruler of the world, the Indians "felt after God, if haply they might find Him." But those faint glimmerings of religion did not constitute the Gospel, and in what a sad condition they had left the red men of the forest, for lo, these many centuries!

On the 13th of June, 1858, Mr Duncan delivered his first formal message to the Tsimsheans in their native speech. Describing the memorable occasion in his journal, he wrote:

"Bless the Lord, O my soul, and let all creation join in chorus to bless His Holy Name. True to His word, 'He giveth power to the faint, and to them that have no might He increaseth strength.' Bless forever His Holy Name!

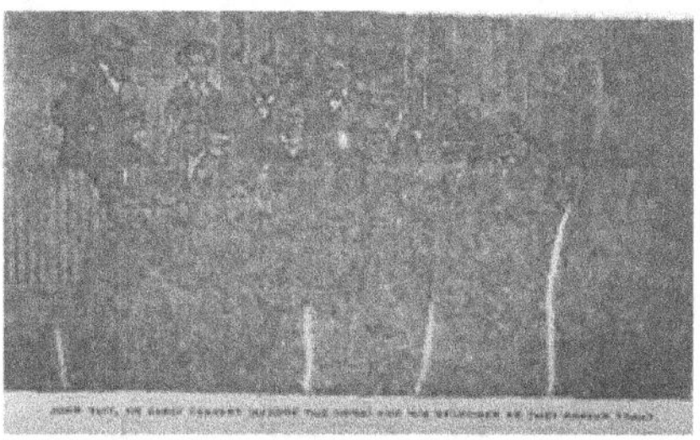

John Tait, an early convert (before the door) and his relatives as they appear today [33]

"Last week I finished translating my first address for the Indians. Although it was not entirely to my satisfaction, I felt it [34] would be wrong to withhold the me»age say longer. Accordingly, I sent word last night (not being ready before) to the chiefs, desiring to use their houses today to address their people in. This morning I set off, accompanied by the young Indian (*Clah*) whom I have had occasionally to assist me in the language. In a few minutes we arrived at the first chief's house, which I found ail prepared, and we mustered about one hundred souls. This was the first assembly of Indians I had met. My heart quailed greatly before the work — a people for the first time come to hear the Gospel tidings, and I, the poor instrument, to address them in a tongue so new and different to me. Oh, those moments I began to think that after .all I should be obliged to get *Clah* to speak to them, while I read to them from a paper in my hand. Blessed be God, this lame resolution was not carried. My Indian was so unnerved at my proposal that I quickly saw I must do the best I could by myself, or worse would come of it. I then told them to shut the door. The Lord strengthened me. I knelt down to crave God's blessing, and afterwards I gave them the address. They were alt remarkably attentive. At the conclusion I desired them to kneel down. They immediately complied, and I offered up prayer for them in English. They preserved great silence. All being done, I bade them good-by. They all responded with seeming [35] thankfulness. On leaving, I asked my Indian if they understood me, and one of the chief women very seriously replied, 'Nee, net,' (yes); and he (*Clah*) assured me that from their looks he knew that they understood and felt it to be good.

"We then went to the next chief's house, where we found all ready, a canoe-sail spread for me to stand on, and a mat placed on a box for me to sit upon. About 150 souls assembled, and as there were a few of the Fort people present I first gave them a short address in English, and then the one in Tsimshean. All knelt in prayer, and were very attentive as at the other place. This is the head chiefs house. He is a very wicked man, but he was present, and admonished the people to behave themselves during my stay.

"After this I went in succession to the other seven tribes, and addressed them in the chiefs' houses. In each case I found the chief very kind and attentive in preparing his house and assembling his people. The smallest company I addressed was about fifty souls, and the largest about 200. Their obedience to my request about kneeling was universal, but in the house where there were over 200 some confusion took place, as they were silting so close. However, when they heard me begin to pray, they were instantly quiet. Thus the Lord helped me through. About 800 or 900 souls in all have heard me speak; and the greater [36] number of them, I feel certain, have understood the message. May the Lord make it the beginning of great good for this pitiable and long-lost people."

Mr Duncan's next endeavor was to establish a school where instruction would be given in both secular and spiritual things. What was his surprise and delight when the notorious head-chief Legaic offered his large house in which to conduct it for a time. About two weeks later it was opened with an attendance of twenty-six children in the forenoon and fourteen or fifteen adults in the afternoon. Everything went happily for a few weeks, until Legaic and his wife departed on a fishing expedition, and the house was closed.

The school was such a success, however, and was proving such an effective means of attracting the Indians, that Mr Duncan set about building a school-house at once. Late in the autumn it was completed and on the 19th of November, the opening day of school, there was registered an enrollment of one hundred and forty children and fifty adults. As the days and weeks passed the Interest grew rather than lessened and the Gospel teaching was making rapid inroads upon the heathen ideas and customs.

Classroom

There was one class of men amongst the Indians to whom the teaching was doubly displeasing; namely, the medicine men. They were the high priests of the heathen religion, and the spread of knowledge and [37] the Gospel meant the deathblow to their calling and the position of honor in which they were now held. Four chiefs had already abandoned their medicine practices and were giving earnest heed to Mr Duncan's instruction.

As the month of December progressed the season drew near for the holding of the annual medicine rites and ceremonies, which were attended by large numbers of visitors from other tribes and were marked by devilish abominations and much debauchery. Legaic and other leading medicine men held a conference and sent notice to Mr Duncan through the manager of the Fort that he must close the school for four weeks while the medicine work was in progress. He declared that such a course was impossible. A little later he received word that the chiefs would be content provided the school was closed for two weeks — and that afterward they would all come to be instructed — while if he did not comply with their request, the pupils would bs. shot as they came to school. Mr Duncan knew that his own life as well as that of the scholars would be in danger if he refused, but his duty in the matter was perfectly plain. Like Daniel of old he determined to do right whether he lived or died. He returned answer that lie could not close (he school a single day in deference to their heathen abominations; that Satan had ruled there long enough and it was time his rule should be disturbed. [38]

A few days later, on the 20th of December, as the children were assembling for the afternoon session of the school, Mr Duncan looked out of the door and saw Legate approaching, followed by a motley crowd of medicine men dressed in their fantastic garb. When they reached the building, Legaic shouted at the top of his voice to the few children who had just come in, ordering them to hurry home at once. He then entered the room, followed by seven or more of the medicine men, and drawing near to Mr Duncan, they tried to intimidate him by their terrorizing language and frightful appearance. Legaic declared the school must be closed four days, at least, or he would shoot at the pupils as they came to school; that if he was unable to stop the school medicine men from other tribes would shame and perhaps kill him;. that he knew how to kill men (drawing his hand across his throat as he spoke); that he was a wicked man and would go down anyway.

God enabled Mr Duncan to stand calmly dating the long harangue, and then to address the intruders with far more fluency than usual. He was enabled to tell them of their sin faithfully, and to vindicate his own conduct. He declared that God was his Master and that he must obey Him rather than men; that the devil had taught their fathers what they were practising and [39] it was bad; that he had come to tell them of God's way and it was good.

During the excited scene, which lasted fully an hour, Legaic once pointed to two men standing near and said they were murderers as well as himself, hence it was useless for them to go to school At this point Mr Duncan broke in, declaring the Gospel was for murderers as well as others; that if they would repent and amend they could still be saved.

Toward the close of the interview, however, two vile-looking confederates went and whispered something into Legaic's ear; doubtless a taunt that he was afraid to kill the missionary. Legaic at once became passionately inflamed and drawing near to Mr Duncan, gesticulated wildly, having a knife concealed in his right hand.

Without doubt, he was preparing to murder Mr Duncan at once. when something occurred, which though human, was also providential and miraculous, and showed that God still watches over His servants, even as in the days of Daniel. [40]

Chapter IV
Planning a Model Village

AS Legaic approached Mr Duncan and was about raising his hand to slay him, he happened t o glance behind him, and saw a person he had not previously observed, standing behind Mr Duncan, silent, yet guarding him with eagle eyes.

It was *Clah*, the faithful interpreter and friend. He had heard of the visit of the medicine men, and hastily securing his revolver had hurried to the school-house, resolved to shoot anyone who attempted the life of the missionary. He had entered the building unobserved by either Mr Duncan or Legaic, and it was not until the latter drew near to Mr Duncan that he saw *Clah* standing behind him. Legaic knew that *Clah*'s hand, which was slipped just inside his blanket, contained a [41] revolver and that the moment he raised his arm to kill the missionary, he would be shot. With the new turn of affairs Legaic realized that his mission was a failure, and in a few moments sullenly withdrew, followed by his disappointed confederates.

Thus was Mr Duncan's life wonderfully preserved and the Gospel triumphant over heathenism. The school was not closed, but Legaic's hostility continued and as his house stood near the school it was difficult for the children to attend. At this Juncture another chief proffered the use of his house for the school, and it being in a less dangerous locality the offer was gladly accepted and the scholars transferred to the new place where rapid progress was made. Mr Duncan's connection with Legaic by no means terminated with this incident. Of his future career we shall hear in detail as the narrative progresses.

The first Christmas spent by Mr Duncan among the Tsimsheans was very different from his later ones. However, he did what he could to make the day notable, and to explain to the people its glorious meaning. In a letter to the Missionary Society he described the day in the following manner:

"Yesterday I told my scholars to bring, their friends and relatives to school today, as I wanted to tell them something new. We numbered out two hundred souls. I tried to make them understand why we distinguished this day from others. After this [42] I questioned the children a little and then we sang two hymns, which we also translated. While the hymns were being sung, I felt I must try to do something more, although the language seemed to defy me. I never experienced such an inward burning to speak before, and therefore I determined to try an extemporaneous address in Tsimshean. The Lord helped me; a great Stillness prevailed, and I think a great deal was understood of what I said. I told them of our condition, the pity and love of God, the death of the Son of God on our account, and the benefits arising to us therefrom, and exhorted them to leave their sins and pray to Jesus. On my enumerating the sins of which they are guilty, I saw some look at each other with those significant looks which betoken their assent to what I said. I tried to impress upon them the certain ruin which awaits them if they proceed in their present vices. Very remarkably an illustration corroborating what I had said was before their eyes. A poor woman was taken sick not four yards from . where I stood, and right before the eyes of my audience. She was groaning under a frightful affliction, the result of her vices."
During the ensuing four years Mr Duncan made slow but steady progress in instructing the people and wooing them from heathenism and savagery to Christianity and civilization; even Legaic often attending school and listening eagerly with the rest. [44]

Nor were his efforts confined entirely to the nine Tsimshean tribes surrounding Fort Simpson. Occasionally he made journeys to interior tribes who had never heard the story of the Gospel. It was on a visit of this character up the Nass River that a most remarkable incident occurred. Let us give Mr Duncan's own narrative of the visit as it was afterwards related by him:

Thomas Eaton and family

"They had heard that I was coming, and the chief, in order to show his great delight at my arrival, put up what they call a large cap. Their cap was an umbrella. They had no idea of preventing rain from falling on their heads by its use, but looked upon it simply as a web-footed cap, and so they used it on state occasions. As soon as I landed I saw the man with the umbrella, and saw the excitement. He sent a message to this effect: 'I would like you to come into my house and I shall send my messenger to tell you so.'

"I immediately encamped upon the bank of the river. By and by I was told that all things were ready and prepared to receive me. I said to my little crew — for in those days I took only boys with me, being afraid to take men, as they might kill me for the, purpose of getting my clothes — I said, 'What are they going to do when I go into the house?'

"'Dance.'

"'Tell them I did not come here to see [45] dancing, and I cannot go therefore.'

"They told the messenger to tell the chief that I objected to seeing them dance, that I had come with a solemn message to them.

"The chief replied, 'Tell the white chief he must come; if he doesn't come to me I won't go to hear his word; but if he will come I will go and hear him.'

"That changed the matter altogether. I had a little consultation with my boys, and they said, "You had better go; if you do not go the chief will not come to hear what you have to say.'

"I walked up to his house, I confess, in a very grum {grim} kind of a spirit. I did not like to attend a dance. But I saw that I had to do it. I was very glad afterward that I did go. When I entered the house there was a person there ready to point out a seat for me. There was a bear-skin spread over a box for me to sit on. The chief had all of his men placed around in different portions of the house, which was a very large one. I observed that he had gotten a large sail and used it for a curtain in part of the room. "Very soon I saw two men step out. One had a rod in his hand beating the floor. They had a kind of theatrical performance. The old man, after stamping his foot and putting his rod down very firmly, said, in his own language, of course,

"The heavens are changing.'

"The other man was there to respond, [45] 'Yes, so it seems; the heavens are changing.'

"A few little remarks of this sort were made, and then the sail was drawn aside and out dashed the chief, dressed in most magnificent costume, his head being completely covered with feathers and other ornaments. He had his rattle in his hand. He [46] shook it before my face; walked up a little way to me and then put up his hand with his rattle in it; he looked through the hole in the center of the roof where the smoke came out, and immediately began a beautiful prayer. I was astonished. This was no dance. If I could only give you his prayer in his own beautiful and eloquent language, you would be astonished also. I can only give you the substance of "it:

"Great Father in Heaven, pity us! Give us Thy good Book to do us good and to cleanse away our sins! This Chief (Mr Duncan) has come to tell us about Thee. It is good, Great Father, we want to hear! Whoever came to tell our forefathers Thy will? No! no! But this Chief has pitied us and come.

He has Thy Book. We will hear! We will receive Thy Word I We wilt obey!'

"When I heard this prayer I felt thunder-struck. I had expected to be disgusted at seeing their heathen abominations, but the people sat solemnly during the ceremonies, even saying amen to the prayer.

"After this the Indians began a chant, clapping their hands. It was an extemporaneous song and I listened to it with a great deal of pleasure. There was a man among them who extemporized the song as they sang it, verse by verse as they wanted it. The chant was a very plaintive one. I found the song was all about God having [47] sent His servant and His messenger to teach the Indians.

"When this was done the chief turned to me and made a short speech to the effect that they wanted me amongst them as they wanted God's Word. They wanted to cast away their evil ways and to be good."

Mr Duncan spent the day visiting a number of houses, and invited every one to hi» tent for the evening address, where he told them as much as possible about the wonderful news of salvation.

The first public reception of Indian converts into the church occurred on the 26th of July, 1861, when fourteen men, five women and four children were baptized on their public profession of faith in Christ. Others also came forward, but it was thought best that they wait for a time; while several who believed in Christ were afraid to come boldly out for fear of their relatives.

As the years had passed since Mr Duncan began his work among the Indians, he had realized more and more the necessity of separating the converts, and especially the children under instruction in the school, from the vices and immorality and heathenism around Fort Simpson. As early as 1859 he wrote as follows to the Missionary Society in London:

"What is to become of the children and young people under instruction, when temporal necessity compels them to leave school? If they are permitted to slip away [48] from me into the gulf of vice and misery which everywhere surrounds them, then the fate of these tribes is sealed, and the labor and money that has already been spent for their welfare might as well have been thrown away. The well-thinking part of the Indian people themselves see this, and are asking, nay, craving, a remedy. The head chief of one tribe (a very well-disposed old man) is constantly urging this question upon me, and begs that steps may be taken which shall give the Indians that are inclined, and especially, the children now being taught, a chance and a help to become what good people desire them to be."

Gradually the conviction grew in his mind that what was demanded for the spiritual welfare of the Indians was a Christian colony, where peace and quiet would reign, where industries would be taught and toil rewarded, and where the terrible evils of fire-water would be unknown. He talked the plan over with his followers and they not only highly favored it, but suggested that the colony be located on the beautiful island of Metlakahtla[23]*, only seventeen miles distant, where they and their forefathers had lived before they removed to Fort Simpson. So glowing were their accounts of the beauty and suitability of the island that Mr Duncan visited it, and found it admirably adapted to the plan in every particular. [49]

Mr Duncan believed such a village .would not only be an infinite blessing to the Indians themselves, but would be a Gospel lighthouse, shedding its radiance throughout the entire northland. In describing the project, he wrote: "All we want is God's favor and blessing, and then we may hope to build up in His good time, a model Christian village, reflecting light and radiating heat to all the spiritually dark and dead masses of humanity around us."

His first step toward the actual realization of the settlement was the drawing up of a set of fifteen rules which all who joined the colony would be required to sign. They were as follows:

1. To give up "Ahlied" or Indian deviltry.
2. To cease calling in "Shamans" – or medicine men when sick.
3. To cease gambling.
4. To cease giving away their property for display.
5. To cease painting their faces.
6. To cease indulging in intoxicating drinks.
7. To rest on the Sabbath.
8. To attend religious instruction.
9. To send their children to school.
10. To be cleanly.
11. To be industrious.
12. To be peaceful.

---

[23] * Metlakahtla means "Inlet of Kahtla." { 'saltwater passage' }

13. To be liberal and honest in trade.
14. To build neat houses. [50]
15. To pay the village tax.

In the winter of 1861-2 active preparations for the embarkation to the new home went forward, but it was not until May 27th that everything was in readiness for the long planned event. For some time previous to the day of departure Mr Duncan devoted himself to visiting from house to house, and to delivering farewell addresses to the tribes in the homes of the chiefs.

Several days before the date set for departure the school-house was torn down and made into a raft on which ten Indians went in advance of the main group, piloting the logs through the sea seventeen miles to the island where it was to be speedily re-transformed into a school-house.

Finally, the eventful day arrived and the party of pilgrims gathered on the shore, ready to set out on their journey. Those who had subscribed to the rules and were ready to leave home and friends for the sake of the Gospel numbered in all about fifty souls; men, women and children. Six large Indian canoes lay at the water's edge ready to receive the pilgrims and bear them to their new home. A large company of Indians had assembled to witness the departure and looked on with solemn and earnest faces, many promising to join the settlement in the near future.

As the heroic band entered the canoes they were filled with solemn joy at the thought of the Christian community in [510] which they were going to dwell Mr Duncan realized fully what an eventful page in the history of the Indians was being turned, and his joy was great when as the canoes left the shore, the sun which had been behind the rain-clouds, broke forth and disclosed to view a beautiful rainbow. It was a happy omen as the pilgrims departed for their new home on the island of Metlakahtla.

A corner in an Indian house today

Chapter V
The Arcadian Isle

THE six Indian canoes freighted with heroic pilgrims had left Fort Simpson in the afternoon and it soon became evident that they could not reach Metlakahtla until late at night. Hence, when they reached a good camping place only a few miles from the Fort, the canoes were headed for the shore, and soon all were on the beach gathering fuel for fires and preparing tents and blankets for the night. After supper all gathered around the camp-fire while Mr Duncan conducted evening prayers. It was a beautiful and impressive sight and one long to be remembered, to see those -Indians, who, only a short time since were degraded savages, sitting quietly around the camp-fire with faces aglow with Christian joy,

Mr David Leask was for many years leader among the Metlakahtla Indians

singing praises to their Creator and King in softly flowing Tsimshean accents. [53]

Early the next morning they broke camp and in a few hours reached the shore of their new island home, where much eventful history was to occur during the coming years.

During the next few days all were actively engaged in selecting sites for their homes and in making preparations to build. Each evening after the labor of the day, they gathered together on the beach, like a large, happy family, for prayer and singing and a short Scripture address by Mr Duncan.

Only four or five days after their arrival others began coming from Fort Simpson, singly and in groups, while on the 6th of June great excitement was created by the arrival of thirty canoes, bringing three hundred souls, with two chiefs.

Scarcely had the exodus occurred when a fearful plague of small-pox broke out at Fort Simpson, which swept away over five hundred Indians and spread up and down the coast carrying death and desolation in its wake. In terror they fled in all directions from the dread disease, many now coming to Metlakahtla and pleading to-be allowed to join the colony. Most of them were admitted, but some who were still steeped in heathenism Mr Duncan was compelled to refuse. Many of the newcomers were infected with the small-pox and Mr Duncan was kept busy day and night tending the sick. The members of [54] the original colony were wonderfully preserved from the plague, only five of them dying, three of these deaths being occasioned by attending sick relatives who already had the disease when they reached the island.

The colonists fervently thanked God for their marvelous escape from the surrounding destruction, and as the plague subsided they set earnestly to work to build up a handsome village which should be a veritable Christian Arcadia.

Since he had left Victoria, Mr Duncan had by no means been forgotten by the governor, Sir James Douglas. The governor took pains to converse with Indians who had been under Mr Duncan's instruction when they visited Victoria, and was delighted at the results observed. He requested Mr Duncan to send him reports from time to time concerning the progress of the mission.

The governor's request was gladly complied with by Mr Duncan, and in a report sent in the spring of 1863, about ten months after the arrival at Metlakahtla, he wrote Sir James a long letter, giving many interesting details of the new settlement. A part of the communication was as follows:

"To many who have joined me, the surrendering their national and heathen customs performed over the sick — ceasing to give away, tear up. or receive blankets, etc., for display, dropping precipitately [55] their demoniacal rites, which have hitherto and for ages filled up their time and engrossed alt their care during the months of winter; laying aside gambling, and ceasing to paint their faces — had been like cutting off the right hand and plucking out the right eye. Yet I am thankful to tell you that these sacrifices have been made; and had your Excellency heard the speeches made by the chiefs and some of the principal men at our Christmas evening meeting, alluding to these and other matters, you would, I am sure, have rejoiced.

"On New Year's Day the male adult settlers came cheerfully forward to pay the village tax, which I had previously proposed to levy yearly, viz, one blanket, or two and one half dollars of such as have attained manhood, and one shirt, or one dollar of such as are approaching manhood. Out of 130 amenable we had only ten defaulters and these were excused on account of poverty. Our revenue for this year thus gathered amounts to one green, one blue, and ninety-four white blankets, one pair of white trousers, one dressed elk skin, seventeen shirts and seven dollars. The half of this property I propose to divide among the three chiefs who are with us, in recognition of stated services which they will be required to render to the settlement, and' the other half to spend in public works.

"As to our government; all disputes and difficulties are settled by myself and ten [56] constables; but I occasionally call in the chiefs, and intend to do so more and more, and when they become sufficiently instructed, trustworthy and influential, I shall leave civil matters in their hands. I find the Indians very obedient, and comparatively easy to manage, since I allow no intoxicating drinks to come into our village. Though we are continually hearing of the drunken festivals of the surrounding tribes I am happy to tell you that Metlakahtla has not yet witnessed a case of drunkenness since we have settled here — a period of ten months. Still, not all with me arc true men. Some few, on their visits to Fort Simpson, have fallen; and two, whose cases were clearly proved and admitted of no extenuation, I have banished from our midst.

"On Sabbath days labor is laid aside, a solemn quiet presides and the best clothing is in use. Scarcely a soul remains away from divine service, excepting the sick and their nurses. Evening family devotions are common to almost every house, and, better than all, I have a hope that many have experienced a real change of heart. To God be all the praise and glory.

"We have succeeded in erecting a strong and useful building, capable of containing at least 600 people, which we use as church and school. We held our first meeting in this building on the night it was finished, the 20th of December last. I have about one hundred children who attend morning [57] photo

[58] and afternoon and about one hundred adults (often more) in the evening. I occupy the principal part oft the time in the adult school, in giving simple lectures on geography, astronomy, natural history and morals. These lectures the Indians greatly prize. "Trusting, by God's blessing upon us, we shall go on improving and continue to merit your Excellency's favor and good-will.

"I have the honor to remain, with warmest gratitude,
"Your Excellency's humble and obedient servant, W. Duncan."

A few weeks later, the Bishop of Columbia visited Metlakahtla to baptize those who were ready to receive the sacred rite, Mr Duncan being a lay, not a clerical missionary. Two full days were spent in examining the candidates, of which the Bishop wrote:

"We were met by the whole village, who stood on the bank, in a long line — as fine a set of men and as well dressed as could anywhere be seen where men live by their daily toil — certainly no country village in England would turn out so well-clad an assemblage.

"At three the bell was rung and almost instantly the whole population were wending their way to church. There were hymns and prayers in Tsimshean. They repeated the answers to a catechism in Tsimshean. I addressed them and offered [59] prayers in English, which were interpreted by Mr Duncan.

"Converts from heathenism can fully realize renunciation of the world, the flesh and the devil. Among these Indians pomp of display, the lying craft of malicious magic, as welt as all sins of the flesh, are particularly glaring, and closely connected with heathenism. So are the truths of the Creed in strongest contrast to the dark and miserable fables of their forefathers and heartily can they pledge themselves to keep the holy will of God, all the days of their life, seeing in Him a loving and true Father, of whom now so lately but so gladly, they have learned to know.

"I first drew forth their views of the necessity of repentance, its details and their own personal acquaintance with it. ' I then questioned them as to the Three Persons of the Trinity, and the special work of each with allusion to the judgment, and the state of the soul hereafter, inquiring into their private devotion to learn their personal application of repentance and faith. I questioned their anxiety for baptism, and demanded proof of their resolution to keep the will of God for their guide, to speak of God, and to labor for God's way, all their life long. I sought to find out the circumstances under which they first became seriously inclined, and to trace their steps of trial and grace. Admitting them to the promise of baptism. I exhorted them [60] to prayer and devotion, as a special preparation until the time came.

"A simple table, covered with a white cloth, upon which stood three hand-basins of water, served for the font, and I officiated-in a surplice. Thus there was nothing to impress the senses, no color, nor ornament, nor church decoration, nor music, The solemnity of the scene was produced by the earnest sincerity and serious purpose with which these children of the far West were prepared to offer themselves to God, and to renounce forever the hateful sins and cruel deeds of their heathenism; and the solemn stillness was broken only by the breath of prayer. The responses were made with earnestness and decision. Not an individual was there, whose lips did not utter in his own expressive .tongue, his hearty readiness to believe and to serve God."

The Christian experiences of the candidates for baptism were most touching and impressive.

Clah, who had saved Mr Duncan's life and was his first friend, testified as follows:

"I have made up my mind to live a Christian. Must try to put away all my sins. I believe in Jesus Christ, the Son of God, who died for our sins. God is good to us and made us. God gives us His Spirit to make us, clean and happy. I pray to God to clean my heart, and wipe out my sin from God's book. It will be worse for us [61] if we fall away after we have begun." *Clah*'s wife was also baptized with him.

The chieftainess of the Nish-Kahs, named Nishah-Kigh, whose sorrow was great when she first heard the message of salvation and who had been seeking God for five years, said:

"I must leave all evil ways. I feel myself a sinner in God's sight. I believe in God, the Father Almighty, and in Jesus Christ, who died for our sins. God sends down His Spirit to make us good. Jesus is in Heaven, and is writing our names in God's Book. We must stand before God and be judged by Him. I feel God's Word is truth. Have been for some time accustomed regularly to pray."

A young man, Kappigh Kumlee by name, thirty years of age, who had been a sorcerer, but found no satisfaction in the calling, said:

"I have given up the lucrative position of sorcerer. Been offered bribes to practice my art secretly. I have left all my mistaken ways. My eyes have been bored (enlightened.) I cry every night when I remember my sins. The great Father Almighty sees everything. If I go up to the mountain He sees me. Jesus died for our sins upon the cross to carry our sins away."
Kappigh Kumlee's wife was baptized with him, and all their family having renounced heathenism, they were doubly united in the bonds of Christian fellowship. [62]

A chief seventy years of age named Neeash-Lakah-Moosh, when asked if he desired to become a Christian, said:

"For that object I came here with my people. I have put away all lying ways, which I had long followed. I have trusted in God. We want the Spirit of God. Jesus came to save us. He compensated for our sins. Our Father made us and loved us because we are His work. He wishes to see us with Him because He loves us." When asked about the judgment he said:

"The blood of Jesus will free those who believe from condemnation."

Vilroauksh, a young man who rescued three of his relatives from the darkness of heathenism, said:

"I believe in Jesus as my Savior, who died to compensate for my sins to God."

One, named Neeash-ah-Pootk, who was converted by losing ten of his relatives by the plague of small-pox, said:

"I have long followed sins which made God angry. I have put away sin, but if I am ever so ignorant in my endeavors I will persevere. Used to be a great drunkard. Have given up magic and display of property. Felt God last summer. We have turned back to our great Father. He see all; His Spirit is with us. The blood of Jesus cleanseth us from all sin. How happy the angels wilt be io see us good, and how they will cry if we are sinful! At the last God will divide us. Lost ten relatives by [63] the small-pox last year, and it opened my eyes to my sins. God's hand was strong to cut down sinners."

As beautiful testimony was given by Kaklp, only thirty-five years of age, who had had a sad and checkered career. When a young man he was captured by the Hydah Indians. Later he was brought back and sold to his old chief, who kept him in slavery several years. The chief's son finally sold him to his own friends, who set him free.
He said:

"I shall fight against my sins. My heart truly says I will turn from sin to God. God is perfectly right in His ways. Whosoever believes in God, the Father, the Spirit of God lives in his heart. Those who die in their sin go to darkness and to fire. I will fear God as long as I live. I pray for God's Spirit and light to lead my own spirit along the path to Himself when I die. Was a slave; was poor in

spirit, and was drawn to cry to God to take my heart."

One of the most touching experiences of all was that given by a boy sixteen years of age, named Kisheeso. It shows how, when the Gospel really fills one's heart, one is willing to forsake all for Christ This boy left his heathen home, and came by himself in a tiny canoe across the sea to join the Christian people. He said:

"A duty to give up the ways of the Tsimsheans. Was very wicked when quite young. Will try to put away my sin. I pray [64] night and morning for God to pity and to pardon me."

These are only a few of the touching testimonies given by these Indians who had for centuries been steeped in heathenism, but had at last seen a great light, had come into possession of the pearl of great price, without which life is a dreary waste, but with which it is a foretaste of the Heaven hereafter.

The most notable of all the Indians baptized by the Bishop was one with whom we have already become acquainted; who from being a persecutor was marvelously transformed into a saint. The story of his conversion and valiant career as a Christian reads like a new chapter in the Acts of the Apostles. [65]

Chapter VI
The Transformation Of Legaic

A FEW months after the settlement had been established at Metlakahtla a thrill of surprise and delight ran throughout the village at the announcement that a notable recruit had arrived at the island, determined to sign the rules and cast in his lot with the Christian party. The newcomer was none other than Legaic, head-chief, murderer and medicine man, who had so nearly succeeded in taking Mr Duncan's life. The Spirit of God had long been working upon his heart until he had come to loathe heathenism and to long for the peace and joy which he saw were the outcome of the Christian life. To openly join the Christian party at Metlakahtla, however, would be to make a tremendous sacrifice, for it would mean the practical renunciation of the headship of the 

Indian boy

Tsimshean nation. But the victory over self was won and Legaic had finally arrived at the village ready to subscribe to the fifteen [66] rules. Accompanying Legate were his wife and daughter, and Mr Duncan and the natives gave them a warm and hearty welcome.

Legaic began building a beautiful home, but was often interrupted by messengers from Fort Simpson urging him to return and resume his position over all the Tsimshean tribes. The temptations were so strong and constant that Legaic finally weakened, and gathering the Metlakahtla Indians together on the beach, he told them that he could hold out no longer, but must return to his old life. He said he knew it was a wrong step and he might perish as the result, but that he was being pulled away by influences stronger than he was able to resist. In deep sorrow, amid falling tears, he shook hands with each one present, then turned and entered his canoe and paddled silently away.

As he disappeared from sight, do you think the Indians went back to their homes criticising him and discussing the weakness of-human nature, as most white people would have done under similar circumstances? Not at all. They knelt on the beach and held a prayer-meeting, imploring God to check Legaic in his backward course and to restore him to his right mind.

The subject of their prayers paddled rapidly toward Port Simpson until night came on and he was compelled to put the canoe ashore. He wrapped himself in his blanket [67] and lay down to sleep, but sleep came not to his eyes. Instead, he tossed and turned in awful unrest of soul. The Spirit of God was wrestling mightily with him even as with Jacob of old. Finally, the torture became unbearable. Such misery overwhelmed him as words cannot describe, until the Spirit conquered and kneeling in the darkness he repented of his evil, and weepingly besought God for pardon. Next morning he turned his canoe about and once more appeared at Metlakahtla, this time a thoroughly saved man. Saul, the persecutor, had become Paul, the apostle. In afterward describing the agony he endured on that memorable occasion, Legaic declared:

"A hundred deaths would not equal the sufferings of that night."

Six months later a visitor to Metlakahtla wrote as follows of Legaic and his family:

"I paid a visit to the wife of the chief, Paul Legaic. He it was who nearly took Mr Duncan's life at the head of the medicine band attacking the school. They were both baptized by the Bishop last April. Legaic was the wealthiest chief of the Tsimshean at Fort Simpson. He has lost everything — has had to give up everything by his conversion to Christianity. It was with many of them literally a forsaking of all things to follow Christ.'

"His house is the nicest and best situated in the village. A very little labor and expense in the way of interior fittings would [68] make it quite comfortable. He and his wife have one child only, a young girl of fourteen. She is a modest looking, pleasing child — very intelligent — one of the first class in the school,. She does not look like one who has ever been 'possessed with a devil', and yet this is the child, whom, three years ago, her teacher saw naked in the midst of a howling band, tearing and devouring the bleeding dog. How changed She who 'had the unclean spirit' now sits at the feet of Jesus, clothed and in her right mind."

Not many months later Mr Duncan paid a visit to Fort Simpson to preach the Gospel to the heathen Indians, who still remained there. He was accompanied by two natives, *Clah* and Paul Legaic. On their return, in a letter to the Missionary Society, Mr Duncan related a remarkable incident which occurred during the trip. He said: "I have just returned from a visit to Fort Simpson: I went to proclaim the Gospel once more to the poor, unfeeling heathen there. I laid the Gospel again distinctly before them, and they seemed much affected. The most pleasing circumstance of all, and which I was not prepared to expect, was, that Paul, Legaic and *Clah* (the one in times past a formidable enemy and opposer, and the other one among the first to hear and greet the Gospel), sat by me, one on either side. After I had finished my address on each occasion, they got up and spoke, and spoke well. [70]

Indian school girls with teachers

"Legaic completely shamed and confounded an old man who, in replying to my address, had said that I had come too late to do him and other old people good; that, had I come when the first white traders came, the Tsmsheans had long since been good; but they had been allowed to grow up in sin; they had seen nothing in the first whites who came amongst them to unsettle them in their old habits, but those had rather added to them fresh sin, and now their sins were deep laid, they (he and the other old people) could not change. Legaic interrupted him and said: 'I am a chief, a Tsimshean chief. You know I have been bad, very bad, as bad as anyone here. I have grown up and grown old in sin, but God has changed my heart and He can change yours.

Think not to excuse yourself in your sins by saying you are too old and too bad to mend. Nothing is impossible with God. Come to God; try His way; He can save you.

"He then exhorted all to taste God's way, to give their hearts to Him, and to leave all their sins; and then endeavored to show them what they had to expect if they did so — not temporal good, not health, long life, nor ease, nor wealth, but God's favor here and happiness with God after death."

Legaic had been known far and wide along the coast, and the traders who heard of his conversion and transformation could scarcely believe it. As time went on he became [71] came of immense service to Mr Duncan in the prosecution of the work, and came to be called "Mr Duncan's Grand Vizier."

For seven years Legaic played a prominent part in the life of the settlement, eager to assist in every undertaking for the betterment of his fellows, and humbly earning his living as a carpenter. In 1869 he made a journey up the Nass River, and on reaching Fort Simpson on his way home, was taken suddenly ill. He at once dispatched a messenger to Mr Duncan, bearing this note:

"Dear Sir: — I want to see you. I always remember you in my mind. I shall be very sorry if I shall not see you before I go away, because you showed me the ladder that reaches to Heaven, and I am on that ladder now. I have nothing to trouble me. I only want to see you."

Mr Duncan wished greatly to go at once to the bedside of Legaic, but his duties at Metlakahtla would not permit him to leave, for a peculiar epidemic was raging just then and there were a score of sick people on the island whom be was attending day and night.
A second and third messenger followed in quick succession, but still Mr Duncan could not leave. Then came the sad tidings of the death of the famous chieftain, accompanied by the following lines, which were still unfinished when the death angel bore his soul to the long home above: [72]

"My Dear Sir — This is my last letter, to say I am very happy. I am going to rest from trouble, trial and temptation. I do not feel afraid to meet my God. In my painful body I always remember the words of our Lord Jesus Christ" —

Here the letter ended abruptly, and in -this triumphant manner ended the life of the Apostle Paul of the Tsitnshean Indians. He was a modern miracle of grace, a striking example of the power of Christ's blood to. wash away the darkest sins and to transform men from darkest sinners into saints.

"During the years from 1863 to 1869 the spiritual progress of the settlement had gone on apace. In 1868 the Bishop of Columbia paid a second visit to Metlakahtla and baptized sixty-five adults, of whom he wrote: "I truly believe that most of these are sincere and intelligent believers in Christ, as worthy converts from heathenism as have ever been known in the history of the church."

In the autumn of the following year Mr Cridge, then Dean of Victoria, baptized 98 adults and 18 Indian children.

The desire of Mr Duncan that the island should be a beacon of Gospel light to the Indians of all the Northland was being happily fulfilled. Wherever the Metlakahtla Indians went on their fishing, trading and hunting expeditions, they carried with them [73] the Gospel message and proclaimed it at every opportunity.

Old Metlakahtla

On one occasion a party of Metlakahtla people visited the Chilkat Indians, who lived on the Alaskan coast, 500 to 600 miles to the north. So impressed were these northern Indians with the wonderful tales they heard of the power of the Gospel and of the material progress at Metlakahtia, that they decided to pay a visit to the island [74] to see the man who had accomplished such marvels. A delegation came down the coast in their handsome canoes, and aa they near-ed the shore they put on their finest apparel and barbaric ornaments to suitably impress the people with their importance. On landing, they approached in solemn state, and Mr Duncan was advised to dress in his best clothes, as the savages might despise him if he appeared in rough garments. He, however, was engaged in some important work which he could not drop just then.

The Chilkats marched through the village well-nigh struck dumb with astonishment at what they beheld; the beautiful buildings, the strange industries, the civilized clothing of the Metlakahtlans.

Finally, Mr Duncan left his work, just as he was, and hastened to greet the visitors. As he drew near and was pointed out to the Chilkats, they looked over and beyond him and declared they could not see him. When he cordially welcomed them they said scarcely a word beyond the formal syllables of recognition, so disappointed were they. Mr Duncan escorted them to his house, and there their pent-up astonishment gave way, and they exclaimed:

"Surely, you cannot be the man! Why, we expected to see a great and powerful giant, gifted in magic, with enormous eyes that could look right through us and read our thoughts' No, it is impossible! How [75] could you tame the wild and ferocious Tsimsheans, who were always urging war, and were feared throughout the whole coast? It was only a few years ago that all the country was a streak of blood. Now we see nothing but white eagle's down (their emblem of peace and amity.) We can hardly believe our own eyes when we see these fine

The interior of Father Duncan's church in New Metlakahtla.

houses and find the Tsiimheans have become wise like white men! They tell us that you have

God's Book and that you have taught them to read it; we wish to see it."

Mr Duncan then brought out a Bible and placed it before them. That sacred book, he declared, contained the Word of God, the Message of the Great King, the Way of Life Everlasting. It was only because the Metlakahtla Indians, had obeyed the words of that Book that they had built such a beautiful city.

Each of the Chilkat delegation then went forward and reverently touched the Bible, exclaiming, "Ahm, Ahm" — "It is good, it is good."

For several days the delegation remained at Metlakahtla inspecting the truly wonder-hit results, which had been achieved by the Metlakahtlans during the few short years of their residence.

As the years passed Metlakahtla became not only a Gospel beacon, but a great light, radiating law and order throughout all the surrounding country. Mr Duncan was [76] appointed a magistrate by the Canadian Government, with jurisdiction up and down the coast for hundreds of miles. In the enforcement of his duties, chief among which was the suppression of illegal liquor selling, many thrilling and perilous experiences were encountered, some of which will next lit related. [77]

Chapter VII
Fighting Against Fire-Water

ONE of the first steps taken by Mr Duncan on his arrival at Metlakahtla had been the: appointment of a body of Indian constables to maintain order. Although he anticipated no trouble, yet he deemed it wise to take time by the forelock, remembering that many who had signed the fifteen rule had had very little training, and had not yet fully surrendered themselves to Christ.

By the year 1866 there were twenty of these constables, "as fine a set of young men as you would wish to see — the very pick of the Christians." The Indians greatly enjoyed their distinction as guardians of the law, and to be admitted into the force was esteemed the highest honor that could be conferred upon a stalwart 'young man'. [78]

In his duties as magistrate and justice of the peace along the Alaskan and Canadian coasts, Mr Duncan found these constables indispensable.

At this period, as today, it was against the law to sell liquor, or fire-water, to any Indian. However, wicked white men and Indians constantly attempted to sell it in, secret, though they well knew that liquor set the red men on fire with evil and led them to commit the most horrible crimes. The influence of intoxicating drinks on white men is sufficiently terrible, but on the Indians it is often two-fold worse.

One of the saddest incidents in connection with his duties as magistrate was the following, which Mr Duncan reported to the Canadian government in 1865:

"The Indian camps about us are deluged with fire-water, and, of course, every kind of madness is rife.

"It is just because our village makes a stand against the universal tide of disorder that we are being threatened on every side.

"In July last I apprised his Excellency, the Governor, that we had in the spring seized a quantity of liquor, which a party of Kitahmaht Indians brought here for sale.

"In revenge for the loss of their liquor (I am sorry to inform you) these Indians, in the summer, stole a little boy belonging to this place, while he was away with his parents at a fishery on the Skeena River. And, horrible to write, the poor little [79] fellow was literally worried to death, being torn to pieces by the mouths of a set of cannibals at a great feast they had made.

"This atrocious deed would have met with summary vengeance from the relatives of the boy had it happened a few years ago. In this case, however, though highly exasperated, they would not allow themselves to do anything until they had seen me. In order to prevent blood being shed at random, I ordered them to wait till the arrival of a ship of war, when I promised to refer the matter to the captain, and hoped they would have justice done them in a civilized way.

"Last week, however, an Indian, (uncle to the unfortunate boy, but not a Metlakahtla man), arrived here from Victoria. where fie had been living for the last two years and a half. On his learning of the Kitahmaht atrocity, it seems he secretly resolved to take the law in his own hands, and for that purpose proceeded two or three days ago to Fort Simpson, .where a party of Kitahmaht Indians had recently arrived.

"This morning at two o'clock, I was awakened and informed that a Kitahmaht Indian had fallen a victim to this man's revenge, and that great excitement was occasioned at Fort Simpson. Nor is it known who will be the next to fall, to feed the stream of blood which has commenced to [80] flow, but every Indian around me is in fear for his life."

Mr Duncan and his heroic band of constables performed valiant service in ridding the coast of the illegal and infernal liquor traffic, and in nearly every case without loss of life. On one occasion, however, one Indian was killed in the attempt to capture a sloop, manned by white men, which was smuggling in liquor to be sold to the Indian camps. Mr Duncan, hearing of the presence of this vessel in the neighborhood, sent several Indians with a warrant for the arrest of the captain. The result of the encounter and the series of events following were thus related by Mr Duncan:

"The sad result was that the five Indians serving the warrant were fired upon by the three white men on board the sloop, one being killed on the spot, three being severely wounded. The sloop got away and it was not till the following day that the Indian unhurt returned to the settlement, bringing his three wounded companions in a canoe. Unfortunately, at the time, I had very few people left in the village, so that we were unable to follow the murderers while within a reasonable distance of us. After I had done all and the best I could for the wounded men, I determined to run down to Victoria, it being unsafe from the unsettled state of the coast to send the Indians alone. [81]

Indian wedding party

"On the 25th of August I started for [82] Victoria in a small boat, and on the 5th of September, by seven a.m, I was in Nanaimi {Nanaimo}, the nearest white settlement, having been brought by a gracious God safely through many perils on the sea and perils by the heathen.

"I need scarcely say that, as soon as possible I communicated the shocking tidings to the Governor of each colony, to Admiral Denman, and to all our friends. All deeply sympathized with us; and Governor Seymour, of British Columbia, lost not a moment of time till all the needful despatches were written, and forwarded to the two neighboring governments, Russian and American, and to the Admiral of the station, calling upon all to do their utmost to seize the murderers and hand them over to justice. The Governor also engaged a doctor to visit the wounded men, and Admiral Denman sent up H.M.S. '*Grappler*' with the doctor and myself on board to the settlement.

"I cannot express to you the anxiety I felt while away and how restless I was to return to the sick men. But God was better to me than my fears. We arrived on the 4th instant at

Metlakahtla and to my great relief I found the wounded men doing well, and all the settlement going on prosperously. I called a meeting of the village on the evening of our arrival, to return thanks to Almighty God. that He had remembered us in our affliction. In my addresses both [83] before going to Victoria and since my return I have been greatly helped in opening to the Indians the passages and truths from the Scripture which this late dispensation of Providence illustrated; and I have been shown by unmistakable signs that this severe chastisement with which it has pleased God to visit us, will be productive of great good to us.

"It would take too long to detail to you the series of Indian laws of revenge and compensation which this sad occurrence and its sequences have revived, met, defeated and dispersed forever; and how the Christian taws on these mailers have been put forward in strong contrast, approved, magnified, and made to triumph; and how for the first time a calamity which would have called forth only savage fire and relentless fury in the Indian as heathen, has only called forth patient endurance and lawful retaliation in the Indian as Christian."

Among the scores of persons brought to justice by Mr Duncan and his constable a notable case was that of Peter Gargotitch who, on account of a grudge against Mr Duncan, had boasted in Victoria that he would make the Metlakahtla Indians drunk.

Some weeks later the Indians reported that there was a white man at Inverness, ten miles distant from Metlakahtla, selling liquor contrary to law. Mr Duncan told his constables to find out definitely the facts in the case add report to him. Accordingly [84] two Indians went to Inverness to gather evidence. While one went into the man's tent and bought some liquor in a bottle, the other looked through a hole in the tent in order to testify as a witness. As soon as they reported to Mr Duncan he sent a white man then staying on the island at the head of several constables to arrest the offender, When the party reached Inverness with the warrant the liquor seller drew a revolver, and brandishing it in their faces, declared he would shoot the man who attempted to serve the warrant upon him. The white man, at the head of the constables, did not wish to risk his life, so he returned, to Mr Duncan with the warrant unserved. Mr Duncan declared that oh no account must the offender be allowed to escape. He asked the man if he would make another attempt at capture, if it were made certain that his life would not be in danger. He consented and Mr Duncan completed his plans without delay. Very early the next morning, a number of large canoes left Metlakahtla, filled with forty Indians, all fully armed, with the white man at their head. When they reached Inverness they found that the liquor dealer had loaded all his kegs into a canoe and set off up the river, accompanied by two companions. The Indians at once started in pursuit after going a few miles they saw the fugitives in their canoe paddling for dear life. When it was seen that the Indians [85] would soon overtake them the canoe was headed for the shore and beached, with the liquor still in it, while the three men took to the woods. They knew that escape was impossible, for the forest was well-nigh impenetrable, and behind them were forty fleet-footed Indians. Hence, they ran only a few rods and hid in the bush. As the pursuing canoes came opposite the place where the leader was hid the officer with the warrant shouted out that he wished to see him. The leader stepped boldly out, prepared as before to defy. his captors. The officer then shouted that he placed him under arrest and ordered him to hold up his hands at once or he would be a dead man. At the same instant the rifles of the forty Indians standing in the canoes were leveled at the dealer with orders to fire if he offered the least resistance. The man saw he was caught and at once held his hands high above his bead.
The warrant was server and the three men, with the canoe and liquor, were brought to Metlakahtla. As the leader was brought before Mr Duncan, who should it prove to be but Peter Gorgotitch, who had threatened to make the Metlakahtla Indians drunk? He was fined $500

which he succeeded in borrowing and paying, and he left the Island a sadder but wiser man. The circumstances of the arrest did not allow Mr Duncan to confiscate Gorgotitch's twenty-three kegs of liquor, each containing [86] ten gallons. A few weeks later, however, about half of it was stolen, and Gorgotitch returned to Victoria burdened by debt and in a pitiable condition. For several years he went here and there, until news .reached Mr Duncan that he had been killed in British Columbia. The activity of Mr Duncan and his constables in enforcing the law became more and more feared by the smugglers and liquor sellers until by 1876 the illegal traffic had almost entirely ceased. During the eight years following the arrival of the pilgrims at Metlakahtla in 1862 great material progress had been made. Between one hundred and two hundred houses had been built, almost every one having a neat garden attached. A large general store had been established, which was patronized not only by the Metlakahtla Indians, but by men from surrounding camps who were thus brought into contact with Christian influences. A court house and commodious school house had been erected and several Industries started, including a soap-house, blacksmith shop, and by no means least, a saw-mill run by water power. When one old Indian heard that Mr Duncan intended to make water saw wood, he' exclaimed:

"If it is true that Mr Duncan can make water saw wood, then I will see it and die."

In 1870 Mr 'Duncan paid a visit to England. where he procured machinery for new industries and spent several weeks learning [87] the arts of weaving, rope-making, twine-spinning and brush-making. In addition, he acquired the gamut of each instrument in a band of twenty-one pieces, which was presented to him for the settlement. On his return tourney he spent nearly three months in Victoria, reaching Metlakahtla once more in February, 1871, after a year's absence. Describing the first evening after his arrival, Mr Duncan wrote:

"At night, after visiting among the sick, I sat down with about fifty for a general talk. I gave them the special messages from Christian friends which I had down in my note-book, told them how much we were prayed for by many Christians in England, and scanned over the principal events of my voyage and doings in England. We sat till midnight, but even then the village was lighted up, and the people all waiting to hear from the favored fifty, what I had communicated. Many did not go to bed at all, but sat up all night talking over what they had heard."

As may be seen from this royal welcome accorded to Mr Duncan. and from events shortly to be narrated, the Tsimshean Indians were far from being a stolid, unemotional race. At times they fairly overflowed with emotion and excitement, and no people enjoyed holidays and festal occasions more than they. At this period there occurred two notable celebrations which were . red letter days in the history of the settlement. [88]

Chapter VIII
Gala Days On The Island

THE island of Metlakahtla being in Canadian territory one of the days most elaborately celebrated by the Indians was Queen Victoria's birthday. On one occasion the date occurred when a British warship, "*The Sparrow-Hawk*," was anchored in the bay off the village. The Bishop of Columbia had come on the ship to Metlakahtla to receive fresh converts into the church, and he and the officers ot the vessel joined heartily in the effort to make the day one long to be remembered.

The day dawned bright and beautiful and at an early hour a party of sailors rowed ashore to decorate the mission house and bastion with flags of all nations.

The proceedings of the early part of the day were spiritual, seventeen children being baptized in the house of God. Later, a distribution of small gifts took place among 140 nicely dressed Indian children.

On the stroke of twelve o'clock a royal salute of twenty-one guns thundered from the ship, and the special exercises of the occasion began. There were sports and games of all sorts which were engaged in most heartily and joyously by young and old. There were foot races, sack races, [89] etc., with such games as blind man's' buff, and a review of the village constables. The most-exciting feature of the afternoon was the canoe race. The course was two miles long around the island. Five large canoes entered for the contest, eight or nine stalwart young Indians being seated in each. Beneath the deep, swift strokes of the paddies the canoes shot forward like birds, and the race was as beautiful as it was exciting.

In the evening a public meeting was held when a number of the officers of the "Sparrow-Hawk" addressed the Indians, and several of the Metlakahtla leaders made brief but eloquent replies. A few of the short speeches made by the Indians were reported as follows:

Abraham Kemskah: — "Chiefs, I will say a little. How were we to hear when we were young, what we now hear? And, being old and long fixed in sin, how are we to obey? We are like tire canoe going against the tide which is too strong for it; we struggle, but in spite of our efforts we are carried out to sea.' Again, we are like a youth watching a skilled artisan at work; he strives to imitate his work but fails; so we: we try to follow God's way, but how far we fall short. Still we are encouraged to persevere. We feel we are nearing the shore; we are coming nearer the hand of God, near peace. We must look neither to the right oor left, but look straight on and persevere." [90]

Richard Wilson; — "Chiefs, as we have now heard, so do ye. Indeed, father" (addressing Mr Duncan) "we arc sinners before you; we often make your voice bad in calling us; we must persevere, we must try, though we are bad; we arc like the wedge used in splitting the trees; we arc nuking the way for out children; they will be better than we, are. The sun does not come out in full strength' in early morn; the gray light at first spreads itself over the earth; as it rises the light increases and by and by, is the mid-day sun. We shall die before we have reached much, but we shall die expecting our children to pass on beyond us, and reach the wished-for-goal.

Daniel Baxter (Neeash-ah-pootk) — "Chiefs, I am foolish, I am bad, bad in your sight. What can our hearts say? What shall we do? We can only pray and persevere. We will not listen to voices on this side or that, but follow on till we reach our Father in Heaven."

Jacob (Cheevost) — "Chiefs, we have heard you. Why should we try to mistake the way you teach us? Rather we must try to follow on; though our feet often slip, we must still try; we have rocks all around us; our sins are like the rocks, but the rudder of our canoe is being held. She will not drift away. We are all assisting to hold the rudder and keep her in her course. What would she be without the rudder? Soon, a wreck upon the rocks; so [91] we must cry to God for help to follow on."

* * *

As the Indians had grown enlightened under Mr Duncan's teaching, and had come to understand the full meaning of Christmas day, they entered as heartily as their white brothers into making it a season of Joy and gladness, and thus fittingly celebrating the .birthday of Him who redeemed the world from darkness and death. The Christmas season of 1873 was especially notable because large numbers of Fort Simpson Indians were invited to Metlakahtla to spend the period with their Christian' brethren. Of the series of events which filled up the days with happy memories Mr Duncan sent the following graphic report to the Missionary Society:

"This is the first season that the heathen customs at Fort Simpson have been generally disregarded, and hence we thought it well to encourage Christian customs in their place. To this end we decided to invite all the congregation at Fort Simpson to spend the festival of Christmas with us at Metlakahtla, that they might receive the benefit of a series of special services, and be preserved from falling into those excesses which we had reason to fear would follow should they spend the Christmas by themselves. About two hundred and fifty availed themselves of our invitation and they arrived at Metlakahtla the day before Christmas in twenty-one canoes, which, indeed, [92] presented a picture as they approached with flags flying.

"According to previous arrangement they alt clustered to the market house, which we at present use for our church and which has been very appropriately decorated. On our guests being seated I gave them a short address, and after prayer, in company with Mr and Mrs Collison, shook hands with them all. They then were quartered around the village and a very exciting scene ensued, all the villagers literally scrambling for the guests. After the scramble several came running to me to complain that they had not succeeded in securing a single guest, while others had got more than their share. To settle matters amicably, I had to send two constables round the village to readjust the distribution of our new friends.

"Our Christmas eve was spent in practicing with a band of twenty young men, new Christmas hymn in Tsimshean, which I managed to prepare for the occasion. About 1:30 on Christmas morning we reassembled, when Mr Collison and myself accompanied the twenty waits to sing round the village, carrying the harmonium and concertina with us. We sang in seven different places and three hymns in each place. The village was illuminated and the singing was hearty and solemn. This was the first attempt of the Indians at part-singing in their own tongue. [93] Brass band [94]

"Christmas day was a great day, houses decorated with evergreen's, flags flying, constables and council passing from house to house in "their uniforms, and greeting the inmates. Now a string of young men, then another of young women, might be seen going

Zobo Girls Band

into this house, then into that; friends meeting on the road, shaking hands everywhere; everybody greeting everybody, hours occupied with handshaking and interchanging good wishes; nobody thinking of anything else but scattering smiles and greetings, till the church bell rings, and all wend their way to meet and worship God.

"The crowd seemed so great that fears were entertained that our meeting house could not accommodate them. I at once decided that the children should assemble in the school-house and have a separate service. Samuel Marsden kindly volunteered to conduct it. Even with this arrangement our meeting house was crowded to excess. There could not have been less than seven hundred present. What a sight! Had anyone accompanied me to the Christmas-day services I held twelve or fourteen years ago at Fort Simpson, and again on this occasion, methinks if an infidel he would have been confused and puzzled by the change; but if a Christian his heart must have leaped for joy. The Tsimsheans might well sing on this day, 'Glory to God in the highest, and on earth [95] peace, good will towards men.'

"The following day the young men engaged in the healthy game of foot-ball, and all the people turned out to witness the sport. Mr and Mrs Collison and myself were present to encourage them. After foot-ball a marriage took place. A young woman formerly trained in the mission-house, was married to a chief. A marriage feast was given, to which between four and five hundred people were invited.

"On Friday, the second day of January, our guests departed home. When ready to start the church bell rang, and they paddled their canoes to the meeting-house, which is built upon the beach. Leaving their canoes, they reassembled for a short address and a concluding prayer. This out, again entering their canoes, they pushed a little from the beach, a cannon was fired, and amid the ringing cheers of hundreds of voices they dashed off, paddling with all their might."

The most memorable events of the next few years were the completion of the remarkable church, and the visits of two distinguished personages, with one of whom our narrative has already been concerned, and whose presence again in their midst filled the Metlakahtlans with the keenest Joy. [96]

Chapter IX
Two Notable Visitors

WITH each passing year the settlement at Metlakatla grew stronger, the village more prosperous and beautiful. On the sixth of August, 1872, there was laid the corner-stone of a massive new church which was to be the crowning glory of the Christian colony. Although part of the cost of the church was given by outsiders; yet the Indians sacrificed largely and often that the work might progress unhindered. A little over two years from the laying of the corner-stone, on Christmas day, 1874, the beautiful edifice — entirely the work of Indian hands — was dedicated to the service of God. It was a time of great rejoicing and gladness. Describing it, Mr Duncan said:

"Over seven hundred Indians were present at our opening services. Could it be that this concourse of well-dressed people in their new and beautiful church, but a few years ago made up the fiendish assemblies at Port Simpson! Could it be that these voices, now engaged in solemn prayer and thrilling songs of praise to Almighty God, are the very voices I once heard yelling and whooping at heathen orgies on dismal winter nights!" [97]

At this period the Governor-General of Canada was the Earl of Duffern. He was one of the great statesmen of the age, and one of the leaders of the English aristocracy. In the year 1876 he made an extended trip through the western part of Canada, in the course of which he planned to visit Metlakahtla, of which he had heard most glowing accounts. The Indians on their part were greatly delighted at the prospect of receiving a visit from so famous a man. As one method of showing their appreciation of his coming, they prepared the following address of welcome, which was presented to him on his arrival:

"May it please your Excellency: We, the inhabitants of Metlakahtla, of the Tsimshean nation of Indians, desire to express our joy in welcoming your Excellency and Lady Dufferin to our village. Under the teaching of the Gospel we have learned the Divine command, 'Fear God, honor the King,' and thus as loyal subjects of her Majesty, Queen Victoria, we rejoice in seeing you visit our shores.

"We have learned to respect and obey the laws of the Queen, and we will continue to uphold and defend the same in our community and nation.

"We are still a weak and poor people, only lately emancipated from the thralldom of heathenism and savage customs; but we are struggling to rise and advance to a Christian life and civilization. [98]

"Trusting that we may enjoy a share of your Excellency's kind and fostering care, and under your administration continue to advance in peace and prosperity.

"We have the honor to subscribe ourselves, your Excellency's humble and obedient servant,

"For the Indians of Metlakahtla,
"David Leask,

"Secretary to the Native Council."

The Governor-General was accompanied by his accomplished wife, Lady Dutferm, and to say that they were pleased with what they saw is putting it mildly. Lord Duffern declared he would treasure their address of welcome above all others he received during his journey. In an address to the Indians assembled in the open air on a beautiful summer day the Governor-General said in part:

"I have come a long distance in order to assure you, in the name of your Great Mother, the Queen of England, with what pleasure she has learned of your well-being, of the progress you have made in the arts of peace and the knowledge of the Christian religion, under the auspices of your friend, Mr Duncan. I have viewed with astonishment the church which you have built entirely by your own industry and intelligence. That church is in itself a monument of the way in which you have profited by the teachings you have received. It does you the greatest credit, and we have [99] every right to hope that, while in its outward aspect it bears testimony to your conformity to the laws of the Gospel, beneath its sacred roof your sincere and faithful prayers will be rewarded by those blessings which are promised to all those who approach the throne of God in humility and faith.

* * *

"Before I conclude I cannot help expressing to Mr Duncan and those associated with him in his good work, not only in my name, not only in the name of the Government of Canada, but also in the name of Her Majesty, the Queen, and in the name of the people of England, who take so deep an interest in the well-being of all the native races throughout the Queen's dominions, our deep gratitude to him for thus having devoted the flower of his life, in spite of innumerable difficulties, dangers and discouragements to a work which has resulted in the beautiful scene we have witnessed this morning. I only wish to add that I am very much obliged to you for the satisfactory and loyal address with which you have greeted me. The very fact of you being in a position to express yourselves with so much propriety is in itself extremely creditable to you, and although it has been my good fortune to receive many addresses during my stay in Canada from various communities of your fellow subjects, not one of them will be surrounded by so many hopeful and pleasant [100] reminiscences as those which I shall carry away with me from this spot."

Church at Metlakatla erected by the Indians

But there was one person whose coming to the island threw it into a far greater commotion of pleasurable excitement than even the visit of the Governor-General. That person was none other than Admiral Prevost, who, twenty-five years before, as Captain Prevost, had been the means of starting the entire work. His visit has been well called "the most joyous and memorable event in the history of the settlement." It was the red letter day of Metlakahtla.

Throughout a quarter of a century amid all the dangers and perils of naval life God had preserved the gallant captain, and had honored him enabling him to reach the exalted station of Admiral. During all the years, however, he had not lost sight of the glorious work he inaugurated, and now at last he was permitted to see with his own eyes the marvelous results of his early efforts. The Admiral spent a full month among the Metlakahtlans, declaring that words could not describe the joy he experienced at witnessing their transformation. He sent a graphic account of his visit to the Church Missionary Society part of which was as follows:

"Three a.m., Tuesday, 18th June, 1878. Arrived at Fort Simpson in the United States Mail Steamer California, from Sitka.

Was met by William Duncan with [102] sixteen Indians, nearly all elders. Our greeting was most hearty, and the meeting with Duncan was a cause of real thankfulness to God, in sight, too. of the very spot (nay on it) where God had put into my heart the first desire of sending the Gospel to the poor heathen around me. Twenty-five years previously H.M.S *Virago* had been repaired on that very beach. What a change had been effected during those passing years! Of the crew before me nine of the sixteen were, to my knowledge, formerly medicine men or cannibals. In humble faith, we could only exclaim, 'What hath God wrought! It is all His doing, and it is marvelous in our eyes.

"It did not take long to transfer ourselves and our baggage to the canoe and at 4:30 a.m. we started against wind and tide, rain, too, at intervals; but having much to talk about of past events and future plans the twenty miles of distance soon disappeared and about noon we crossed the bar and entered the 'inlet of Kahtla.' On the north side of the inlet stands on an eminence the church of God;' on either side of it spreads out the village of Metlakahtla, skirting two bays whose beaches are at once a landing-place for its inhabitants and a shelter for the canoes. As we approached the landing-place two gun« were ' fired and flags displayed from house to house — conspicuous by a string of them reaching the Mission House verandah, [103] inscribed, 'A Real Welcome to Metlakatitla.' Near to this were assembled all the village — men, women and children — gaily dressed.

"'After twenty-five years' absence God had brought me back again amidst all the sundry and manifold changes of the world, face to face with. those tribes amongst whom I had before witnessed only bloodshed, cannibalism and heathen deviltry in its grossest form. Now they were sitting at the feet of Jesus, clothed, and in their right mind. The very church-warden, dear old Peter Simpson, who opened the church-door for me, was once the chief of one of the cannibal tribes * * *

"Before my departure from Metlakahtla I assembled the few who were left at the village, to tell them I was anxious to leave behind some token both of my visit to them after so long an absence, and also that I still bore them on my heart What should it be? After hours of consultation, they decided they would leave the choice to me, and when I told them (what I had beforehand determined upon) that my present would be a set of street lamps to light up their village by night, their joy was unbounded. Their first thought had a spiritual meaning. By day, God's house was a memorable object, visible both by vessels passing and repassing, and by all canoes as strange Indians traveled about; but by night all had been darkness, now this was no longer so — as the bright light of the [104] glorious Gospel bad through God's mercy and love shined into their dark hearts, so , would all be reminded by night as well as by day, oi the marvelous light shining into the hearts of many at Metlakahtla."

But the narrative of the Admiral's visit would by no means be complete without relating the sequel to the beautiful action which had occurred on the Queen Charlotte Islands a quarter of a century previously. One day a well built canoe containing two stalwart Indians was seen approaching Metlakahtla. When the occupants landed they proved to be Edensaw, the head chief of the Hydahs, and his son. They had heard of Admiral Prevost's visit and had made the long journey through the open sea to see his face once more. Their meeting with the Admiral presented a beautiful scene, which reached its climax when Edensaw put his hand into his bosom and drew forth a little book which he handed to the Admiral. The heart of the venerable commander overflowed with wonder and praise to God when he saw written on the fly-leaf these lines: "From Captain Prevost, H.M.S. '*Satellite*' trusting that the bread thus cast upon the waters may be found alter many days."

Truly it had been found after 'many day' indeed! The son of Edensaw was an earnest Christian — the first person among the Hydahs to come out boldly on the Lord's side. Edensaw himself was [105] convinced that Christianity was the right way, but he was a proud man and had not yet been willing to sacrifice his power and wealth as chieftain in order to follow Christ. But who can estimate the part played by that small testament in preparing the heart of the son to receive the Gospel? Doubtless scores of times as a boy he had heard his father relate the story of how be received "The Letter of God" from the great white Chief, and he had without doubt longed earnestly to know the meaning of the message contained in the strange English book. Hence when the missionary came to the Queen Charlotte Islands it was natural that the son of Edensaw should be the first convert.

And now once more in .this world, father and son stood 'face to face' with their spiritual benefactor, after a full quarter of a century had passed, whitening the hair of the Admiral and bringing wrinkles into the face of the old chief. It was a memorable meeting worthy of the brush of a great painter; It was a strange and wonderful illustration of the glorious fruitage that results in the far distant future from the .good little deeds of today.

* * *

But ere long the idyllic life of the colony was to be shattered to pieces, only to spring up again more beautiful than ever on an isle of paradise under the glorious banner of the stars and stripes. [106]

Chapter X
In Quest of a New Home

EARLY in the eighties when the Christian colony was in the lull bloom of its vigor and prosperity a cloud appeared on the horizon, which grew larger with each passing year until the Metlakahtlans finally left their dearly loved island, and, in company with Mr Duncan, set out in search of a new home. The trouble began soon after the death of the great Henry Venn, secretary of the Church Missionary Society, who had most heartily approved of Mr Duncan's methods and plans for the conversion and education of the Indians. Following his decease, however, a Missionary Bishop was appointed to oversee the work at Metlakahtla and other missions in British Columbia. He decided that the Indians should conform more closely to the customs of the Church of England; that the Lord's Supper should be instituted with the use of real wine in the service; and that much of the ritual and ceremony of the English church should be introduced among the red men. Mr Duncan strongly objected to these changes. He knew the inordinate

111

passion of the Indian for intoxicants and felt it would be wrong to use fermented wine in the communion service; [107] while in addition the law of Canada prohibited any Indian from touching wine under penalty of imprisonment.

With regard to the elaborate ritual of the Church of England, Mr Duncan believed it entirely unsuited to the worship of the Indians, and felt that if introduced it would seriously weaken and undermine their spiritual life.

The Bishop, however, still insisted on the changes being made. But Mr Duncan was accustomed to adhering to principle at whatever cost, and rather than submit to what he believed was wrong, he left the Church Missionary Society and started an Independent Native Church. All but a few of the Indians at Metlahahtla followed him and joined the new church. The Missionary Society, on the advice of its Bishop, but against that of several of its missionaries in the vicinity, still continued to carry on a mission among the few who remained, and claimed the ownership of the two most central acres of land in the village on which the mission buildings stood. The Canadian Government supported the Society in this claim, to the Indians' astonishment and dismay, for the land had been, theirs for ages past.

Mr Duncan and his followers carefully considered the situation and rather than have discord and disunion in their Arcadia determined to set out for the second time in quest of a new home. [108]

A short time later a band of Metlakahtla set out in their canoes in search of another island upon which they could erect a new and more beautiful Christian city. They went northward into Alaska, exploring the land carefully as they went. At last, about one hundred miles north of Metlakahtla, they found an island which even surpassed the old one in beauty and natural advantages. When the Indians saw it they unanimously exclaimed that they would look no farther, for it was certainly an isle of paradise they had found, with its marvelously beautiful harbor, its virgin forests, its purple mountains, and its silvery waterfall. As the scouts approached Metlakahtla on their return, they signalized the success of their mission by singing the "Canoe-song," the moat beautiful of all the native melodies.

Mr Duncan now started for Washington to secure permission from the United States Government to settle on the land. The case of the Metlakahtlans was carefully considered by President Cleveland, the secretaries of the Interior and Treasury, the Attorney-General and others. Many distinguished people earnestly seconded the cause of the Indians, among them being the Governor of Alaska, Henry Ward Beecher and Dr. Sheldon Jackson. By the advice of the Attorney-General, the Secretary of the Interior finally decided that the Metlakahtlans could settle [109] upon any unoccupied land in Alaska, but that no reservation could be set aside for them, as land laws for the territory had not yet been made. He also declared that when Alaskan land laws should be formed "ample provision will be made to meet the necessities of all law-abiding inhabitants."

With this assurance of fair treatment from the United Stales, Mr Duncan was fully satisfied. He mailed the good news to the Indians and during the summer of 1887 a small number of them journeyed northward in their canoes to fell the forest and prepare the way for the remainder. On the 7th of August, Mr Duncan reached the new island, having been absent in the United States nearly nine months. His. welcome was most hearty as he stepped upon the beach of the New Metlakahtla, which was to be the future home of the colony. A memorable service, like that the Pilgrims must have held on landing at Plymouth Rock, was at once arranged, which a newspaper correspondent who was present described graphically as follows:

mission buildings

"The day was a perfect one and the visitors were at once put on shore. A more lovely place than this harbor it is impossible to imagine. It is semi-circular in shape, opening out through a number of small islands to the westward. On the east and, north were wild, rugged mountains, coming down to the water's edge, and on the south is a low, green shore skirted by a [110] gravel beach that winds in and out in beautiful curves. The place was entirely uninhabited except by thirty or forty of the men of Metlakahtla with their families who had come on as an advance guard. The remainder, in all about one thousand people, men, women and children, will come as soon as provision can be made for them and the [111] means of transportation shall arrive.

"The exercises were impromptu and Mr Duncan first addressed his people in their native tongue. He told them of his trip to the United States, and concluded by introducing Hon. N.H.R. Dawson, the U.S. Commissioner of Education then upon an official tour of Alaska, who had kindly consented to make an address upon this occasion. In Mr Dawson's address, interpreted by Mr Duncan into the native language for the benefit of those who did not understand English, they were impressively told of the power and glory of the great American Government, under whose protection they were coming, and were assured that when its flag was raised over them. they would be protected in their lives and liberties, that their , homes and lands would be assured to them, and that their education and welfare would be the cherished care of the great Government, to which they had intrusted themselves.

"When he concluded, the flags were raised, the ship saluting them as they went up [112] with its battery of one gun. The natives then sang 'Rock of Ages' exquisitely in their native tongue. Rev. Dr. Fraser of San Francisco, in a touching prayer, then commended the new settlement to the protection of Divine Providence, after which all united in singing 'Coronation.' One of the principal chiefs or selectmen, Daniel Ne-ash-kum-ack-kem, then replied to Mr Dawson's address in a short speech as follows:

" 'Chiefs, I have a few words of truth to let you know what our hearts are saying. The God of Heaven is looking at our doings here today. You have stretched out your hands to the Tsimsheans. Your act is a Christian act. We have long been knocking at the door of another government for justice, but the door has been closed against us. You have risen up and opened your door to us. and bid us welcome to this beautiful spot, upon which we propose to erect our homes. What can our hearts say to tills, but that we are thankful and happy. The work of the Christian is never lost. Your work will not he lost to you. It will live, and you will find it after many days. We arc here only a few today who have been made happy by your words; but when your words reach all of our people, numbering over a thousand how much more joy will they occasion. * * * We come to you for protection and safety. Our hearts, though [113] often troubled have not fainted. We have trusted in God, and He has helped us. We are now able to sleep in peace. Our confidence is restored. God has given us His strength to reach this place of security and freedom, and we are grateful to Him for His mercy and loving kindness. We again salute you from our hearts. I have no more to say.'

"At the conclusion of this reply, which was delivered in the musical intonations of his native tongue, with a grace and eloquence that did credit to the picturesque forum in which he stood. Dr. Fraser gave the benediction."

During the autumn of 1887 the remainder of the colonists removed to their new home, and throughout the following winter and spring building preparations went rapidly forward. Mr Duncan drew up a beautiful design for the streets and homes and public buildings of the new village, so that it should be a model city in every respect. A new set of rules, or declaration of principles, was also drawn up in harmony with the present enlightened character of the people. It read as follows:

"We, the people of Metlakahtla, Alaska, in order to secure to ourselves and our posterity the blessings of a Christian home, do severally subscribe to the following rules for the regulation of our conduct and town affairs:

"1. To reverence the Sabbath and to [114] refrain from all unnecessary secular work on that day; to attend Divine Worship; to take the Bible for our rule of faith; to regard all true Christians as our brethren, and to be truthful, honest and industrious.

"2. To be faithful and loyal to the Government and laws of the United States.

"3. To render our votes when called upon for the election of the Town Council, and to promptly obey the by-laws and orders imposed by the said council.

"4. To attend to the education of our children and keep them at school as regularly as possible.

"5. To totally abstain from all intoxicants and gambling, and never attend heathen festivities or countenance heathen customs in surrounding villages.

"6. To strictly carry out all sanitary regulations necessary for the health of the town.

"7. To identify ourselves with the progress of the settlement, and to utilize the land we hold.

"8. Never to alienate — give away — or sell our land, or building lots, or any portion thereof, to any person or persons who have not subscribed to these rules."

In the land of the tree, in the midst of unsurpassed natural landscape, a new and more beautiful village sprang into existence under the skilled and willing hands of Mr Duncan, and his devoted followers. A salmon cannery and saw-mill were erected, [115] numerous stores opened, and after months of faithful and loving toil a large and beautiful church was built. Peace and joy dwelt in the hearts of the people; industry, purity and harmony guarded the homes; and the spot became indeed Paradise Island, a bit of the garden of Eden regained.

Sixteen years after the foundation of the new village it was the good fortune of the writer to make a 3,000 mile journey across the continent and up into the Northland, solely to obtain the strange and inspiring history of these red men and to observe their present condition. The story of the journey and Of some of the remarkable things seen and heard at Metlakahtla will next be related. [116]

Chapter XI
On the Isle of Paradise

AS the Queen of Sheba traveled far to pay a visit to the court of King Solomon to see for herself the marvels of which she had heard so much. so the writer made a round-trip journey of

6,000 miles to sec the wonderful model city of Metlakahtla inhabited by red men, who yesterday were wild savages, today are well-dressed exemplary Christians. The trip from Chicago occupied nine days. Leaving the inland metropolis on Monday evening the writer reached Seattle Friday afternoon, and the following day arrived at Victoria, the old English city on Vancouver Island, which is so frequently mentioned in our narrative. Here I saw the naval station which was the headquarters of Admiral Prevost halt a century previous, and called upon the venerable Bishop Cridge, who entertained Mr Duncan upon his arrival in the city in 1857, and has ever since been a staunch friend and warm supporter. A delightful Sunday was spent in this quaint English city where the Sabbath is observed far better than in the United States. Early Monday morning I embarked on the swift steamer, *"Cottage City,"* and for two days. u we sped northward, enjoyed a changing [117] panorama of sea and land scenery which is probably unparalleled on the North American continent. At five-thirty Wednesday morning we reached Ketchikan, Alaska, a gold-mining town fifteen miles from Metlakahtla, where it was necessary to change steamers. It proved to be a typical frontier village with less than a thousand inhabitants and eight saloons into whose coffers, I was informed, went two-thirds of the wages of the miners.

But fortunately I had not long to wait in the town. At nine a.m. a large steamer approached, which proved to be *"The Dolphin,"* carrying the United States Senatorial Committee of five members, appointed to inspect Alaska (or the purpose of framing laws for the territory. The vessel was just returning from a special visit to New Metlakahtla to enable the committee to see (lie famous Indian settlement and to obtain Mr Duncan's views on the needs of Alaska. As the ship touched the dock I hastened on board and greeted Senator Dillingham, chairman of the committee, whom I had met in Seattle a few days previous. He took me into the captain's cabin and there introduced me to the man I had come three thousand miles to see — William Duncan! And yet, could it be possible that the vivacious, ruddy-faced man with whom I was shaking hands was the missionary who had spent forty-six years of toil and privation among the red men? [118] His hair and beard were white, but at seventy two years of age he had the energy and vigor of mind and body of a man of fifty.

Mr Duncan had come from Metlakahtla to Ketchikan as the guest of the Senatorial party, and was accompanied by two leading members of the Indian community, Mr John Tait and Edward K Mathers. After several hours of waiting the luxurious excursion steamer *"Spokane"* reached Ketchikan on its way to Metlakahtla; which it visits on every trip to Alaska, and Mr Duncan, the Indians, and myself, were soon speeding rapidly toward the village, whose fame has reached round the world.

As we came into the bay — which I have never seen equaled for beauty at home or abroad — and beheld the quiet, peaceful village, set like a jewel between the blue sea and the purple mountains, I was filled with amazement and awe and could only inwardly exclaim: "'Fifty years ago savages and today this!" What a tremendous power is contained in the Gospel! No other force on earth or above or beneath it could have transformed those savage tribes into that tranquil Indian village! Truly I was looking upon a modern miracle of the Gospel and it was marvelous beyond the power of description.

Eleven delightful days I spent at Metlakahtla as the guest of Mr Duncan. Needless to state, there is no saloon on the [119] island, and during my entire stay I saw no one intoxicated and heard no profane nor angry word! Instead, a spirit of peace and quiet contentment broods over the island and fills the heart with satisfaction, and one realizes as never before of what little account are the riches and honors of the world compared with the true riches of living right with God!

The village lies on a right-angled point of land so that two sides of it face the sea. The houses of the Indians are on the average considerably finer than those in an American village of eight hundred inhabitants. They are mainly two stories in height, plentifully supplied with windows and usually have a verandah. The village sidewalks are wide and well built.

The church stands on an eminence just at the back of the village and is far the most handsome and pretentious building in the town. It was constructed entirely by the Indians themselves under Mr Duncan's direction. The interior is finished in spruce and cedar, and the large arched auditorium, capable of seating over seven hundred people, is most impressive. The handsome pews and ornamental pulpit, with the painting of the Angels at Bethlehem above the pulpit, — indeed, everything save the pipe organ, is the result of native handicraft. The church is the largest in Alaska and has fitly been called "The Westminster of the Indians". [120]

The combined school house and town hall stands next to the church and has the unique distinction of being equipped with a gymnasium. Next to the school is a commodious building designed for a boy's home or boarding school, and next that a girl's boarding school. At present there ire only nine girls in the school, but it is expected the number will be shortly increased to fifteen or more.

The two most important industries in the village arc the salmon cannery and the sawmill. 'During a recent season the former turned out over 800,000 cans of salmon, while the latter employs a considerable number of people the year round. It any of our readers wish a good can of salmon and at the same time a souvenir from Metlakahtla let them ask their grocer for salmon put up by "The Metlakahtla Industrial Company." The chief occupations of the 800 inhabitants are salmon fishing in the summer and logging in the winter. There are nine stores in the town, the largest being owned by Mr Duncan, the other eight by natives. The saw-mill and most of the stock of the salmon cannery are also owned by Mr Duncan. some of the shares, however, being held by the Indians. There is no doubt but that Mr Duncan is simply acting as trustee for the people in conducting these enterprises and that at his decease the profits, if there be any left, will be given to the village. Today Mr [122] Duncan pays

Metlakatla from church tower

the salary of his assistants in the work, Dr and Mrs Boyd, and supports the girls' school, which is conducted by the doctor and his wife. Last year, as previously, Mr Duncan personally taught the public school, in addition to all his other duties, but he finds the burden very severe and is desirous of securing a young minister and his wife to undertake this work and to assist in the spiritual training of the people. [121]

Mr Duncan is still the active pastor of the church, serving without salary. He preaches twice on Sunday, conducts the children's Sunday School, and the midweek prayer-meeting. He is also the spiritual and temporal adviser and counselor of his people, and his office, where he spends many hours daily as active manager of the cannery, saw-mill and store, is the natural resort of anyone in trouble or difficulty. I spent considerable time with Mr Duncan in his office, and sometimes there would be a stream of callers which would occupy his attention for hours together.

The home life of the people is beautiful and affectionate. Among strangers they appear stolid, for they hide their feelings, but among themselves they are often most lively and gay. I saw considerable of the nine girls in the boarding school, and they were constantly bubbling over with fun of some sort and frequent bursts of hearty, wholesome laughter filled the air. Some of

[123] the homes are furnished very attractively, two houses in the village containing pianos.

The energy and natural talents of the people are amazing. Many of them earn double wages by doing double work. For example, the blacksmith at the cannery, Mr Edward K. Mathers, works at night at his home carving queer figures on silver spoons. Going to the native stores on several occasions I found them locked, until I discovered that the proprietors worked at the cannery or saw-mill during the day, and opened their shops after a hasty supper in the evening. The village photographer, Benjamin A. Haldane,[24] does not hesitate to work in the cannery when it is running and looks after his picture-making and developing after or before working hours. Mr Haldane is a versatile and talented young man. In addition to being an excellent photographer, he is leader of the village band, and plays the pipe organ in the church. One of the two pianos in the town is in his home, and one evening he displayed much skill in playing several difficult selections for my entertainment. It is typical of the people that they learn any art or trade with astonishing ease and rapidity. There are several excellent silversmiths in the village, and at least one skilled wood carver. In addition most of the older women weave handsome baskets out of a certain kind of bark which find a ready sale to tourists. [124]

The two Sundays spent in Metlakahtla were red letter days in my experience. On Sabbath morning all is peace and quiet throughout the village, and the spirit of worship permeates the atmosphere as strongly as the spirit of gladness fills the air of our land at Christmas-tide. At ten o'clock I stood on the church steps and watched the streams of people coming from different directions, all converging at the church door. They were dressed in the bright colors they love, and the sight of the happy people and the quiet village, with the sea and mountains for a background, made one of the most beautiful pictures I have ever seen. I was especially struck with the large number of Indian boys and girls who accompanied their parents to church, and with the sight of the very aged coming to the House of God as long as they were able to walk. One old woman, probably nearly or quite ninety years of age, bent over a large staff as she slowly approached the church. After going up a couple of steps she sat down to rest awhile, and then found strength to enter the building and worship her Creator.

Part of the church service was in the native Tsimshean language and part in English. Following the organ voluntary played by Mr Haldane, came a song in soft, flowing Tsimshean accents. Mr Duncan then offered prayer in Tsimshean, at the close of which all repeated the Lord's [125] Prayer in the native tongue. The beautiful song, "He Leadeth Me," was next sung in English by the congregation,

---

[24] {j His 163 glass negatives rescued from the Metlakatla dump, Mique'l Askren Dangeli, PhD, a Tsimshian Tlingit from that community has devoted her academic career to his talented work. https://web.archive.org/web/20120306171344/http://travelpeapod.wordpress.com/2010/04/16/bringing-our-history-into-focus/}

followed by a short prayer in our language by Mr Duncan. A passage of Scripture was then read in English by Mr Duncan, followed by the sermon, which is always delivered in the native tongue. A short prayer in Tsimshean closed the service, an organ postlude being played as the people passed out of the church. The order of service in the evening varies little from that in the morning.

But two services during the whole of the Sabbath day cannot at all satisfy the energetic Indians. At three o'clock in the afternoon they gather in the church again for an "Adult Sunday School," the children's Sunday School being held in the school house. Here there are often more than twenty classes all taught by native teachers.

At the conclusion of the Sunday School Mr Mathers, the blacksmith and silversmith, invited me to attend a "Sing Practice" which he holds at his home on Sunday afternoons. It is an informal gathering of ten or a dozen friends and neighbors in his parlor to learn and sing Gospel hymns. I gladly accepted and greatly enjoyed hearing the old familiar hymns in a new tongue. Some of their favorite songs are: "There's a Stranger at the Door" "There's a Land That is Fairer [126] Than Day," "I Will Tell the Wondrous Story," "I Must Tell Jesus", "Nearer the Cross."

Mr Mathers is an elder in the church and a native evangelist. Whenever he is away fishing or on any business he gathers the people together and preaches to them. One day he showed me a large account book, in which he kept a record of every preaching service he held and of every prayer-meeting or sing-practice he led. The record was headed thus: "Record of God's Work Done by E.K Mathers, Lay Preacher." He set down accurately the date, place and number of people at each meeting. There are sixteen elders in the Metlakahtla church and each gladly grasps the opportunity to preach and exhort when he is absent from the island and can gather a few Indians together. Family worship is held in most of the homes, and daily Bible reading is the rule. I asked one young man how he read the Bible, and he said it was his custom to read it through yearly, reading three chapters each week day and five on Sunday.

One of the wisest and most devout men now living at Metlakahtla is Mr John Tait. He is over sixty years of age, was one of Mr Duncan's early converts and has been one of his staunchest friends and followers. One day I asked Mr Duncan if he would [127] again become a missionary if he had his life to live over. In reply he said: "I have enjoyed my work and would gladly go through it again if necessary. Looking back over my career I have nothing to regret in regard to my plans and methods of conducting the work, and it called upon to begin again would follow the same program." Mr Duncan believes all missions would be more successful if they would follow the "Christian village" plan. He said:

"I firmly believe that missionaries all over the world should adopt the Christian settlement plan of procedure. Just as soon as a small group of Christians have been won from heathenism they should remove and form a, separate and distinct colony. The converts wilt in that way grow and develop far better and faster than when living in daily contact with all sorts of vices common among the heathen.

"Why, suppose I had never removed my people from Fort Simpson, I could never have obtained the result you see today in this village. In one house there would be living a Christian family and in the next a heathen one. The Christians would constantly be in trouble, enduring slanders and seeing and bearing evil things that would mar the beauty of their characters.

"Now, if it were necessary for the converts to come into daily contact with all kinds of evil the plan of separation would be unwise, but no good purpose is served by it. [128]

On the contrary the departure of the Christian from evil surroundings has been the divine plan from the beginning. God called Abraham to come out from Ur and remove to a place where a separate people could be trained up into holiness. Again the Children of Israel were led out from Egypt and given a land where they would be separated from other nations and where they were given an opportunity to become a light unto all the world."

* * *

Such is the strange and remarkable story of Metlakahtla. Its lessons of zeal and heroism, of faith and devotion, are many and inspiring. If those poor red men with their meagre advantages can produce such a beautiful Christian life in a single generation what ought not we to be and accomplish with our countless advantages and our generations of Christian ancestors!

There are other red men. and yellow men, and black men, and white men in all parts of the earth living and dying without the Gospel. Let us arise and carry the news of salvation to them. or help others to do so by giving largely of our earnings!

The End

Better images added to this text come from

Devil and Mr Duncan Peter Murray Vivtoria: Sono Nis Press   1985

Metlakatla The Holy City Phylis Bauman   Chilliwack   1983

Many Voyages of Arthur Wellington Clah Peggy Brock   UBC   2011

Story of Metlakatla Henry Welcome Saxon & Co, London   1887

THE SHOREY BOOK STORE
Facsimile Reproduction 1964 1966 1968
815 Third Avenue Seattle, Washington 98104 SJS # 19

From Potlatch to Pulpit

Being the Autobiography of the

REV. WILLIAM HENRY PIERCE

Native Missionary to the Indian Tribes of the
Northwest Coast of British Columbia.

Edited by REV. J.P. HICKS

Published by
THE VANCOUVER BINDERY LIMITED
VANCOUVER, B.C. 1933.

CONTENTS

PART II.

[7]

Chapter I
Early Days and Conversion

MY father, Edward Pierce, was a Scotchman and an apprentice in the service of the Hudson's Bay Company. He came out from the Old Country in the year 1835, in a sailing vessel named *The Columbia,* owned by that company, and was employed by them to come to this coast to prospect for coal.

In company with my father was a young man named Simpson, a house carpenter, also in the service of the Hudson's Bay, who afterwards became known as Captain Simpson, and who died on the Naas River while superintending the erection of the Fort there. When the company moved the Fort to a more suitable location thirty-seven miles farther south, the settlement became known as Fort Simpson* in memory of Captain Simpson. His remains were brought down from Fort Naas and buried, there. [8]

[*British Columbia Coast Names,* page 394 (Walbran), states that Fort Simpson was named in memory of Captain Armitage Simpson, lieutenant in Royal Navy, seniority March 2nd, 1815, later an officer of the Marine Service of the Hudson's Bay Company on this Coast, and a chief trader of the Company, who died September, 1831, at the trading post on the Naas, this known as Fort Naas. His remains were subsequently removed to the new fort — Fort Simpson. — *Editor.*]

After spending some time around Nanaimo, my father sailed for Fort Simpson on the old steamer, *Beaver*, which was the first steam vessel ever to appear at that port. When the *Beaver* first appeared in the waters of Cunningham Passage a great fear came upon the 4,000 Indians who resided there. The older people fled to the woods, for they could not understand this strange object. They thought it was the devil and that the smoke pouring from the funnel came from the regions below. To the old men and women on shore it appeared that the blocks in the rigging were human heads, and, altogether, the *Beaver* was a fearsome object. The younger ones were not quite so much afraid of the steamer, for they had heard of its expected arrival from the whites — the Hudson's Bay men at the Fort.

My father married an Indian woman of the Fort Simpson tribe and in a short time they moved down the Coast several hundred miles to the Hudson's Bay post at Port Rupert. It was there I was born on the 10th of June, 1856, and three weeks after my birth my mother died. My father cared for me until my grandfather, to whom had been conveyed news of my mother's death, came and took me away. He had paddled all the way down the Coast in a large war canoe and, going to my father in the Fort, announced his intention of taking me away. What could my father do? It was useless for him to resist, so I was taken from him. He told me afterwards that he went down to the shore and watched and cried as the canoe bore me away. Little did he think then that twenty-five years [9] would elapse before he would ever hear of or see me again. We went to Port Simpson, my grandfather and I, and I was brought up amongst the Indians who were the tribesmen of my mother.

My grandmother used to light the fire in the early morning and she always prayed as the smoke went up. I used to like to hear her pray to the Great Spirit. One morning there was a great wind and when my grandmother lit the fire she did not pray. Being very curious, I asked her why she did not do so. "Oh," said she, "There is no use praying now, it is too windy and the smoke does not go straight up. My prayers would be lost." I imagined that her prayers went to the

Great Spirit in the mountains or up in the air, and her explanation naturally seemed good reasoning.

At nights when all was quiet, several of us used to gather around my grandfather and listen to his advice. He impressed us very strongly to be good boys, always to work well and never be lazy. Every night he would instruct us in this way and he never forgot to warn us to keep away from bad company.

Things went on in this way till one day my grandfather said: "Get your best clothes on and come with me to the Fort to see Mr. Duncan. I dressed and we went to the Fort. Even then I could understand a little English and I knew when Mr. Duncan asked me what my name was, but could not answer. Mr. Duncan patted me on the head and my grandfather informed him that my name was William. Mr. Duncan then asked my grandfather to bring me to the Fort every Sunday, and I often went, Mr. Duncan had only then [10] come to the Fort and he remained inside for nearly three years while he learned the Indian language before mixing with the people to teach them. When he had mastered the language sufficiently he opened a little school and I was one of those who attended.

The Man-eater and the Dog-eater dancers were very much opposed to Mr. Duncan, and they did everything in their power to drive him out, but they could not succeed. Finally, one day — it was Sunday and we were at Sunday School — the man-eater dancers, half a dozen of them, came in and they told Mr. Duncan that they were having a celebration in the village and the noise of the church bell disturbed them. They did not wish the bell to be tolled any more that day. Mr. Duncan came down from his desk and told the Indians who were crazy with whiskey, that the bell would be rung twice more that day.

"Well," said one of the Indians, angrily, as he stepped up to Mr. Duncan brandishing his scalping knife, "I have killed twenty-six men and you will be the twenty-seventh."

At that, all the Indians closed around Mr. Duncan. He was a brave man, however, and never flinched. He informed them that if they killed him there would be three missionaries come to take his place.

While this row was in progress and just as one of the Indians, inflamed with passion, was about to strike Mr. Duncan down, *Clah*, my uncle by adoption, came into the building. He was armed with a revolver and ordered all who were threatening Mr. Duncan to leave. That revolver did the work and Mr. Duncan has often [11] said that my uncle saved his life. All this time we boys were huddled together in a corner and locked in the room. We were crying through fear. After the Indians had gone, Mr. Duncan went back to his desk and cried for a long time; then he told us to take our seats and the lesson was continued. The bell rang that day and for many another Sunday.

Just as I was learning my ABC's and getting along with my figures, my grandfather ordered me before him and told me while it was his desire that I should attend school, it had been ordered by the chief of the tribe that I should not. There was nothing to do but obey, so I left Mr. Duncan's school. During the whole of the next winter I did nothing. One night I was taken by my grandmother to a big house where a number of boys were to be taught the mysteries of the Dog-eaters' dance. That dance was a ceremony by which the boys were to become identified with the tribe. I had no knowledge of the dance, but it was impressed upon me by my grandmother that I should learn. A number of boys, myself among them, were initiated into the preliminaries and then we became probationers, as it were. All the following winter we were kept by ourselves and not allowed to associate with others of the tribe. We were isolated in preparation for the part we were to take in the actual Dog-eaters' dances. However, I never graduated. Circumstances willed otherwise.

One day when I was twelve years of age, while playing on the beach, the steamer *Otter* came in. I may say that the Otter was the second steamer to ply the Coast. It followed the *Beaver*. Both boats belonged [12] to the Hudson's Bay Company and were built in the Old Country. Captain Lewis was master of the *Otter*, and as he was going up the beach towards the Fort, he noticed me, and on coming up to me asked if I would like to go with him on the steamer. I said I would. So he told me to get my things and wait for him, and on returning from the Fort he would take me on board. He promised that I should receive $12.00 a month for my services. Very quickly I got together what little I had and went on the *Otter*.

Captain Lewis instructed me in my duties, told me I was to be cabin boy and that I was to keep his cabin clean. I worked on board that boat for two years and a half. Part of the time I was cabin boy and then I became second steward, and when the chief steward was away I acted in his place.

One day Captain Lewis called me in to him and said: "My boy, the Hudson's Bay Company have been watching you for a long time. You have not acted as other boys have done. You have not mixed up in bad company and you have not turned around as others have done and sold whiskey to the Indians. ! shall teach you your lessons and afterwards the Company will give you money and send you to school, and finally you will be given a clerkship or appointed to the charge of some station. Now I want you to come to my cabin every night and I will teach you for an hour."

I owe a great deal to Captain Lewis. Every night, except when the weather was too rough to permit, I went to his cabin for instruction. [13]

After spending two and a half years on the Otter I left and shipped on a steamer running between the Sound and Sitka. I went as second steward and received $45.00 a month. It was big pay then and the money was what attracted me. However, I only made three trips on that steamer, because I could not stand the rough company. The language was frightful, and although at that time I knew nothing about the Bible, it hurt my feelings to listen to the jests and oaths which came from the mouths of the men with whom I was compelled to associate.

I returned to Victoria. There were a great many Indians there when I arrived, for revival meetings were being held. Indians were here from all over the Coast. One night I attended the service and listened to the words of Rev. Thomas Crosby, and that night I gave my heart to God. I felt that a great weight had been lifted off my shoulders. I went back to the meetings and the more I saw of them the more t liked them.

On the night of my conversion, I felt that I wanted to tell the good news to somebody, and while walking along the street it occurred to me to go to see my friend, George Edgar. I knew that he was not leading the best of lives and, prompted by the feeling that was in me, I went right out and found him. He was in bed. I asked him to get up and let me in as I had something very important to tell him. After speaking to him of my conversion, I asked him to accept the truth also. We knelt down and prayed. After that George gathered together his belongings and came with me. We lived together many months. We both attended [14] ed the services of the Rev. Wm. Pollard, a Methodist preacher, who was then pastor of Pandora Avenue Methodist Church.

George Edgar

After attending his Church for some weeks, Mr. Pollard came to us one night and asked us to remain after the service. We did so, and he informed us that he had noticed our devotion and had concluded to teach us. Every day we had to go to his house and receive one hour's instruction. In that way we learned a great deal. Afterwards his daughter, who later became Mrs. Burgess, of Victoria, taught us. She gave us two hours each day, and we learned rapidly.

Some time after Mr. Pollard received a long, strong petition from the Tsimpsheans. He then decided to open a mission at Fort Simpson and he asked me to go north with him as interpreter, which I did.

The mission at Fort Simpson was opened and hundreds of Indians used to come to hear Mr. Pollard preach. Finally he went away, leaving me in charge of the mission until Rev. C.M Tate arrived to take Mr. Pollard's place. Mr. Tate was succeeded by Rev T Crosby, and I stayed with him as interpreter. Thus began my career as a missionary.

After staying with Mr. Crosby six months, I went down to Victoria again to attend school. I attended both day and night sessions until my funds gave out. It was then necessary that I should seek some means of earning more money. Accordingly I decided to try the American side and went over to Port Laidlow. At this place a large saw-mill plant was in operation. Several hundreds of Indians from all parts were [15] employed. They came from Queen Charlotte's Island, Port Simpson, Naas, Bella Bella, Kitamaat, and other points. My first Sunday spent here was a revelation to me. All hands were paid every Saturday, and as the saloons were open to the Indians without any restriction, they spent most of their money at those places, with the result that there was drunkenness and fighting all day on Sunday, and when Monday morning came nobody was in a fit state to begin work, or if they turned up at their post, nothing was satisfactory.

I felt that if I was going to stay there a while, there must be some effort made to change the conditions, so I determined, by God's help to take my stand the following Sunday, Accordingly, when Saturday came I visited every house, informing them that there would be service on the following day, the manager having given me permission to use the white church which was only used for service by the whites occasionally. All were surprised, some were angry, others jeered at the idea, and a few thanked me. All wanted to know who was to be the preacher and were much surprised when told who was going to make the attempt.

On the second Sunday we launched the idea of a temperance society. The manager, I found out afterwards, was a temperance man, so I invited him to come in and write down the names of those who joined. He did so, and brought a number of pledge cards with him. It was a solemn time. Many wept their way to the table where the pledge was signed. The movement was a success. The manager was well pleased with the results at the mill. The owner himself was moved, and [16] he told the manager to give me promotion.

From this place at this time sprang a few of our faithful native workers. Phillip McKay, who became a burning light as a missionary in Alaska and who died there, was one. Charlie Amos, of Kitamaat, who was the first one to introduce Christianity amongst his people, was another. Bella Bella Jack also was converted and was the first one to proclaim to the Bella Bellas that Sunday was God's day by hoisting a flag in front of his house. George Tait, on the Naas, became a local preacher and was one of Rev. A.E Green's councillors there when that mission was first established. That was a revival, but we did not realize it at the time. God's Spirit spoke to the hearts of the people in such a manner that they could not resist.

It was while working here that I became convinced that my life work was to be a missionary among the natives. After spending four months at the mill I returned to Victoria to continue my studies. It was while there that I received a letter from Mr. Crosby saying there was urgent need of workers up north and he asked me to go and receive an appointment as missionary teacher on one of the mission fields. [17]

Chapter II
My First Mission Field

Some months after receiving Mr. Crosby's letter, a sloop, *The Georgina*, belonging to a chief named Alfred Dudoward, of Fort Simpson, came down to Victoria to buy goods for a store he had started up there. This I thought was my opportunity to accept Mr. Crosby's invitation, and I went with him on the return trip. This was in 1877. Owing to strong head winds we had to take shelter at Alert Bay and remain there for some days. We were not sorry for this delay aa we had heard that man-eater and dog-eater dances were being held there and we were anxious to do what we could to stop them.

While there, two warships, one of which was large and the other small, cast anchor in the bay. I learned that Lord Dufferin, the Governor-General, and Lady Dufferin were on board. The next morning, after the ships had anchored I was on the beach and Lord and Lady Dufferin came ashore. Lord Dufferin asked me to act as interpreter, and through me he told the Indians assembled that he had heard a great deal about their dances since he had come to the Coast and now that he had found them at the practice he was going to stop their performances. He offered the Indians their choice of going to Victoria as prisoners, or accepting Christianity. They chose the latter.

After this address to the tribesmen. Lord and Lady Dufferin made a tour of the village. Lady Dufferin [18] wanted some curios, and when she found what was to her liking — I forget what it was — she asked the Indians the price and they said five dollars. Her ladyship had no purse with her, so she asked Lord Dufferin for some money and he had none, so they both fell back on me, I had five dollars, which I handed over to Lady Dufferin. His Excellency said he would repay me before the ship sailed in the morning. Just after daylight an officer came ashore and handed me six dollars — an extra one for interest. In this unexpected manner I became banker to Lord Dufferin and this event was quite an interesting incident on my journey north.

In about one week from that time we arrived at Fort Simpson. It seemed that Mr. Crosby, who was chairman of the district, had been urgently invited to visit Port Essington, and during the previous year he had done so at intervals. Mrs. Cunningham, the wife of the trader, rendered valuable assistance in carrying on the Sabbath School and holding evening service until some one should be sent to take charge. To that field Mr. Crosby now proposed to send me. Accordingly I left Fort Simpson and went down to Port Essington, a distance of about fifty miles, to begin work on my first mission field, my salary being paid in part out of Mr. Crosby's own pocket. This was in the fall of the year. Everybody gave me a glad welcome. The two tribes of Kit-sumkalum and Kitselas, having now moved down from their old villages in a body, renounced heathenism and became christianized and civilized, thus forming a Christian village.

School was taught and services were held in a [19] building kindly loaned by the trader, Mr. Cunningham. However, right after Christmas, it was decided that a place of worship should be erected. All felt the need to be great. Every man subscribed very liberally and volunteered to go for lumber, a distance of about forty-five miles, in their canoes, alt at their own expense. Before many more weeks had passed the lumber came to hand and the building was under way. During that year, 1877, the church was finished, and the work had all been done free of charge-

Since then the building has been repaired and for many years served as the mission school house. At the present time it is used for week-night services and on Sundays during the year, when the people are few. After the church waa built the mission was organized. A council was formed and by-laws were made to govern the village. New houses were built and a good road was made which extended from one end of the village to the other. Bible class and evening services were conducted and all who were anxious for baptism were instructed at certain hours during the week.

Many couples who had been married according to their heathen rites now desired to be married as Christians and they, too, were instructed. Some of them were nearly eighty years of age, but they, becoming Christians so late in life, felt that nothing ought to be in the way of their fulfilling God's commandments. When all were sufficiently instructed, the chairman of the district, Rev. Thomas Crosby, was called down to officiate.

During the next winter there were indications of a revival. Those who had become followers of Christ [20] were anxious to see God's work spread amongst the strangers who were then living there from outside places, as Metlakahtia, Port Simpson and the Naas. Many of these had been disgraced in some way and had come to Port Essington for shelter. Amongst the crowd were husbands and wives who had been separated for years. After the preaching of God's word and much heart-searching in answer to prayer, a mighty revival came and swept the place, reaching even to Metlakahtia, Port Simpson and the Naas. Wonderful conversions took place during those six weeks. The chiefs of the Kitsumkalum and Kitselas tribes — *Kitkon* and *Scaugumzeush*, with their people, were amongst the converts, as were also all the man-eaters belonging to those tribes. After these chiefs and leading people had been converted, their influence was so great that it was felt on the Upper Skeena, amongst the heathen tribes there, that heathen power had given way, as it were, under their feet. The news so spread even as far as Kitamaat and Bella Bella.

Quite a number of young men began to study their Bibles with the missionary and some of them became exhorters and local preachers. Moses Hudson, Cornelius Hudson, William Young, James Smith and Jonah Roberts are the names of some of these who from that time continued to live good, faithful lives until the end. For a period of six weeks the time was given up entirely to religious work. Three services were held every day, the evening service often continuing till quite late. Between the services the people met together to learn a number of Sankey's hymns and had them [21] translated into their own tongue. It was often difficult for the missionary to keep the church closed at night after the service was over. One night at the close of the service, I told them the hour was very late and advised them all to go to bed, for we were tired and needed a good rest. The door was locked and the key in my possession. It was not long, however, before my rest was disturbed. Some one awoke me, saying there was singing in the church. In a few moments I was on the spot, anxious to discover how any one had entered. The building was full, and all had entered by the windows, using short ladders for that purpose.

On unlocking the door, my eyes beheld a great sight. Men, women and children were all on their knees, sobbing, and praying most earnestly, while above it all arose the cry of a woman, "Here comes the missionary!" After spending a short season of prayer and. testimony together, all were dismissed and went home feeling satisfied that they had been able to put in an extra service before morning dawned.

It seemed as if they were feeling for and reaching out for something. Often a text or a prayer, or it might be the verse of a hymn newly translated, touched and moved their hearts strangely. This excitement, of course, had to be checked by the missionary, in order that they might not depend on their feelings instead of having faith in a living Christ. It was while learning the hymn, "The Half Was Never Told," that their feelings were moved in a special manner. I told them of the Queen of Sheba who, on hearing of the widsom and greatness of King Solomon, paid a visit to that [22] monarch in order to see for herself whether alt the reports that had gone abroad were true, and that when she did behold all the grandeur and prosperity, she was so amazed that she exclaimed that the half had not been told. I explained to them that from this incident the hymn in question was written. After learning this grand old hymn, the hour was quite late and we were all dismissed for the night. It was not long, however, before my rest was disturbed by a loud knocking at the door, and the sound of many voices outside. On inquiring the cause of this disturbance they replied:

"We want you to come outside; come now, didn't you hear us singing?" In a few minutes I had joined them when they said: "We have come to you to tell us the other half". You have told us of King Solomon and all his riches, but as we have only heard the half, you will please tell us the other half." This was unexpected, and for a moment I hesitated, wondering how best to satisfy their curiosity. At last I replied: "Dear friends, keep on praying and believing; serve God faithfully to the end of your lives, and then when you reach Heaven you will hear the other half." The explanation was quite satisfactory. The outdoor service was concluded and all went to their homes feeling quite happy and content Afterwards, whenever that hymn was sung at any service it never failed to touch their hearts. It always seemed to have a deeper meaning to them than any other hymn they aver sung. [230]

Chapter III
Opening Up of Mission Work in Alaska

Early in the spring of 1877 it was ordained that I should leave Essington and move to a new mission at Fort Wrangel, Alaska. It was in 1876 that Phillip McKay, with three other Tsmpsheans, left Fort Simpson for Alaska to work at their mines there. However, they never got any further than Fort Wrangel. On reaching that place they found the natives in such a dark, degraded condition that they longed to remain amongst them and preach the old, old story. Fortunately they found plenty of employment, so their hearts' desire was granted in being able to proclaim the glad tidings of salvation. Phillip McKay was the leader. For many months he continued the good work and led many souls to Christ. At last he sickened and died. His loss to the people was great. They were then left without help of any kind. A letter was sent to Rev. T. Crosby at Fort Simpson urging him to send some one. He called for volunteers, but no one responded to the call. Finally it was impressed on my mind that I should offer myself for that field. There was no salary in the bargain, but that did not trouble me. I believed that if God were leading me there He would supply all my needs.

The schooner *Kate*, loaded with lumber, was just about ready to start for that port, so I boarded her and went. Before we had travelled far we encountered a [24] very bad storm and instead of arriving at our destination in three days, it took us a whole week. Quite a number of the natives were down at the wharf when we landed, but all were perfect strangers to me and I was a stranger to them. However, everybody was delighted to know that a missionary had arrived and one chief welcomed me very cordially to his house and told me that I was to stay there. He showed me a bag of gold which I was to share with him. His house he offered to be used for service at any time.

The next day I called all the people together and explained to them what I wanted. All responded and said they would be with me. It was arranged that the Sunday services should be held in Chief Doo-yak's house.

On the first Saturday spent in Wrangel I was invited to have dinner with Captain Jocelyn at the Garrison. I accepted the kind invitation and found about one hundred soldiers there, also Captain Jocelyn's wife and children. The Captain and his wife were Christians, as were also some of the soldiers. After dinner the Captain asked many questions and made a nice speech. He said that he did not wish me to feel a stranger and promised that just as he had helped Phillip McKay so he would do what he could for me, and, said he, "If you do not receive proper treatment from either whites or Indians, let me know. I will attend your services whenever I can, as will also my wife and children." These words were most encouraging and made me feel that my Lord and Master was indeed opening up my way for His work. [25]

My stay in Alaska lasted six months. During that time many changes took place. Heathen homes were forsaken and new civilized ones built. There was no more desire to break the law of the land. Many of the worst characters now acted as peacemakers. All were anxious to learn about God and whenever we gathered together for worship we were sure of a good congregation, Every Sabbath we held four services. The day began by holding a prayer meeting at 7 a.m. At 9 a.m. there was Bible School, followed by a preaching service. In the afternoon we had Sunday School where both young and old joined together. Again in the evening we had preaching services followed by testimony meeting. At every service God's power was felt and many conversions took place.

Every Saturday each family was urged to clean up their home and prepare a good supply of wood to last over Sunday. This they did gladly, and it soon became a custom which still exists today.

The chief with whom I stayed was anxious that I should accept ten or twenty dollars each week from his bag of gold. This I refused, for did I not receive food and shelter from him, therefore I told him more than that was not necessary. However, this did not satisfy him, and he bought me a new suit of clothes.

After six months among this people, I received a letter from Mr. Crosby asking me to return. There was an urgent cry from the Naas river for a missionary and, as they stated to Mr. Crosby that they must have me, I was asked to leave Alaska. This news was a great surprise and shock to the people and they urged me to [26] remain. I could not bear to think of it. However, the farewell Sunday came and we had a great time. The house was crowded. Indians, soldiers and miners were all present, as were also Captain Jocelyn, his wife and family. The captain made a speech. He said that the United States had built a garrison and stationed a number of soldiers there for twenty years past in order that the law of the land might be maintained. The law had been broken very frequently; punishment had been meted out, some were hanged and others were sent to jail to serve a number of years or a life sentence. But in spite of every effort that was made to check the many evils, wrongdoing went on just the same. Often extra soldiers had to be called out in order that peace might be maintained. "Now," said he, "I am glad to be able to witness the mighty change that has come about through the preaching of the Gospel. We shall not be needed here any more." Three years later all the soldiers were recalled to the States by order of the Government, and the garrison was pulled down.

At the close of the service, the Captain handed me a ten-dollar bill for my own personal use, and the storekeeper gave me fifteen dollars. The collection, amounting to forty dollars, was also given me, and the chief with whom I stayed added a twenty dollar bill, making a total of eighty-five dollars.

A few days later the old *Otter* came along and I went on board. Captain McCulloch, being a Methodist from Pandora Street Church, Victoria, told me that I was to have a free passage. So I certainly proved the truth of the promise, "My God shall supply all your needs." [27]

The whole tribe was on the beach (there was no wharf in those days) to say goodbye, and all sang very impressively, "Shall We Gather at the River," before we parted. Many tears were shed. Some urged me to stay, offering to pay me a good salary. In the meantime our chairman, Rev. T Crosby, had communicated with the Mission Rooms in Toronto, urging them if possible to send a man to Alaska, that I was to be called away to another field. The reply stated that funds were low and that it was impossible to keep the work going in Alaska. Mr. Crosby then wrote to the Presbyterians in the States and explained to them the situation, urging them to take up the work if possible and send a missionary to that field. His appeal was successful and the first missionary to succeed me was Mr. McFarlane. In later years Rev. Mr. Young was sent to take charge at Wrangel. The work then began to spread amongst the tribes and other missions were formed. A large boarding school built by the United States Government, was erected for the natives at Sitka. [28]

Chapter IV
Beginning of Naas Mission

After leaving Alaska, I remained in Fort Simpson about two weeks waiting for a canoe to come down from Naas to take me to my new field there.

I had agreed to build a mission at Lak-al-Zap, and we arrived there one week after leaving Fort Simpson. This was early in September 1877*. At that time there were only three Indian houses built on that site and two other shacks, owned and occupied by two white men, both of whom were miners and old timers. These two white men gave me a hearty welcome when landing on the beach, promising to give me various kinds of food and help in every way possible.

[*In Chapter 1 in this story, Mr. Pierce states he was appointed to Essington in 1877, completed a church in that year. Later he states he was sent to Alaska "early in the Spring of 1877," remained there six months and moved to the Naas "early in September, 1877." These dates rather conflict, and it is probable the second and last cases should read "1878." — Editor.] [29]

Lak-al-Zap is situated on the right bank of the Naas River, almost at the mouth, and four miles above Fishery Bay. This village derives its name from the fact of its being the chief seat of the councillors of the chiefs belonging to the lower tribes of the Naas River. Here they would congregate to discuss their own affairs once during each year. In former years the Hudson's Bay Company opened up a small store at Lak-al-Zap, as it was a central place for all the tribes to meet. Behind the village runs a small stream — a tributary of the Naas — called Koha-Zip, which means "Bone stream.

One of the homes at Lak-al-Zap was occupied by a chief who kindly offered his house to be used for services just as long as we needed it. My first Sunday service held there was attended by six Indians and two whites. At the evening service there were a few strangers present who had come from other places purposely to attend. At the close of this service, an invitation was given to those who wished to Join the Christian life, to speak. Four responded and said, "We are the ones who wrote to Mr. Crosby and invited you to come here. Now we are going to pull down our old heathen homes at the other villages where we have hitherto lived and build new Christian homes and move our families down here."

On Monday morning a day school was opened for the children. During the week those who had made up their minds to become Christians and move from their heathen quarters, came down in their canoes loaded with goods. Some had come all the way from [30] Kit-wun-sikh. which is a distance of about fifty miles farther up the river.

Before I had been at Lak-al-Zap many weeks, a letter came from Rev. T Crosby, informing me that a missionary had been appointed by the Mission Board, Toronto, to be in charge of this mission, and I was to remain with him to act as teacher and interpreter. The late Rev. A.E. Green, who labored with much success amongst the Naaa tribes for twelve years, was the name of the missionary referred to. This was cheering news to the people, and towards the end of November Mr. Green arrived. Week-night services had been held during the time that I had lived amongst them, and quite a number had professed Christianity. As soon as the missionary arrived it was arranged to build a small frame mission house, consisting of two rooms, just large enough to accommodate the two of us. Mr. Green's room was heated by a box stove and my room was heated by a very small cook stove. When the north winds began to blow and the snow was drifted through the cracks, we did not find our quarters any too warm. Drips came through the boards and icicles formed on the inside. It was necessary to keep both stoves going all night in order that we might obtain any degree of comfort and sleep.

Towards Christmas our provisions gave out and as we were new on the ground, we had no idea of what the Naas River was like in winter time. The nearest store was at Kincolith, a distance of about twenty-five miles lower down, but it was impossible for any canoe to travel there, and our supplies dwindled down to [31] almost nothing. The natives, knowing of our plight. brought us a little of what they could spare from their own. It was not till quite a while after New Year that we were able to replenish our own stock from the store at Kincolith. Our Christmas dinner consisted of boiled turnips and potatoes, with boiled porcupine, and a dessert consisting of boiled rice without any milk. As a substitute for bread, we had hardtack and no butter. We were inexperienced cooks as far as porcupine was concerned, and in spite of its long cooking of several hours, it was too tough to eat. Next day it re-entered the pot and after a few more hours of boiling it was very palatable, and we then really enjoyed our meal.

Before we had finished our meal I noticed my friend brush away some tears and on inquiring the cause he burst out sobbing and exclaimed, "Whatever would my mother and father think if they saw me in this plight on Christmas — nothing but procupine for my Christmas dinner!" I tried to he cheerful and said that better times were coming and that as he was the leader he should do his utmost to be brave instead of making me feel weak-hearted. Instantly the tears were dried and we continued our meal with a greater measure of contentment.

About the middle of February some of the natives volunteered to haul their canoes over the ice and make the trip to Kincolith in order that some supplies might be purchased. They made the journey successfully and returned bringing sufficient food to last us till spring.

Early in March the people from the Upper villages moved to Fishery Bay in order that they might make [31] preparations for the oolichan fishing, which usually begins towards the end of March. As there was quite a big crowd at that place, it was arranged that I should go and stay with the people there and open up a day school. Mr. Green was to visit us every second Sunday. During this period there was always an unusual amount of excitement. While staying here Rev. T Crosby, with a number of his people from Fort Simpson, paid us a visit and we were glad to learn from him that the Missionary Society in Toronto had promised a grant to build a mission house at Lak-al-Zap, also that the Indian Department at Ottawa were willing to give a sum of money towards the expense of erecting a schoolhouse. This news greatly cheered and encouraged the hearts of the natives. They felt that when both the Society and Government were taking such an interest in their behalf it encouraged them in the steps that they had taken in forsaking their old heathen homes and customs, and building up a Christian community.

At the close of the fishing, some men were employed to haul out the timber and hew the logs for the foundations of the school and mission house. Other timber required was brought from Georgetown sawmill.

During the fishing time, conversions amongst all classes were taking place right along. The services were all well attended. On a Sunday morning when the tide was suitable, there would be two or three canoes from the Tsmpshean camp at Red Bluffs, a distance of about eight or ten miles, come to help us out in the services on that day. [33]

In the month of June the mission house was finished and occupied and one month later the schoolhouse was completed.

Those who had come down from Kit-wun-sikh, now returned up there again, so that they might secure all the salmon they needed for their winter food. It was planned that I should go along with them and stay for the remainder of the summer to conduct services and open up a day and Sunday School. A few years ago I was much surprised when visiting Port Essington to be presented with a case of canned roast beef by a young man who, at that time was conducting a store there. On inquiring the reason he said, "Several years ago when I was a young boy on the Naas River, you used to come to my father's house at Kit-wun-sikh and urge me to attend school, which I did, and what I learned then has helped me to be what I am today. I give you this — it is not much — but I want to show you how much I appreciate all that you have done."

In the fall of that year the work was beginning to spread and we needed more help. Rev. T Crosby sent a young man from Port Simpson, George Edgar by name, to take my place at Kit-wun-sikh, and I was to move on to Kit-lik-damuks, a distance of about six miles. On reaching the lower end of the village, I stood still wondering just where I should stay. Just then a young chief named *Nahoogh*, nephew of the head chief *Skadeen*, came along with an invitation for me to remain at his house until I could find better accommodation. He took my pack and I followed him. His house was of small size, consisting of one room [34] with a fireplace in the centre. The roof was covered with cedar bark, having a hole left in the centre in order that the smoke from the fire might escape. There was no floor other than the bare ground. There were three other families who, besides himself, occupied this room. A special table, both small and low, was provided for me and I had my own dishes which were always kept separate from the rest. After supper the chief's wife showed me the corner that I was to occupy. Clean straw was spread on the ground which was to take the place of a mattress and over this was placed my cedar mat and blankets. Several young people came in to have a peep at me and to inquire what kind of work I was going to do. I told them that on Sunday afternoon next there would be a Sunday School for both old and young, and in the evening preaching service would be held. For any of the bigger ones who were not able to attend school during the day I would have an evening session. This arrangement seemed to please them very much. As there were still two days ahead of us before Sunday came, I, with some others, made the most of our time by hauling in sufficient wood to last us over the week-end. But when the young people saw me at work, they did not like it and said that in future they themselves would get all the wood that was necessary, that my work was to teach. From that time on, all through the winter they kept their word and we always had plenty.

About a mile from the village there was a store which was kept by an old Scotchman, named John Matheson, who was living with an Indian woman. The [35] young chief took me down there and gave me an introduction. The old man was very friendly, particularly so when I told him my father was Scotch, too. He allowed me to take what provisions I needed, on credit, and he also promised to attend the Sunday services.

During the week Chief *Skadeen* had threatened to shoot any one who would attempt to ring any bell calling the people together for service. He strongly objected to having a missionary in the village, or to any of his people becoming Christians. He knew that this would change all his old heathen customs and, in his opinion, weaken his power as a chief. After this threat I thought it advisable to send a messenger around and call the people together quietly, and thus prevent any unnecessary ill-feeling or disturbance. However at the time appointed for afternoon service John Matheson was on hand and he offered to take all risks and go through the village with the hand bell himself. When John passed *Skadeen*'s door, he saw the man standing there with two rifles, but not a word was spoken and no trouble occurred. Several of the women and children came to the service around by the back of the village, through fear of the old chief. They knew he was watching every movement. The attendance was very good for the first time and some stayed behind afterwards to learn the text or to sing a hymn.

At the evening service the attendance was better. It was dark then and everybody knew that Chief *Skadeen* could not be on the watch. We had a very interesting service — after preaching, a fellowship service was [36] held and any who wished to become Christians were invited to do so. Chief *Nahoogh* and his wife, John Matheson and his wife, and a few others decided to forsake their old life and become Christians.

Thus Christianity began at this little village. On Monday morning a day school was started which was well attended, but the only clothing worn by the pupils was a blanket or cotton shirt. On Friday night we had prayer meeting and singing school. During this time heathen dances of all kinds were raging through the village, but they never attempted to come into the house where I stayed. On Sundays they were very quiet. Somehow it was whispered around that if there was any nonsense on the Sabbath day I would surely send in a report to the Government and that would be the means of ending their heathen rites.

Joshua Moody, the young man who had walked with ,me, carrying my blankets from Kit-wun-sikh to Kit-lak-damaks, offered to stay a while and assist me. He stayed about three weeks and then returned to Lak-al-zap. When he told the good news, Mr. Green decided to take the trip and see for himself. He came, bringing with him a few of his men. During the time of Mr. Green's visit, a very sad affair occured in the village. One of the young men who had been caring for and supporting his aged grandmother for a number of years, became tired of her and decided to end her life. Early in the morning, before anyone was astir, he took a club and knocked her senseless. At noon, while eating our lunch, we heard the sound of fire crackling and on opening the door to investigate, we [37] detected a very disagreeable odor. On making inquiry, we were informed that the body of the old lady was being burned. We both left our food and went out to the spot. The sight we beheld was truly awful. Four men, each with a stick in his hand, were to be seen j poking at the burning body. Mr. Green requested them to stop but they replied that they must have the heart. In the early days, it was customary to burn the dead but the heart was always taken out and preserved. It was wrapped in a dry cedar mat and buried under a log or tree. After the men had gathered all the bones together and piled them in a heap amongst the ashes in the middle of the fireplace, Mr. Green asked them to stand still while he offered a prayer. He spoke to the men telling them that after they became Christians, all these old customs would be abolished. We then returned home and finished our meal but the dreadful sight we witnessed we could never forget. "Surety," said Mr. Green, "these people need the Gospel." After Sunday Mr. Green returned home leaving Joshua Moody with me to give assistance.

In the beginning of March, everybody moved down to Lak-al-zap and Fishery Bay for the oolichan fishing, and of course Joshua and I moved with them. The heathen chiefs in their big meeting, decided that all must try to keep the Sabbath during their stay down the river. There was to be no fishing and no work of any kind done on that day.

They were now nearer to the villages that were civilized and were afraid of the law. When all the people were congregated at Fishery Bay, the sounds [38] of rattles and drums belonging to the heathen doctors could be heard each evening during the entire season. In the month of April, I left the Naas river for good. Mr. Green and a teacher remained at Lak-al-zap and George Edgar at Kit-lak-damak. [39]

Chapter V
How the Bella Bellas Accepted Christianity

Jack, a Bella Bella native, during a visit to Victoria, was converted there. On his return home it grieved him sorely to see the whole tribe living in heathenism and darkness, and every day he prayed very earnestly that God would send a missionary to show them the way of life. He had brought with him from Victoria, a Bible which he prized as the word of God, but he being unable to read could not teach any of its truths to his people.

He had also bought a flag and this he always hoisted in front of his house every Sunday morning, afterwards walking through the village telling everybody that this was God's day and all work should cease.

At this time Mr. Crosby made a trip to Bella Bella by canoe — steamers were very rare in those days — and Jack gave him a very cordial reception and urged him to do his utmost to send a missionary. After Mr. Crosby's return to Fort Simpson it was arranged that should go to Bella Bella and commence work at that place.

In June, 1883, I boarded the Steamer *Grappler* and went. Captain Myers instructed his men to place all my belongings on the beach above high water mark. [40] Some of the older men came down to inquire my business and when I told them they went away and left me. While keeping watch over my goods Chief Charley came along and on finding me there welcomed me most heartily. He had known me when on board the *Otter* some years before. At once he invited me to his house and ordered some of the young people to pack my goods up there. He told me that his house was at my disposal either for school or service both on week days and Sundays. I appreciated his kind offer very much, but having noticed an empty warehouse on the beach belonging to a white trader I thought if I could obtain permission from him to use the building for school purposes I could do better work than in Charley's house which was occupied by five families besides himself.

On interviewing the trader, Mr. Clayton, he assured me that I was quite welcome to use the place free of charge, providing I could get it cleaned and fixed up. Several of the young people gladly rallied to my assistance and after a thorough cleaning we managed to find a few boards with which we made some benches. The building was large enough to accommodate only about twenty. Sunday services were held both morning and evening in Chief Charley's house, but Sunday and day schools were carried on in the warehouse.

I lived amongst them three months before the chiefs and people were all agreed to accept Christianity and until they did arrive at that point I could not succeed in accomplishing very much. Both day school and [41] Sunday services were attended by a few, but there was no real interest taken in anything relating to Christianity. However I worked and prayed and had faith in God that an answer would surely come in His own good time.

During that three months there were several councils held, but no decision could ever be made. Then one day when all the people had come home from their fish camps, Chief Charley said to me, "Today there is going to be another council and I want to let you know that it will be the last. Whatever decision is made tonight, will stand. If they all agree not to accept Christianity you will have to leave, but if, on the other hand' they are all united to forsake their old heathen customs and become Christians, you will have a very big congregation on Sunday." This was on Friday. The meeting was to last till midnight. I said to him, "How shall I know what the decision is? I shall want to know to night." "Well," said he, "if the decision is in your favor, we will fire two shots. If you hear nothing, you will understand what has been done." Sure enough, about midnight, two shots were fired and shortly afterwards Charley, with all the other chiefs, came into the house to shake hands with me. Two of the chiefs made a speech, Said they, "It has taken us all this time to get the people united. We wanted to be quite sure of what we were doing before taking the step. We did not want to change and then repent of our action and return to the old life. Now we are ready to listen to you and you can preach to us tonight. If you send word out, this house will soon be filled." [42] When I told him the hour was late, one of them said, "Well, nobody is going to sleep tonight and we might just as well begin." Accordingly two messengers were sent around and in a short time the house was full. I can never forget with what eagerness they learned their first hymn. The beginning had to be simple and I thought nothing more suitable could be found than the old familiar hymn, "Come to Jesus." The words were repeated over and over and then the time was taught. And how they did sing. Truly God's presence was felt. The service lasted two hours. That night quite a number of the leading men, with their families, declared then and there that their old rites were given up and they surrendered themselves to God.

Thus Bella Bella mission began. In "a few weeks many changes were noted. Each family selected a lot on which to build his Christian house and instead of wearing blankets as their only article of clothing, the men desired to buy suits of clothes and boots. The women bought shawls and some material to make dresses for themselves and the children. Week by week the change became more apparent and in a short time the village became transformed. Those who did not make a start during our first service, did so week by week, until the whole band were on the Christian side. Those who were away from home at the time united with us as soon as they returned. We held four services each Sunday and three services during the week. All were very much in earnest and nobody ever thought of staying away. A number were anxious to have their children baptized and several couples who had been [43] married according to their heathen rites, desired a Christian marriage. Mr. Crosby came down from Fort Simpson to attend to this. During his stay arrangements were made to build a church and mission house. The people themselves suggested this and said that they were quite willing to do their part.

Each chief gave fifty dollars and their wives twenty. The others subscribed in cash from ten to twenty dollars and upwards. In one day we collected from the Bella Bellas over one thousand dollars. Other small surrounding villages promised to help also. When Mr. Crosby returned home he took with him the money collected, promising to send down the lumber by next steamer. This he did. When the steamer arrived, lumber, nails, windows and doors were put ashore. Peter Pollard, a native carpenter of Fort Simpson, came also. This caused much rejoicing among the people, and when they saw that such headway was being made, their interest in God's work became greater than ever. When the foundation was laid, we had a special service and two of the chiefa gave an address. As soon as the roofs were on both buildings, the Rev. C.M Tate arrived to take charge of that mission.

Acting on Mr. Crosby's instructions, I remained with him a few weeks and then returned north to Fort Simpson.

How the Gospel Reached Bella Coola

After leaving Bella Bella I was only in Fort Simpson a short time when Mr. Crosby decided to open up the work at Bella Coola where the entire population of [44] two hundred were wholly pagan. No one had ever gone there to proclaim the Gospel of Peace and Love. They had received no teaching of any kind. Accordingly he arranged to make one of his trips and to take me along in order that he might leave me behind at Bella Coola to open up the work.

It was in the fall of 1883 when we left Fort Simpson by canoe. On reaching our destination the chiefs informed us a white trader had told them that the Anglicans were to open up work in their village. Acting on that information, Mr. Crosby withdrew. Next morning before leaving, the chiefs told him that if the Anglicans did not enter that field they would welcome us.

On our return trip we called at Bella Bella and as the new missionary there. Rev. W.B Cuyler, was in need of assistance it was agreed to leave me there with him for a time.

Before Christmas Chief Tom of Bella Coola, with his family, came down to spend Christmas and New Year at Bella Bella. When leaving his home he told the people that he was going to try to find a missionary and if he succeeded he would fire two shots on his return, if he arrived in the night. By this sign they would be certain that he had a missionary on board.

I accepted his invitation and went back with him as their missionary. We reached the village before midnight and sure enough Tom kept his word. Two shots were fired and immediately following were shouts and great excitement on both sides of the river. Tom placed his house at my disposal to be used during the day for [45] school and to hold services there on Sundays. One corner was set apart for my own especial use and there I lived during the whole of my stay at Bella Coola. This dwelling was a very large heathen house having just one room which was big enough to accommodate everybody. There were no windows and not even a lamp, but a large fireplace in the centre of the room piled up with huge blazing logs furnished us with all the light we had.

Because of Tom's kindness to the missionary, he was greatly persecuted by all the other chiefs. While the young people were anxious to have a missionary and learn the new way, the chiefs and older people were strongly opposed to having any change whatever. This opposition made him all the more determined to become a Christian. After his conversion he became very anxious to burn all his idols which he said he had been serving for thirty years. Accordingly, one Saturday he informed me privately that it was his intention to destroy them all that night after everybody had gone to bed, and he requested that I remain up with him to be a witness to the deed. At midnight two boxes were brought in, both filled with heathen treasures of all kinds, such as the secret whistle which belonged to the man-eater dances, dog whistles, wild dance whistles, aprons, head dresses, leggings, etc. These boxes he told me, had been handed down for several generations and had travelled from place to place during the heathen dances. Their frequent use could easily be detected by looking at the top and bottom of each box which had worn so thin that they would [46] bend with the slightest pressure. One of the secret whistles belonging to the man-eater dances which he showed to me was in the form of five fingers at one end while at the opposite end was just one piece where the blower was. He told me that the Kitamaat man-eaters had offered his grandfather one slave for this special piece. This offer was refused, it being against their rules to sell at any price. So when Tom decided to part with these treasures, it was to him a great sacrifice. It meant that the traditions of his family would be wiped out. At two o'clock in the morning, everything had perished in the flames. We then knelt down to pray — there were five of us — Tom and his family and myself. I asked Tom to lead in prayer, which he did. This was Tom's first prayer in public.

When Sunday morning dawned, the news spread through the village like wild fire. Everybody knew on that day Tom and his family were going to take a stand on the Christian side. At the evening service the house was full. All the heathen chiefs, wearing their blankets and with painted faces, were present, anxious to see and hear. They saw Tom and his family stand up and heard them declare that they had done with the heathen rites for ever. Tom had always been one of the chief leaders in the old life, so this change was a big blow to the heathen heads. He was now the leader in the Christian way and I am glad to say he continued to be faithful throughout his life. Often he found the struggle very hard, especially when tempted by other tribes to attend the Potlatch, but he always found God's grace sufficient to keep him from falling. [47] During that winter several families accepted Christianity and Joined the Church.

The services both on Sundays and week days were well attended and the children and young people came to school regularly each day, anxious to learn all they could.

After spending nearly one year among these people, I was appointed to a new field and never had an opportunity of visiting them again for nearly forty years. It was in 1920 the opportunity came and I went. It was a source of delight to note the many improvements that had taken place during that time. It all seemed wonderful. I was cordially welcomed to the mission house by the missionary and his wife, Mr and Mrs Gibson. and it was quite a contrast having the privilege to enjoy my stay in such a pleasant and comfortable home, compared with the heathen dwelling I had occupied in the early days.

It was a pleasure to visit the neat church building which had been erected, also the nice schoolhouse, the latter having been built by the Government, a good teacher being in charge — another contrast from the time when I taught the children their A B C's in the old heathen house, using the floor as a blackboard.

It was early Sunday morning when I landed at the mission house and at the usual hour we went to church. As I glanced around my eyes detected a face that seemed familiar, which I knew at once to be my old friend Tom of long ago. He was delighted to see me again and it seemed too good to be true that after an absence of nearly forty years we had been permitted [48] to meet again. Said he, "When our issionary, Mr. Gibson, told us last Sunday that you were coming, I could not sleep that night. My mind would travel back to the time when we used to take our canoe trips down to salt water and up the river." Less than fifty miles away were two other villages, Kimsquit and Taliome, having a population of less than two hundred. The language spoken was that of the Bella Coolas. These people have never accepted Christianity. Attempts have been made to instruct and help them by frequent visits of the missionary from time to time. with but little apparent success. They seemed to have no desire to accept the new teaching, consequently have made no progress and have decreased very rapidly. Today the population is about one quarter of what it was then.

The Glad Tidings Mission

It was in 1895 that I was appointed to the *Glad Tidings* Mission under the direction of our chairman, Rev. T Crosby.

During that year we travelled altogether about seven thousand miles. A few native workers were chosen to accompany me on these trips to assist in holding evangelistic services at any suitable point we might touch.

I shall not forget some of the sad sights we witnessed around Cape Scott, Cape Cook and Cape Beale, on the West Coast of Vancouver Island. The heathen [49] dances, potlatches and wickedness were too dreadful. Sometimes we would find nearly the whole village under the influence of liquor, and I was told that the whiskey had cost them six dollars a bottle. We spent one Sunday at Nootka Sound and at the close of the evening service sixteen men came forward expressing a desire to lead a new life if a missionary could be sent to help them.

During the round trip we reached about three thousand heathen Indians, and held one hundred and sixteen religious services. The total number of villages visited was thirty-two. The following spring, at the close of our District Meeting, held in Port Simpson, the *Glad Tidings* left for Conference, having several missionaries on board. During the trip she struck a rock and was badly damaged. This accident caused a delay of four days. Naturally our friends became alarmed and a rumor went abroad that the mission boat with all on board was lost. This report had even been wired to the Mission Rooms in Toronto, when the General Secretary suggested that the Dominion Government be asked to send out a search party for the missing boat. While patching up the *Glad Tidings* as best we could the Steamer *Danube* happened to come along, so we all, with the exception of the captain and engineer, went on board. When nearing Victoria we met the Steamer *Maud* which had been sent out with the search party. The *Glad Tidings* reached Vancouver safely, when she was thoroughly repaired and put in good running order, capable of doing as much work as before. [50]

However, this proved to be my last trip on board this staunch little craft. It was during this Conference that I was appointed to leave the boat and take charge of Kishpiax Mission on the Upper Skeena. [51]

Chapter VI
How The Work Began At Kitzegucla
On The Upper Skeena

When in the fall of 1885, our chairman, Rev. T Crosby, decided to commence work amongst the different tribes on the Upper Skeena, he asked me to accompany him on his trip with the intention of leaving me there, if the way should be clear to open up work amongst those benighted tribes. Mr. Crosby had received several letters from some of the young people up there, urging him to send them a missionary. Lack of funds was the only reason for the long delay. It was getting rather late in the season to make the trip We could not get off before the first of November and in that month there is always danger of the river beginning to freeze over at any time. There was no other way of taking the journey except by canoe which required a crew of five men, besides Mr. Crosby and myself.

With everything in our favour we could not expect to reach the Forks of the Skeena (known as Hazelton), in less than ten or twelve days. However, we made a good start, six of the Tsimpsheans having volunteered to take us up the river free of charge.

We loaded up our canoe with provisions, sufficient to last about three weeks and left Fort Simpson early [51] in November. The weather was not very favourable and our progress was slow. The days were short and we had to camp early.

After several days journeying we reached Kitwun-gah which was the first large village to call at. The Church of England had just commenced mission work at this point and it was here where we spent our Sunday. Some of us visited Kit-wun-cool on that day which was a distance of about five hours' walk. These people were entirely heathen and we found them all engaged in poliatching and dancing. Our appearance amongst them was a big surprise. However we held one service and had a good attendance, although several were present just for the purpose of making fun.

We returned to Kit-wun-gah that night and proceeded on our journey next morning, reaching Kitzegucla the same evening — a distance of seven miles. Here the whole tribe was engaged in potlatching and dancing.

As soon as we landed we held a service in front of the village and while singing, a dog-eater rushed out and threw a dead dog right in our midst, some of the blood splashing our clothes.

Next morning we passed on to Hazelton, a distance of fourteen miles, which place we reached in the evening. The Church of England had established a mission here a few years before. We stayed two nights and held two services which were given both in English and the native tongue. Several miners from the Omineca district who had congregated there for the winter. attended both services. [53]

On Friday we reached Kishpiax. This was the largest village on the Skeena, and ten miles above Hazelton. We found everybody at home. Heathenism was raging. Nearly every house had a heathen doctor. There was no observance of the Sabbath and no school. Chief Kaal, kindly gave us permission to use his house during our stay.

Next morning when Mr. Crosby informed them that we had brought a teacher, they replied that Rev. R Tomlinson, who had just started a Church of England mission about four miles above Kishpiax, had visited them and had promised to build there the following year; but should they fail to do so, then they would gladly welcome me as their missionary. Accordingly, I had to return with Mr. Crosby, badly disappointed.

The following morning we departed. A cold north wind was blowing, accompanied by a heavy snowstorm. About noon we reached Kitzeguda and held a service in Chief Cooksun's house. At the close, Mr. Crosby said, "My dear friends, if you wish this young man to remain with you and be your missionary, he will be glad to do so. If not, we will both return." At once Chief Cooksun replied that it was their wish that I should remain and he kindly offered the loan of his house both for Sunday services and day school. One corner of his house was to be set apart for my own personal use. This house was quite large, and consisted of one big room about 60x50 feet, with a huge fireplace in the centre, the smoke escaping through a hole in the roof. As a substitute for shingles, split boards and cedar bark were used. Five families, besides the Chief, [54] were the occupants and there was abundance of room for all. Children and young people began to attend school at the very beginning and came regularly all winter. Some of them wore no clothing whatever, except a loose blanket pinned on. One little boy came entirely naked, so I cut out the lining from my own overcoat and made him a little tunic, which he proudly wore all winter.

Early in December, Judge Graham of Hazelton paid us a visit. He was so delighted to see the change and note the interest of the young people in trying to learn the new way that he promised a Christmas donation and when at his invitation I visited Hazelton a little before Christmas, he presented me with provisions of various kinds, such as rice, raisins, pilot bread, tea, coffee, and canned milk, to make a Christmas dinner for the school children. On Christmas day the feast was spread and was thoroughly enjoyed by all. Never at any time, in any form had Christmas at Kitzegucla been observed before. Two of the chiefs, Cooksun and Haask, made speeches. Both urged the young people to do their utmost to learn the white man's ways and become clever. This good advice from the chiefs was very encouraging and the increased attendance at school after Christmas was no doubt due to the effect of those two speeches. On Sundays we had four services. Early prayer-meeting at seven, preaching at eleven, Sunday School at two and evening service at seven. Little by little, Christianity began to spread and the people began to have a desire to erect a mission building. As there was no lumber to be bought in [55] those days, logs were cut and hewed, and shingles were split for the roof. All work on the entire structure was done by the people free of charge. Doors, windows, nails, hinges and locks were supplied by the Missionary Society. Wives of the men collected food from each family in the village and did the cooking for the workmen, The upper part of the house was to be occupied by the missionary, while the lower floor was to be used as church, school and council room. This was built during the following fall and we had the opening at Christmas time. This was quite an important event. We had chiefs present from all the surrounding villages Each night during Saturday, Sunday and Monday, we held special service, urging those who had come from other villages to accept Christ. Several accepted the invitation and promised to lead a new life.

Since the starting of the mission, just over one year previous, many of the Kitzeguclas had renounced heathenism and were enjoying a change of heart and life. Their happiness was so great that they had a longing desire to proclaim the Saviour's love to all their brothers and sisters in other villages, who were still living in darkness. So right after New Year's we left Kitzegucia — twenty of us, men and women — to make a trip right through to Kishgagass, the farthest village on the Skeena and a distance of seventy miles from Hazelton. Calling at Kishpiax on the way, Edward Sexsmith, native teacher, and his wife joined us on the trip.

The cold was intense, and as there was no other village to call at, we had to camp in the woods. But those [56] were happy days; nothing was counted a hardship. All the Kishgagass people, both men and women, attended our services during our stay there, and the only article of clothing worn by each one was a blanket. No missionary had ever been amongst them and they were purely heathen. They urged us to leave some good singers behind, so that the services we had begun could be continued. Accordingly, we left two of our best men there for two weeks. These they promised to provide food and shelter for during their stay. On our return journey, while at Hazelton some of the miners there suggested amongst themselves that it was their duty to give us a little help. Quite a number of them attended our services and enjoyed the singing very much. Early recollections were revived. Some of them requested us to sing hymns which were their special favorites, having learned them from their mothers while young, when living in the Old Country.

At the close of the last meeting, we received a big surprise. One man stood up and said that they had decided to help along the good work by contributing either cash or provisions. This announcement was much appreciated and very encouraging, for during our long tramps in the cold weather our appetites were not small and our stock was pretty well exhausted. The spokesman donated ten dollars and another fifteen. The Hudson's Bay trader kindly gave us fifteen dollars worth of provisions. This was the beginning of revival work amongst all the different tribes on the Upper Skeena. Kitzegucla was the starting point.

During the winter of 1887 a very severe type of [57] measles broke out at Kitwungah, and spread to all the other villages on the Upper Skeena. Potlatching was strong at the time. Consequently the children were neglected. A number of families lost every child. Even grown-ups were attacked. Altogether there were over two hundred deaths. The potlatchers moved along from one village to another, carrying their sick babies and thus the disease spread. At Kishpiax every house was crowded with strangers who had come from other villages. There was no doctor in the country and no medicine. While so many were congregated at this place, deaths became so frequent that it was impossible to obtain sufficient boards to make coffins, so a large bonfire was started right in the centre of the village where the dead were cremated. One day as I walked p to Hazelton I passed two or three women lying under the trees, their babies strapped to their backs. They had been too sick to proceed farther, and while resting had frozen stiff.

This state of affairs I spoke of in one of the Toronto churches during my trip east in 1900. Dr. Wrinch was then preparing to go out as medical missionary to China, but after hearing these stories he told me at the close that he had decided to go to the Upper Skeena and open up medical work there.

At Kitzeguda there was no potlatch that winter, so the children who were at home received better care. Several of the families who were attending the potlatch elsewhere lost their children while away. Two very sick girls I took up to the mission house and cared for them is best I could. Both recovered. I was kept busy making [58] gruel. Twice each day I went from house to house giving all the help I could.

Towards spring the Kitwuncools had another time of feasting and the Kilzeguclas were invited. All attended. At this time Kitwuncool Jim, one of the young chiefs, had a quarrel with his wife who was a Kitze-gucia woman. During the measles, two of their sons died and the mother, a very strong heathen woman, accused the Kitzegucia doctor of using witchcraft. She said to her husband, "You are very anxious to fight me, but you have no courage to kill the one who has killed our sons. You are just like an old woman, saying much and doing nothing, except to fight me."

At once he got up and quietly left the house. During the night he returned again and went out the second time without being seen. He walked along the road between Kitwungah and Kitwuncool and met the same doctor who was accused of witchcraft and shot him right there. During that afternoon the body of the old doctor was brought into the village. The news soon spread everywhere. The Kitzeguclas left Kitwuncool quite hurriedly and arrived at Kitzegucla towards morning. The following day about midnight war songs with the beating of drums woke me up. At once I got out of bed and dressed, then walked down to the house where everybody was congregated. On entering the door their songs and beating of drums stopped immediately. On inquiring of them their intentions, they replied, "Kitwuncool Jim has killed Neatsque, one of our chiefs, and we are going out in a body to attack Kitwuncool village." At once I told them that to take [59] such a step would be foolish and advised them not to take the law in their own hands, but to lay their complaint before the Government.

As they were all in readiness to depart, it was quite a while before they could decide to change their plans. I explained to them that the surrounding tribes were all in heathenism and darkness and that they, having had a missionary for nearly three years, ought to be able to show that Christianity had taught them better things. Finally one chief spoke on behalf of the crowd, thanking me for coming and stopping their movements just at the right time. After offering prayer, all dispersed to their different homes, feeling thankful that bloodshed had been avoided.

All the guns and spears that were piled up in the house were given in charge of two men who were not to allow them to be handed out to anyone.

In the month of April our District Meeting was held at Port Simpson, and in order to be present I had to start off in March, having to travel on foot as far as Naas River. So, taking one man along with me as guide, we left Kitzegucla for the Naaa by way of *Grease Trail.* The trail was unbroken and we had to use snowshoes all the way. This took us six days.

On the second night out we camped at Kitwancool village. Immediately after supper Kitwuncool Jim, having heard that we had arrived in the village, sent a messenger inviting me to go to his house in order to have a little talk. Accordingly we both went. Phillip, my man, was rather afraid to venture and before entering the door he offered up a prayer for protection. [60]

Jim received us very cordially and we had a long conversation. Amongst other things he said, "I want to talk to you as a friend. If a teacher is sent here I will repent and join the church. I do not want either constables or magistrates to hunt for me. Tell them what I say and if they do come I will shoot every one." At the close of our interview, I promised him that I would deliver his words to the authorities at Port Simpson. After praying with him we left. I never saw him again.

On arriving at Port Simpson, I informed Mr. Hall, the magistrate. He then brought out an old shirt which he asked if I recognized. I did not. Then he pointed out two bullet holes and some stains off blood. This, he told me, had been sent through the mail to him by the niece of the chief who was shot. In the early part of that summer a man-of-war, with five hundred soldiers, was landed at Port Essington. The Captain came ashore and inquired for me. He was anxious that I should give him all the information about the murder. He said that the Government had given them instructions to march right up the Forks of the Skeena and arrest Kitwuncool Jim. I told the captain that, in my .opinion, such action would be a waste of time and money. Most of the people, except the old and infirm, were down at the Coast and there was nobody left up there who could fight. My suggestion was that a special constable should go up there and arrest the man.

About three miles above Port Essington is a piece of land known as Soldier's Point, and is so named from this time when the Captain of the army chose this site [61] as their camping ground during their stay.

In those days, the only boat that plied up and down the Coast carrying passengers and freight, was the *Boscowitz.* This boat the Government chartered to bring up a special load of supplies and war implements for this expedition. It was said that the entire cost was sixty-four thousand dollars.

In about three weeks the man-of-war received word from the Government to return with all the soldiers. The goods were to be sold to the highest bidder. In the fall poor Jim was shot by a special constable at Kitwungah.

The District Meeting was over. We left for Victoria in May, 1887, to attend the first Methodist Conference ever held in British Columbia, and it was at this time that the first ordination service was held. Rev James Calvert and Rev G.F Hopkins, along with myself, composed the first ordination class. Dr John Williams, of Toronto, came out to organize the Conference. Rev. Ebenezer Robson was appointed as President and Rev. Joseph Hall as Secretary. Two years later is was my good fortune, when down the Coast, to meet a young lady who promised to be a partner with me in the trials and triumphs of missionary life. Miss Margrave had come out from Toronto as a missionary teacher, first to Port Simpson, then to Port Essington. In August, 1890, we were married in the church at Port Simpson, Rev. T Crosby performing the marriage ceremony. For about two weeks afterwards we were guests at the mission house, waiting for a chance to get up the Skeena. The Hudson's Bay [62] Company's freight canoes were up the river at the time and we had to wait until their return.

Early in the morning of September 1st, we left Port Simpson. The weather being exceptionally fine, we made a quick trip and reached our destination, New Kitzegucla, in eight days. Those who were at home gave us a very glad welcome, for some of them had told me more than once that a missionary without a wife was only half a missionary.

During the previous winter the Christian families had decided to move away from their old village and build a new site seven miles above where they could have good gardens and grow their potatoes and vegetables and be removed from all heathen surroundings. The place was surveyed and lots were marked off by the Indian agent, each family who went to live there claiming one lot. Logs were hewed for a church and the building was erected and partly finished. The following winter it was ready for use. Several small log houses were built as a beginning and each one was occupied. It was expected that as the heathen families accepted Christianity each one would follow their example and thus build up a good Christian village. This site was named New Kitzegucla. Old Kitzegucla was to be visited regularly by the missionary. This plan seemed to work all right for a time, but as the heathen were practically left to themselves; they gained more power and gradually some of the young people began to attend their gatherings. Thus, little by little, God's work was undermined. Those who had mixed with the heathen rites felt condemned and stayed away from [63] God's house. After a two years' trial, the change did not prove to have been successful, so the majority decided to return to the old village and build up a mission there, retaining their lots on the new site for gardening purposes only. Two or three families objected to move away then, but all the rest went back. Those who refused to leave at that time followed later. During that same year, 1895, I was appointed to the *Glad Tidings* Mission, and thus my work at Kitzegucla ended.

Rev. Thomas Neville, now in Manitoba Conference, was my successor, and stayed there for one winter. Since then other missionaries have been in charge, and much progress has been made. Heathen life has all disappeared and modern, neat-looking, little homes have taken the place of the large, old, heathen houses.

There is an up-to-date school house which was built by the Government, with a good teacher in charge. During this year, a fine new church has been erected, the entire cost to be about $2,500. The sum of $700 was contributed by the Missionary Society, the balance being raised by the Kitzeguclas themselves.

Truly there is wonderful, transforming power in the Gospel of the Lord Jesus. [64]

Chapter VII
Kishpiax Mission

It was in August, 1895, that we left Port Simpson by the Steamer *Caledonia,* for our new appointment at Kishpiax on the Upper Skeena, succeeding Rev. J.C Spencer, who had been stationed there for four years previous. Both as pioneer missionary and school teacher, he was very successful and had the joy of leading some of the heathen to renounce their old degraded, dark, superstitious lives and accept Christianity.

As the steamer went no farther than Hazelton, it was necessary that we should travel the remainder of our journey by canoe. We had no difficulty in securing two good canoes which were soon loaded with our cargo. After breakfast next morning we started off, reaching Kishpiax towards evening. Although the distance was not far — only about ten miles — travelling was necessarily very slow. The current being strong and in most places very shallow, the canoes were pushed slowly along, the crew having to use poles and tow-line.

Most of the people were still away, but those who were at home received us very cordially. Willing hands quickly carried up all our goods to the mission house and before bedtime we had made ourselves quite comfortable. [65]

Our first Sunday services were well attended. Nearly everybody who was in the village, both heathen and Christians, were present. As soon as the different families returned home the attendance at church increased and it was soon very evident that the small log building which had been built by Brother Spencer at the beginning of the mission and which had answered for both religious services and day school, hitherto, was now much too small. As the weeks passed by our congregations increased. In all the services held, both on week days and Sundays, much interest was manifest. Week by week new recruits from the heathen ranks were added to our list. It then became necessary to enlarge the building and during that year quite a number of feet were added to the back, the labor all being done by willing hands, free of charge.

A few weeks after our arrival on this mission my heart was cheered to see an old chief enter the church one Sunday evening. His name was Chief Kleumlaka, which means "Walking between heaven and earth." He had spent all the summer months on his hunting ground several miles away. When he entered the church we noticed that one of his arms was bandaged the whole length. A bear had attacked him during his trip and he had a very narrow escape. This is what he said:

"My dear friends, listen to me and look at my arm. This came as a punishment from God, who sent the bear to attack me and bring me to my senses. While struggling with the bear on the ground and feeling that my limbs were going to be torn off piece by piece,, I called upon God for help and promised Him right there [66] that if he would spare my life I would give myself to Him and confess Him publicly before my people. As I was praying and promising, my son Joseph shot the bear and I was saved. Now, my people, as you look at my arm I want you to acknowledge God's power and yield yourselves to Him as I have done."

A strong influence rested upon the congregation while they listened to that story and at that service several gave themselves to God. Shortly afterwards the old chief was baptized and received the name of Paul. Paul was a chief indeed — a gentleman — and his influence was felt everywhere. He was a wise counsellor amongst his people and during his whole life his advice was always accepted and appreciated. Amongst the whites he was highly respected at all times.

Our Epworth League, which had its beginning in 1894, the year before we went to Kishpiax, had become very strong and now numbered eighty-six active members, all striving to help along God's cause. Every Sunday morning the first religious service of the day — the early prayer meeting — began at seven o'clock. The church bell rang at six o'clock, which was a signal for the Leaguers to assemble there to prepare for a march through the village with their drum and banner. Thus, with songs and exhortations, they invited the heathen to come to the Saviour. This outdoor exhortation was repeated before the afternoon service and again in the evening. Instead of meeting together once a week, as is customary amongst the whites, these Leaguers had service every Monday, Wednesday and Saturday evening. The officers were elected every twelve months, by [67] vote. At the end of two years it was unanimously decided to erect a new building and call it the Epworth League Hall.

Our congregations had increased so much that we were over-crowded at every service. To buy lumber up there in those days would cost a good sum of money, so the active members agreed to spend over two weeks in the woods and saw lumber themselves, all by hand. Their wives volunteered to cook all the food which they required and take it up to their camp on the mountain side each day, in pails and boxes. In less than three weeks sufficient lumber had been cut and packed down to the site, and in a very short time a very good building 40x25 feet, was completed. At the opening services there was much rejoicing. Mr R.E Loring, Indian Agent, kindly consented to act as chairman. Hazelton, Kitzegucla and Kitwungah Christians were invited to attend. On Sunday the hall was crowded four times and the collections were good. In addition to this offering, the women donated the lamps and gave as a special subscription their jewelry, silk handkerchiefs, etc. The entire cost of the building was $600. This was the beginning of a blessed revival which lasted three months. Numbers of heathen came out from darkness into the glorious light of the Gospel. Not many years previous had these same people gone about in bands from village to village, under the influence of the evil spirit, wounding and murdering one another. During the revival they went from place to place preaching the gospel of peace and telling their heathen friends what God had done for them. [68]

One of our old chiefs, named *Shak-geant*, which means "Camping without fire," who all his lifetime had been a leader amongst the heathen doctors and wild dancers, decided to come out from the old life and be a Christian. He ordered his nephew to pull down his house to the ground, the totem poles also — he did not wish to see a vestige of darkness and cruelty left behind. At his baptism he took the name of Enoch Williams. Some time afterwards he thought it only right that he and his wife should be married according to the Christian rites and although they were nearly seventy years of age, nothing would satisfy him but to go through the ceremony and have a display in a Christian style, as if they were a young couple just starting out in life.

The bride was dressed in white muslin over a green skirt, and, in imitation of her white sisters, wore a long white veil made out of muslin. Three chiefs acted as best men. There were also three bridesmaids arrayed in various colors. Right after the ceremony a marriage feast took place in the Epworth League Hall. Rabbit soup, made from fifty rabbits, bought biscuits, plain and fancy, with tea, were heartily enjoyed by everybody. This aged couple did not live a great while to to enjoy their changed life, but they were faithful to the end. Well might the heathen exclaim as they watched his daily life, "God's work has changed this man."

Another old man who had always been a noted character along the Skeena river, was converted. In witchcraft and dog-eating dances he always took the [69] lead. His name was Do-ga-gish, which means "Hair grabber". In old times that was the way they fought each other, not with the hands as white people do. This old man used to do a good deal of hair pulling during his dances and that was how he got his pet name. When he professed conversion there was great astonishment everywhere. One day one of our Epworth League workers visited him in his home and talked to him about Nicodemus. which was the first time he had heard the story. He was deeply interested and at the close said, "I should like to have that name when I am baptized. Will you tell me what is the name of his wife, for I should like my wife to take her name."

"Well," said the man, "I cannot tell you her name, but I will ask the missionary."

When he came to inquire, I had to confess that I could not answer that question either, so the old man chose for his wife the name Cecelia. The old couple were both baptized and enjoyed their new life every day.

As the heathen renounced their old life, it was their desire to move out from their old surroundings and build Christian homes at the other end of the village. This meant both money and hard work. After the logs had been cut and hewn, lumber for flooring, doors and windows were required, and as it all had to be done by hand, progress was slow. It was just at this time that the missionary suggested the possibility of their having a sawmill all their own. Three miles below the village was a splendid location for a mill, and if they were willing to put up their money it was thought it could [70] be done. To them this was a big proposition, but after much careful thinking and planning every man decided to make the venture. Fifty dollar shares were called for and during that year sufficient money was raised. The machinery, with planer, moulder and rustic attachments, were bought in Ontario. From Port Essington at the mouth of the Skeena, it had to be freighted up the river by canoe. Four canoes were required to carry the entire plant. Two white men who were supposed to be first class millwrights, were engaged to build the penstock and frame. Just when everything was in readiness to give the mill a trial, to everybody's disappointment, the penstock burst. Therefore all operations had to be suspended for that year. The Indians had been cheated by worthless labor and the work had to be done all over again. The two men, after receiving their wages, had made good their escape, so Mr. Robert Tomlinson, of Menskinisht, was engaged to put the mill in good running order the following year. When the first log was put through there were many natives looking on with intense interest. Some of the chiefs who were present suggested having a prayer meeting right there to thank God for the wonderful waterpower.

This mill not only gave employment to many of the Kishpiax people, but supplied them with lumber to erect new and comfortable dwellings for themselves, which took place of the old heathen houses. In addition large orders came from the Indians and whites at Hazel-ton and other villages below, as well as from the settlers in Kishpiax valley. Large orders, many of them for lumber of different cuts, were filled without error. [71] During the construction of the Grand Trunk Pacific, the demand for lumber was greater than at any other time. The following is an extract from The Missionary Bulletin, dated December, 1909:

Kispiax sawmill, which has now been in operation for ten years, finds this to be far the busiest time of all. Two shifts of men have been employed all summer, in order to keep the mill going day and night. This will continue as late into the season as the weather will permit. The demand for lumber is so great now that it is taken away as fast as it is cut. Some improvements too have been made this summer. A splended new dam has been built, also a new penstock. The old saying, 'that the only good Indian is a dead one,' is certainly not true in this part of the country. Without that Indian sawmill, the Upper Skeena would not be able to obtain any supply at all."

About one year after the mill was in good running order, it was decided to build a church. A good site was selected and lumber was bought from the mill. The Missionary Society donated a grant of $300 towards the cost, the natives promising to meet all other expenses by contributing either cash or labor. During the winter when the thermometer registered over thirty degrees below zero, all hands went up the mountainside to camp for several days to make shingles. It was their delight to do this work. On their return they packed sufficient to cover the entire building.

In the Missionary report for that year we read as follows: "The year 1901 closed with the opening services of our new church. That event will always be a [72] memorable" day in the history of this mission. At the close of the morning service three persons were baptized. It cheered our hearts to see the heathen and christian friends from the other missions come forward with their money. Collections on Sunday were good, amounting to $369.55. The Indian Agent of the district, Mr. R.E Loring, was present and manifested considerable interest on the occasion. Five of our best men were appointed to act as trustees. As soon as they found out that a debt of $100 still remained, they met together and said to the missionary: "This debt on the church hangs over our heads like a heavy weight, and when we pray our hearts are sad." They suggested a plan in order to raise that amount and in two weeks the debt was all paid." A few months later carpet and matting were put down and the people felt quite proud of ils improved appearance. This improvement was all due to the efforts of the Ladies' Aid, which had been organized the previous year. The lamps were kindly donated by the Methodist Church of Norwood, Ontario. A letter of thanks sent to Rev. R Taylor, who was then stationed there, was published in *The Guardian,* and reads as follows:

"Dear Brother in Christ:
	"We, the Christian chiefs of Kishpiax Methodist Mission, in behalf of all the other Christians here, wish to send our warmest thanks to you and others of your church for so kindly rememebring us in our need. It was a great surprise when our missionary informed us that our new church was to be lighted with a beautiful chandelier sent by the trustees of the Methodist Church [73] at Norwood as a gift. Our white friends who do not understand the Indian have often said that Indians have no gratitude. Of course, we cannot send thanks of that kind to you, but we assure you that whenever the lamps are lit, our hearts will remember your kindness to us. We often look back upon the time when the darkness was unbroken in our village and our people were sunk in heathenism and its abominations, but we thank God, through the preaching of His everlasting gospel, the light has come, and we are enlightened, and education is advancing amongst our young people.

"Yours in Christ,

"Abraham Kaal, Paul Klepumptaka, Jonah Kshumgalth,
Enoch We-Bowak, Eli Skolst, "Chiefs."

	After working over five years amongst these people, our hearts were greatly cheered and encouraged by the arrival of a medical missionary in our midst. We were all delighted to welcome Dr. and Mrs. Wrinch, who had come all the way from Ontario to open up medical work on the Upper Skeena. Until a suitable location for the hospital could be secured, the doctor decided to live in Kishpiax and help on the work there. He rented an Indian house close by the mission, and with a few alterations, made it quite comfortable for their temporary abode. Indians from all the surrounding villages came to him for treatment and advice. He was ably assisted by Mrs. Wrinch who had previously received special training as a nurse in Toronto.
	Besides his medical work, the doctor rendered valuable [74] able assistance on this mission in various ways, and Mrs. Wrinch was not behind. At this time a Junior League was organized with Mrs. Wrinch as Superintendent. These young people met together weekly for religious instruction, in her home.
	The girls she taught various kinds of needlework and knitting. A folding organ that she had brought with her from the east, added interest to the musical part, not only in these small gatherings, but also in the church services on the Sabbath.

Two years passed away and then the doctor moved down to Hazelton. He had secured a suitable location for a building site about one and a quarter miles from the town, and it was necessary that he should live where he could superintend building operations. For a long time afterwards, he continued to make weekly visits to Kishpiax, having rented part of an Indian house which he fitted up for a dispensary. This journey meant that he had to walk a distance of ten miles each way over the trail, and return home the same day. Weather conditions were not always favorable but the doctor never failed to keep his appointment. However, when the new hospital was an established fact, and everybody had become accustomed to the benefits received from that institution, those visits were discontinued and all who desired medicine or treatment of any kind, went to consult the doctor down there. To show the development of the medical work, I will quote an extract from a letter published in the Missionary Bulletin, of April, 1910.

"Just nine years ago our first doctor came. You all [75] know Dr. Wrinch and have heard of his splendid work. At Hazelton he has a fine hospital and his work has increased so much that last year he had to get an assistant. Now we have two doctors instead of one and their hands are full. Both whites and Indians have highly appreciated the treatment and attention which they received during their stay in the hospital. The head chief of the Wolf Crest here (Paul Kleumlaka) had to undergo an operation this winter. He is an old man and the operation was a serious one, but old Paul, who is a good man, said good bye to all his friends and told them that if he died the hospital would be the Gate of Heaven to him. The operation was successful and old Paul did not die. After a few weeks spent there he returned home with a beaming face and a heart full of gratitude for what had been done for him. I called to see him, and these are his words, 'I have had every attention and plenty of good food, but my stomach is not made like a white man's stomach and I miss my dry salmon. I am just going to eat some, and, Missionary, will you eat a little with me while we talk? I feel that I should like to give the doctor a great deal of money. He deserves it, and if I Were a young man I would work hard and pay him more than he has asked. To me the hospital was like heaven and the nurses like angels. In our dark heathen days we could obtain no help like this. This is the fruit of the preaching of the Gospel of Christ.'"

More than twenty years after the arrival of Dr. Wrinch the following appeared in the Vancouver Sun, and shows the remarkable progress made in that period [76] of time. "One of the many hardships, perhaps the greatest, for those who dwell in the far corners of the Dominion, remote from civilization, is the lack of a doctor. In case of accident the men must trust in Providence and luck, the women must go through life bearing families with their lives in their hands.

"More than twenty years ago, Hazelton, that most northerly point on the whole of the Canadian National railway tines, was an important packing centre for the interior of British Columbia, with a heterogeneous collection of Indian tribes all around. The nearest doctor was at Prince Rupert, 177 miles away; the trails were rough, the going was hard and the Skeena River, then as now, a dangerous passage both in winter and summer.

"When the twentieth century was still young, there came to these parts a certain doctor with a wide vision and a large heart. He saw the dire need of the country, so he settled at Hazelton and founded a hospital, which has been a godsend and a rock of hope to Indians and whites alike throughout the years.

"With assistance and grants from the Methodist Mission Board, from the Indian department at Ottawa and from the provincial government, Dr. Wrinch bought 300 acres of land up on the hill behind Hazelton, a few acres of which was Indian reserve, the rights being donated by the Indians. He cleared it little by little, and made of it a productive farm which now keeps

the hospital entirely in garden and dairy produce-
"Sixteen acres have been cleared, not in the all-too-frequent method of slashing and burning everything in [77] sight that reduces a beautiful spot to a bleak and treeless waste, but with an eye to the future and an appreciation of natural beauty.

"With the rugged, majestic heights of Rocher Deboule for a background, is seen the hospital buildings set among the trees in the middle of a parklike meadow-land, green and fertile. The whole place has more nearly the look of a well-kept private country estate in England than anything else I have seen in British Columbia.

"In 1903 the doctor's private house was sufficiently finished to take in the first patients. In the following year the hospital itself was completed, since then it has been added to and improved in every way that modern science can suggest.

"It makes a great story of achievement, of hard work and a fight against every sort of difficulty, the history of the Hazelton hospital, which is also the history of Dr. Wrinch. If you want to know more about him you ask the mothers of Hazelton who it is that has brought all the babies roundabout into the world these last twenty years: ask them who drove out to meet them on the trail on bleak winter nights, when they had driven endless miles and could not make the hospital in time, and would have died right there on the road — they and their babies — but for Dr. Wrinch. Ask the Indians, brought in mauled to pieces by a grizzly, or blinded by disease, who it was that healed their hurts and sent them away with new hope in their hearts.

"The main building has twelve wards, six of them [78] private ones, with room for thirty-three patients, nine nurses and assistant doctor. It is central-heated and all wired for electricity. There is a Fairbanks-Morse gasoline electric power plant, especially built for steady power to operate the X-ray, so it will be seen that the doctor is an engineer as well as a farmer and land clearer, but there is also a resident engineer on the spot to take care of it alt.

"There are two other buildings besides the doctor's private house and in the farmyard there is a silo and stables to house the twelve head of cattle. Included in the hospital grounds is a thirty-five acre lake covered with water lilies in the summer and ice in the winter, which latter is cut and stored for the year's use in the hospital.

"Down in the basement you may see rows upon rows and shelves upon shelves of canned chicken and chicken broth, of every sort of canned vegetables and fruit, all produced on the farm and canned under the personal supervision of the doctor himself. Two women cooks have charge of the kitchen and of course the ubiquitous Chinaman has care of the laundry.

"It will be a difficult matter for Dr. Wrinch to tear himself away from his beloved hospital, but leave it he must for at least three months in the year, as the people of that widespread and scattered district have just shown their liking and respect by returning him as Liberal member for the provincial legislature. "

As time went by, we became aware that several heathen, in a secret way, were doing their utmost to upset God's work by fermenting liquor from the juice [79] of berries, and we felt that something should be done to counteract this evil. First we started a Band of Hope amongst the children, so now the Junior League and Band of Hope were all in one. In a letter to the *Missionary Bulletin*, dated January 15th, 1904, is found the following account of the temperance work: "In my last to you I told you that we had started a Band of Hope amongst the children. Now \ want to tell you about our Temperance Society which we have organized amongst the grown people. I had often thought of starting a Society of this kind amongst the people, but somehow it never seemed to fit in until now. And it seems as if God is working with the people through this means.

"You will no doubt think of this movement as being similar to, or just like, what you have seen amongst the whites. But I think if you could have stepped into our service on Sunday evening, December 20th, and have seen the altar filled several times with those who were anxious to take the pledge, you would imagine yourself to be in a revival meeting.

"For some time previous to this, I had preached temperance and talked about it, but when the Sunday evening on which we had planned to start this Society came and your missionary gave the invitation to those who desired to take the pledge, to come forward, he was surprised at the number who responded and who, amid tears and sobs and prayers, made their promise. God seemed very near, all felt His presence, and we trust and pray that the promises made may be faithfully kept. They all look upon this movement as the most serious thing that ever happened in Kishpiax. [80]

"Now I do not for a moment want you to imagine that we have a lot of drunkards up here, or even moderate drinkers, but amongst the heathen they have recently begun to make fermented liquor from the juice of berries and other things. This, of course, was done secretly and yet they were always trying to trap the Christians unawares. Sometimes liquor would be obtained secretly from a steamboat. We all felt that this thing was growing and that instead of the potlatch and its evils being a snare to the Christians whisky was now taking its place and that the Temperance Society, of which we had talked, would be just the same thing to check it. Then the railroad is coming and along with it will come the terrible evil — fire-water. So we trust that this movement started, wilt be the means of helping our brothers and sisters to stand firm. The number who have joined our Temperance Society is seventy-seven, and the Band of Hope thirty-six.

"In 1905 by-laws and a council were established. The Council consisted of twelve chiefs and five councillors. All fines collected were to be used for the improvement of the village. The missionary was chosen by the Council and appointed by the Indian agent to act as chairman. During this fall it was the desire of the Christians to have a flagpole, so one was erected, and stood fifty-eight feet above the ground. In the first place this was to be an object lesson to the heathen, for when the flag was hoisted on the Sabbath it would remind them of how the day was to be kept. Besides, it was to be used on special occasions such as Christmas, New Year's Day and Weddings, etc. The flag was kindly donated [81] by our warm-hearted friends of the Cranbrook Epworth League.

"In those days the Sabbath was strictly observed. No one ever thought of working or travelling on that day. Two of our men were engaged in packing supplies for three white men. When Saturday night came one of the men informed these whites that they did not work on Sunday, that it did not pay to do that. One of them replied, 'We tike you all the better for that. We too, have been taught not to work on Sunday. Tell us what church you belong to.' 'We belong to the Methodist Church,' said the Indian. 'Well,' said the white man, "I am a Methodist.' The next man said, 'I am a Presbyterian,' and the third man said, "I am a Presbyterian, too.' When breakfast was over on Sunday morning, the Indian suggested that they have a little service. But the white man wanted to know who would conduct it. 'I can do that,' said the Indian, and to his surprise he found each of these whites in possession of a Bible. For the Indians to come in contact with white men who cared enough for their Bibles to carry them in their packs instead of whiskey and tobacco was a surprise indeed."

During the fall of 1907 the Skeena river became noted for steamboat wrecks. The Hudson's Bay boat, *Mount Royal*, was the first to go to pieces. A letter, dated October 19th, 1907, written to the *Missionary Bulletin*, describes the losses thus:

"That accident was so sudden and unexpected that it came as a great shock to everybody. All the passengers were saved by jumping on a rock, and in five minutes [82] the boat was gone. Six of the crew found a watery grave. How this brings to our mind the Saviour's command, 'Be ye also ready, for in such an hour as ye think not, the Son of Man cometh.' This accident meant a great loss to everybody living on the Upper Skeena. The *Mount Royal* was the only boat on the river at the time, the Hazelton having been put on the Stickine river for the summer. Supplies and freight of every description were lying at the mouth of the river, and storekeepers, missionaries and everybody else had their patience sorely tried. Then the North West. a boat run by a new company, was put on the river. This was cheering news to all on the Upper Skeena. She was rather too large and clumsy for the river and made slow time, but she could carry one hundred tons of freight. A few weeks ago, while making her fourth trip, she got on a sand bar and was totally wrecked. Several white passengers who were on board, returned to Essington by canoe. A great number of the Indians were on board returning from the canneries with their winter supplies, bedding, etc. The poor people lost everything. They tried their best to save what they could, but after they had piled their sacks of sugar on the beach it all leaked out like water. Their beans swelled and burst the bags leaving the beans strewed on the beach in every direction. Their biscuits (pilot bread) swelled too and burst the boxes. Their bedding was either soaking wet or totally lost. Can you imagine what a plight these poor people were in? Besides all this, they, themselves were left stranded on the beach without any means of getting either up or down the river. Some chance canoe coming [83] along would take one, or perhaps two, on board and they would be left at some village to wait there for another chance. Others would walk to some point where a canoe would catch them.

"About the time that the North West was wrecked the Hazelton made a trip, but on the way down struck on a rock and got on a sand bar. She was badly damaged and was there two weeks or more before she could get off. She is now on her way up again, but the water is very low, and it is doubtful whether she will be able to get up. Some of our people just home from the North West wreck, and having four weeks' toil to get here, say that they feel God is speaking both to the whites and Indians. We are praying that a mighty revival wave may strike the Upper Skeena this winter and that those who are lingering in the heathen life may be swept into the Kingdom."

Not many weeks after the above was written we felt that our prayers were being answered. An extract from a letter dated January 20th, 1908, reads thus:

"Since I wrote my last letter to you, great changes have been taking place on this mission. God's spirit has been working on the hearts of the people in a way that went beyond what we had hoped for them. His mighty power has been felt, and heathenism has been shaken to its very foundations. There have been no Special services and no undue excitement, but God has been speaking to many hearts and ever since about the middle of November there have been conversions from the heathen ranks right along. To Him be all the praise! [84]

"It will interest you to hear about Louis, the leading potlatcher amongst the heathen on this Upper Skeena. He haa always been the head chief of heathenism and a man of influence, one to whom everybody looked up. He has always worked hard and earned lots of money — perhaps more than any other man — and certainly he has spent more than any other man on that great evil, the Potlatch. On Saturday morning, November 16th, he came to the mission house and said, 'I want to give my heart to God. I have been thinking about it for a long time and now I want to make a start tonight. i Will it be right for me to hoist my flag today as a token of my intention, so that the whole village may know?' 'Certainly,' I replied, 'and I will hoist the mission flag in response.'

"As soon as the people saw the flags inquiries were made, and when the explanations were given there was great excitement and rejoicing. Everybody who had a flag hoisted it. That night Louis came to the services, and made a start for the Kingdom. His conversion means so much to Kishpiax and the whole of the Upper Skeena. It means death to the potlatch. Thank God we have lived to see the day when that abomination has been destroyed in this village. Abraham Kaal, our head chief and uncle of Louis, has been a Christian for some years. He is very old and feeble and may not live long. His heart has long been troubled that his nephew, who will take his place at his death, was opposed to what was good. Now that i such a change has taken place, the old man rejoices greatly. He feels that this means a great deal to Kishpiax people. [85]

"The next day was our Temperance Sunday, and it was a day long to be remembered. The whole family of Louis, all grown up, and his son-in-law, were converted, also two other leaders in the heathen life. From that time the heathen have kept coming, one or two at a time. We always have the last Sabbath of the old year for our missionary services. We had a blessed day. In the afternoon Louis gave us his first sermon. He took for his text, 'Go ye into all the world and preach the Gospel to every creature,' and spoke very earnestly. He urged the people to make a united effort and give. 'For,' said he, 'if we are not united, we shall not do much. If we want the gospel to spread, we must have money. Without money, no gospel would ever have come to us.' We raised the sum of $105 in cash and more was promised."

In the following year Conference decided to move us away from Kishpiax. It was thought that Mrs. Pierce's health required a change. During the fifteen years spent on that mission, preaching, teaching and helping the people in the new way of living, we saw some wonderful changes take place. There were discouragements, trials and difficulties to be met, but when, glancing back at the past and reviewing what the Gospel of Christ has done for this once benighted people, we were filled with renewed hope and courage to press forward.

It was in the month of September, 1910, that we bade good-bye to Kishpiax and took up new duties on my old ground at Port Essington. [86]

Editor's Note

[*Editor's Note*: This brings us to the end of what may be called — to use the apt term coined by the late Rev. C.M. Tate — the "auto-sketch" of the Rev. William Henry Pierce, as contained in the interesting manuscript which came into our hands. What follows in that manuscript is devoted to Indian legends, traditions and customs of the pre-white man period — a wealth of information which the future, perhaps even more than the present, will value. But the biographical section here concluded brings Mr. Pierce's story down only to his return to Port Essington in 1910. That was twenty-three years ago, and much water has gone over the wheel during the intervening years; for Mr. and Mrs. Pierce, happily, are still with us in 1933, and until a year ago were continuing their active missionary work. Some explanation, perhaps, may be given; and in any case it is felt something should 'be written of those later years.

The reason why the story stopped in 1910 seems to be that it had been written at that time, by request of the missionary authorities at Toronto, who hoped to arrange for its publication. For one reason or another publication was not proceeded with and the manuscript was held in suspense. When the present publishers became interested they suggested to Mr. Pierce that he write a concluding chapter. Impaired health, and advancing years made him shrink from the task; but [87] recognizing that something should be done about it, he furnished the present writer with incidents of the period and certain other data with the hope that he prepare some suitable concluding material.

The material at hand, however, is both fragmentary and meagre, and nothing we could write could be regarded as a continuation of the story as Mr. Pierce, himself, would have written it. No general review of the period has been attempted. We have sought rather to furnish a few glimpses of the character and devotion of this distinguished missionary and of his work during those more recent years which should not be permitted to go unnoticed. — J.P.H.]

Port Essington Again

It will be recalled that Mr. Pierce's first mission station was at Port Essington (in 1877). When he returned there, thirty-three years later, he noted great changes. In the earlier day the Indian people did not feel permanently settled there. They were there at certain times of the year when trading or fishing — or, perchance, feasting — made it necessary to pass that way; a fact indicated by the native name for the place, which was "Spookshoat" (or Spookshute) meaning "a fall camp." Now, thirty-three years later, with the development of the salmon-canning industry, not only had the Kitselas and Kitsumkalem tribes moved down from the Upper Skeena and built their villages there, but — more marked still — the white population had [88] increased and made many changes: New streets, new houses and stores had been built; also a public school for white children, an Anglican Church and rectory, and the railroad had come "across the river" — with benefits and banalities much interwoven. "But," he apostrophises in one of his letters, "I am very sorry to say that the saloon and the pool room, with al! their evils came also. I need not say," he added, "that these places are a snare to many of our young people. It is too bad that the poor Indians have to learn all these different forms of vice from the whites, who, instead, ought to have been able to show them a good example from the first."

The Indian mission was now, of course, long established; for twenty years or more it had been under the pastoral care of the Rev Dennis Jennings, MA, and then for some years by the Rev BC Freeman, whom Mr Pierce was succeeding; a branch of the Port Simpson Hospital had also been built by that self-sacrificing man, Dr AE Bolton — the first medical missionary on the Coast, and who undertook his work at his own charges. There was thus a strong background of Christian sentiment which Mr. Pierce evidently was not slow to arouse; especially to resist the evils associated with whiskey; for, writing two years later he remarked on the peaceful Christmas season just past: "There was scarcely any whiskey drinking to be seen, either amongst the Indians or the whites during the holiday." This he attributed to the temperance meetings held in the previous July when over one hundred signed pledge cards. And when, later still — as is always [89] happening where the liquor traffic is concerned — there was a resurgence of the vicious elements, with whiskey, as he tells us, causing the trouble, the moral and Christian forces in the town were still active, until the Government suddenly closed all the poolrooms and the Council of Chiefs closed the dance halls — a strange picture of, until lately, pagan aborigines maintaining moral standards against the sordid greed or vicious indulgence of men familiar with Christian teaching and atmosphere as an inheritance of many generations. This type of warfare was now inevitably involved, and courageously waged, year after year, in the changed conditions at Port Essington during the later period of Mr. Pierce's ministry there. It may be assumed by the reader as underlying the whole story, a few incidents of which only we give here.

Early in 1914 a cloud of sadness came over the Indian population of the town; as indeed, over the entire native population of the Coast; for news had come of the death, at Vancouver, of two of the beloved early missionaries who had brought the gospel to them — the Rev. Thomas Crosby and the Rev. A.E Green.

"We cannot yet realize," Mr. Pierce wrote, "that they have really passed away from our midst, but we do feel that our loss is great. All these years they have seemed to be a part of our lives and we have always looked to them for advice and help. God has honored their efforts in proclaiming the gospel to the different tribes both along the Coast and in the interior. Their names will never be forgotten."

The effect of this news upon the Indians was very [90] great. They thronged the Church for the memorial service. Mr. Pierce preached from "How shall they hear without a preacher; and how shall they preach except they be sent?" Then followed touching testimonies, often with tears, from chiefs and others whose lives had been changed by the preaching of those godly men in the earlier years. The oldest man of the mission spoke: "Mr. Crosby was the means of my becoming a Christian," he said. "In the early days when he made a trip here, he found me and my wife and family all pure heathen. At that time my wife belonged to the man-eaters. He came into my house and urged us to become Christians. In a short time we left our old heathen life behind and began to serve God. Then, acting on Mr. Crosby's advice, we were married by him according to the Christian rites, and since that time have never looked back. My wife went to heaven a few years ago, and it will not be long now before I, too, shall follow her. When I get to heaven the first thing I shall want to do is to hunt up Mr. Crosby and shake hands with him."

Another spoke as the first convert in Port Essington: "I remember the time, over thirty years ago, when Mr. Crosby first came to Essington on a revival trip. We were all in heathen life at that time. As we listened to his preaching God's Word changed our hearts. I was one among several who were baptized by him at that time, and I shall never forget the feeling that passed through me when he laid his hand upon my head. My heart was strangely warmed and I felt God's presence very near. I have had many trials and [91] troubles since that time, but I am still looking to God and serving Him."

These and many such tributes suggest that the ministry of those devoted missionaries was not merely an intense emotional appeal, but a something which resulted in permanently changed lives — even from savagery to noble Christian character.

The recalling of these simple, direct testimonies induces the reflection that everyone of these pioneer missionaries was really a flaming evangelist, impelled by the love of Christ which had come into his heart to go and tell others the story. The religion of Jesus was no mystery to him; it was a glorious experience. Man was born in sin, some in heathen darkness. All needed to be "born again." There could be no real happiness or peace without conversion. He rang the earnest, forceful changes upon forgiveness of sins; justification by accepting Christ; the danger of being lost; the possibility of being saved, and of being adopted as God's sons. This was the Gospel they preached They distinguished naturally between morality and spirituality; between reformation and regeneration; between assent of the mind and change of heart. They declared that God loved mankind; that He "so loved the world that He sent His only Son that whosoever believeth in Him should not perish but have everlasting life." This was their message, and it was this message only which changed the lives of the Indians to whom they went. And as soon as the Indian himself was changed he went out and told of what had come into his heart and life. It was this simple story of God's [92] love and the sacrifice of Jesus which changed the "man-eater" and the "dog-eater" into a kindly, earnest Christian; which substituted the prayer-meeting for the potlatch — the pioneer missionary preached no other gospel but salvation through the sacrificial blood of Jesus Christ.

But while he regarded himself simply as an evangelist, he naturally saw the implications of this Gospel; and so became the counsellor and guide of the converts he won. To him they came for advice and leadership on social advancement in the habits of life and improved environment; and for changing ideas in industrial possibilities and a new civilization. Gradually their villages were transformed as they became Christians and self-imposed rules for law and order were respected. And in all this Mr. Pierce was as fully and shrewdly a leader as any of his early colleagues. An outstanding instance will illustrate this phase of his missionary activity:

In 1914 there was considerable discouragement among the natives, who are not naturally industrious or by erstwhile conditions of life fitted to compete with more highly organized peoples. They were realizing that they were being gradually crowded out of the fishing industry by Japanese and white men. By the leadership of their missionary they organized a Native Fishermen's Association which aimed to unite all the tribes into one body for mutual protection of what they considered their natural native rights. Mr. Pierce was chosen President, and a bright young Essington Indian, William Starr, Secretary. Later the organization was [93] incorporated, and a charter was obtained from the Government. Writing of this in 1919, Mr. Pierce was able to speak of its success and of how far it had extended among the Coast tribes. He said:

"For some time previous there had been a spirit of carelessness among most of the fishermen, which, of course, caused the cannerymen to dislike them; and naturally they preferred to employ Japanese, who would persevere in all kinds of weather, whether salmon were plentiful or scarce. As soon as the natives saw that they were gradually being left out, they began to think, and wondered how they could make good again. It was just at that point the Association was formed-Port Essington, being the central place, was chosen headquarters, and it is here the Annual Meeting is held. At the present time there are 1,800 members and 23 branches among the different tribes, from Rivers Inlet to Skeena, Naas and Queen Charlotte Islands.

The Cannery men are now loud in their praises of the work done by the Indians, also of their improved conduct during the fishing time. Both on the Skeena and the Naas the natives were high boat this summer, and at some of the canneries they were high boat last year. All the managers at the different canneries have already engaged them for next year's fishing. This has never been done before. All this means much thought and planning, and I can assure you that your missionary has very little chance to be idle."

The outbreak of the Great War in 1914 disturbed and not a little perplexed many of the Indians. One of the Christian chiefs expressed the thoughts of others [94] when he asked Mr. Pierce how such dreadful fighting could break out among the very people who had been anxious to send the Gospel of Peace to them and had taught them to lay aside all their warlike implements — the scalping-knife, spear, stone hammer and clubs. There were white men, of alien sympathies who sought to exploit the native perplexity in the interests of the enemy; telling them, among other things, that if the Germans won the war they would give all the land back to the Indians. This caused a good deal of unrest among the Indian people.

Mr. Pierce had his own quaint way of dealing with it. Speaking of it recently to the writer he said: "I listened to their statement and saw there was trouble ahead. The following questions were put to me:

" ' What is the reason that the first missionaries who came out to us — like Mr. Duncan and Mr. Crosby — preached Thou shalt not kill. Thou shalt love thy neighbour as thyself; and now some of our missionaries send their own sons out to the war to kill the Germans?'

"I told them I would answer that question tomorrow.

"During the day I made a sketch on the blackboard in the schoolhouse and covered it from view. The next night when the chiefs came together, I unveiled the blackboard, and they saw a house fenced around. Inside the fence was the man's stock, such as cows, chickens, pigs, etc. Amongst them was a big wolf that had jumped the fence to kill and destroy. The man took his rifle and killed the wolf, thus saving his family and his possessions. [95]

"I said to them, This picture you now see is my answer to your question of yesterday. Now you have to answer my question: Who is right, the man or the wolf?
"'The man is right!' they replied.

"I said to them, 'Suppose the Germans do win the war, your lands will never be given back to you. It will belong to them, and you will be their slaves.' "
Following this, with a true spirit of patriotism, Mr. Pierce acquired suitable slides for his magic lantern and gave lectures, not only at Essington but at distant Indian villages, on the subject "Why Britain Went to War." The steadying effect among the people was everywhere evident, and many readily contributed towards the hospital ship and the Red Cross.

In 1900 and the Spring of 1901, Mr. Pierce, at the wish of the Missionary Board, spent several months in Ontario and Eastern Canada, on missionary deputation work. In *The Christian Guardian* the following reference was made to the visit:

"A British Columbia Missionary"

"Rev. W.H. Pierce, of Kishpiax, Fort Simpson District, British Columbia, called at *The Guardian* office this week on his way out to his field of labor in the far Northwest. Bro. Pierce, who is a native of British Columbia, of Indian and Scotch descent, has been spending six months in Ontario and Quebec. During that time he has delivered, in the bounds of the [96] five Conferences, 124 missionary addresses, besides numerous Epworth League and Woman's Missionary Society talks, and has travelled over 7,186 miles. His earnest addresses have done much to awaken an intelligent interest in the mission work among our Indians. He speaks hopefully of that work, and is greatly rejoiced at the prospect of Dr. Wrinch's going to establish hospital work among the Upper Skeena Indians. He is desirous of expressing his thanks to the people of the East for the warm reception given him during his stay. His visit has greatly enlarged his own ideas of the work of the Methodist Church. It will take him a year. he says, to tell his own people of the wonderful things he has seen."

Later, when he was one of the missionaries supported by the Epworth Leagues, on different occasions arrangements were made for similar deputation work in different districts of the British Columbia Conference, and everywhere he was hailed with enthusiasm, with fine results following his work.

More recently Mr. Pierce was sought — and most naturally so — as the special guest and preacher, for the Jubilee celebrations of the missions at Bella Bella (in 1930); Bella Coola (in 1931), and at Port Essington itself, in 1927. These celebrations were carried out on an important scale, covering several days in Joyful festivities; only passing reference being necessary here. In conversation about these events, Mr. Pierce told us the following relating to Bella Coola:

"During the Jubilee celebrations at Bella Coola some of the chiefs said to me: 'Fifty

years ago you [97] brought us the Gospel and we now see the wonderful change that has taken place in our surroundings and amongst our people, both young and old, which is the result of Christianity. Now, at this special time, we would like to hear of some other plan that would help us to go forward and make more progress and advancement in the Christian and civilized life, during the next fifty years. Now, what do you suggest?"
To the writer Mr. Pierce paused to explain that when a question in any important connection is thus pointedly put to one recognized as a leader, he must be ready at once with an answer, or suffer some loss of prestige in their eyes. He was ready.

"1 replied: My plan is to form a Temperance Society amongst all the natives on the Coast and in the Interior, and to make the start during this Jubilee time at Bella Coola."

"They said: That is a good word; that is a great plan,' and at the gathering that night one hundred and thirty-two signed the pledge."

His Shrewdness and Quaint Humour

Only the merest glimpse has been here given of the more recent years of Mr. Pierce's ministry — which he did not record in his manuscript — though it may not be necessary to write more. Only those who have met him, heard him give addresses, or in conversation relate his experiences and his views on life — Christian life, his own field of labour, public life, and the Church's [98] responsibility, can really form any idea of the picturesqueness of his accent and speech — and of his approach to any subject; his shrewd observation; his unconscious, but compelling humour; or the intensity of his Christian devotion. His original, quaint illustrations are captivating, though impossible of realistic reproduction.

Speakng at one time at a Conference of his Church, about the show and display and expenditure on its own vanity a Church is apt to indulge, rather than on its real work, he spoke of the first steamer built by the Northern Indians. Its first trip was to be a great event and many were invited as guest passengers. Loud and long the great whistle was blown, and the start:
But the steamer would not move — the whistle was so large and so much steam had been used in the vanity of blowing it there was not enough left to move the boat. Churches are often like that, he declared, too much whistle, too little real work.

After church union had been achieved he said the Indians were not enthusiastic at losing the old name and asked what was the advantage. He said, Which is the stronger and faster, two small canoes with five men each paddling or a bigger one with ten men paddling? They were convinced.

As illustrating both Mr. Pierce's sense of humour and the Indian rather dubious appreciation of the material evidences of civilization, the following sent us by our friend may here be included. Mr Pierce writes:

"I was amused the other day, while listening to one of our people here relate his experience of a journey on [99] the train. He is an old man, and is able to compare all these changes in the present day, with life as it used to be in the earlier times. His conversation was something like this:

" "Well, I have heard so much talk about the train, that I could not be satisfied until I had taken a trip, so I started off for a short visit to New Kit-se-las. For my part, I prefer to travel by canoe. We were on the train about nine hours, and could do nothing but sit still or sleep. To me, travelling by train is a very lazy way of moving along. When I have gone up there before, we have had to pole and paddle until our foreheads would be covered with perspiration. But we could joke and laugh and enjoy ourselves in the fresh air as we went along. The journey was much slower, of course, but it was pleasanter. How we used to enjoy eating together at our camps. A whole salmon was not considered too much for one man, besides rice, tea and berries. On the train a man came around carrying a tray of bread cut in small squares, with a small piece of meat between, which only made two bites, and a cup of tea for which he charged 25 cents. I suppose this is all white man's style, but, for myself, I prefer our own style, and the canoe."

STERLING CHARACTER

The following incidents from Mr. Pierce's public addresses, recalled by the Rev. S.S. Osterhout, further illustrate his alertness of mind and quaint angle of insight: [100]

The Law Which Cannot Be Enforced

At a Conference in the City of Kamloops, a resolution was presented whereby the former Methodist Church was to be asked to contribute $9.00 per member towards an Endowment Fund for the building of Ryerson Theological College. Mr. Pierce, in characteristic fashion, was on his feet in a moment and at the front of the Conference haranguing the members, in opposition to the motion. In his unique English he said:

"I will not let you pass that resolution, because you cannot enforce it. The Ottawa Government passed a law against the Potlatch years ago, and the Indians are potlatching still, because the Government cannot enforce its law. You pass this resolution today, but you cannot compel my Indians to pay $5.00 each because they haven't got it, and your resolution will die for lack of enforcement. Besides," said he, "that baby is not born yet!" referring to Ryerson College. His last sentence defeated the motion, and in it is clearly discovered Pierce's keen intuition in regard to questions of such a nature, as the public well know that Ryerson College was not "born" for many years after this incident.

Intemperance and the White Man

At a Conference in Nanaimo, Mr. Pierce was one of the speakers at the public meeting on Temperance night. His argument against intemperance was based [101] mainly on the fact that while intemperance is a disastrous vice among the Indians, it is more so among the Whites, as the white man falls from a higher elevation than the Indian in his ignorant and more or less primitive condition. In his own phraseology: "The Indian falls with intemperance, it is true, but when the white man falls he comes down with a terrible whack'" His illustration was from a pioneer in the Cariboo who was so addicted to drink that he was unable to drive his faithful horse home. The usual occurrence was that when the old settler was thoroughly intoxicated, he was placed in his buggy by the hotelkeeper and the reins tied around the dashboard, and the old horse started off home. He invariably brought his master to his destination and in front of the stable door. On one such occasion, in the morning, his faithful wife looked out, to behold the horse with an empty buggy. On investigation she found her husband, by the little instinct that was still left in him, huddled with a drove of pigs in a mound of straw in the yard, where he was trying to keep himself warm. His illustration brought down the house to the extent that he was unable to complete his address that evening, more than to say as he retired from the platform; "That was a white man and intemperance!"

The Burning Heart

At a more recent meeting of the Conference of the United Church in Vancouver, Mr. Pierce heard an [102] address by Dr. W.H. Smith on "The Burning Heart," which made a profound impression upon him. He went hack up the Coast among his Indians to give them the benefit of the address, urging upon them the great need of modern church members for a heart aflame with love for God and His Kingdom. His illustration was a comparison between old-time navigation on the Coast and modern methods. "In days of old," he said, "we were entirely dependent upon favourable winds and tides. If the winds were contrary we camped for one day, two days, three days or more, as the case might be until a favourable wind arose, when we hoisted our square sheet in our canoe and set off on our journey. But now," he said, "it is different. We now have boats with fire in them, and all that is necessary is to start our engine and, in spite of contrary winds and tides, continue our journey. So," he said, "it is with the United Church, the great need of the day is a membership with "Burning Hearts," hearts so full of love and loyalty and enthusiasm that no matter how adverse the storms and tempest and tides of life may be, we can, in the name of God, march forward and attempt great things for Him."

In conversation with the present writer recently, one who formerly was interested in a large way in the salmon canning industry on the Skeena River, related an incident, which at the time revealed to him Mr. Pierce's sincerity and courageous fidelity to principle, when it might have seemed he stood to lose something by doing so. In brief, the incident was this: The [103] canning season had commenced; definite agreement had been made with the Indian fishermen as to price to be paid them — an agreement, all considered, fair to both parties. Then the men struck for higher price, greatly hampering and jeopardizing the season's business. The Indians were numerous, determined and menacing, and local opinion made a show of sympathizing with them. Mr. Pierce, who was their missionary and had to live with them, and would naturally have no desire to displease them, came into the breach courageously and, addressing the Indians, told them plainly that they were doing wrong; that as Christian men and honourable men they should stand by their agreement, which they knew was just and fair between man and man. It was not right to take advantage just because they thought they had the chance or power to do so.

His address was so plain and so disinterestedly honest and their confidence in him was so implicit that the Indians, by common consent, abandoned the strike and went to work. My friend said the incident gave him the highest appreciation of Mr. Pierce's sterling, Christian character, as well as of his great influence as a Christian missionary.

To the present writer, who has known a good deal of him and his work over long years, William Henry Pierce is an outstanding figure among a noble band of heroic missionaries. Brave men who, on our own shores, laboured under conditions already difficult for us to visualize, who travelled great distances by canoe or mountain trail; who suffered privation, exposure and danger, for no [104] earthly reward, but solely to bear the glad news of the gospel to their fellowman, when that fellowman was scarcely other than a savage. The names of Crosby, and Tate, and Green, and Jennings, and Bolton, and Large, and Spencer, who have passed on — and the names of some who are with us still — will be held in honoured remembrance in missionary annals, for the greatness of their sacrifices, adventures and achievements; and among them will be found the name of William Henry Pierce held in equal honour and affection. Indeed his career is surely unique. When one recalls his birth, his bringing up in a heathen village with the most pagan influences about him, separated from his father, and his mother dead. Confronted almost daily with the most savage and cruel scenes — what a marvel that he became what he did become!

"It was a common thing in the dusk of the evening," he writes, "to hear the report of guns. As a boy I used to listen eagerly to the questions put after the report was heard. Some one would ask: 'How many shots were fired?' The answer might be, 'One,' or it might be 'Five,' or less, which meant that for every person killed one shot was fired. Sometimes the persons were shot while their spoons were in their hands eating their meals. At once the leading men of the house commanded that the children should be put in a hole under the house and kept there during the night for safety while the fighting was going on in the village. In those days each house had one of these hiding places dug out underneath for the purpose of sheltering the children. Had anyone gone through Port Simpson in [105] those days and then paid a visit there now, neither the place nor the people would be recognized, the change from darkness to light has been so great.

Looking back it seems a short time, in that so much has been accomplished through the preaching of the everlasting Gospel."

Again he remarks of taking a visiting friend "to the very spot where one winter morning I had seen a woman slave killed and eaten up by the man-eaters. Her body was cut into four quarters, but as there were five men to have a share, one of the number had to be content by licking up the blood."

Imagine a little orphaned, heathen lad, brought up in such environment as this, and yet ultimately emerging into a renowned missionary whose name is known from end to end of this great Dominion. How meagre his equipment! How far-reaching the fruits of his consecrated life! The road he travelled in this emergence he has outlined, in simplest terms, in his own story, and all he ascribes to hearing "the gospel message." His "auto-sketch" is truly a marvellous story, and it is not half of what might be told. In the pages which now follow, also, he has collected and compiled a valuable anthology of Indian myth and legend; has given written form to a native folklore that is far too precious to have been lost.

At the time of this writing William Henry Pierce, in advancing years and in declining strength, has laid down the active responsibilities of missionary labour; and with Mrs. Pierce, who has shared his fortunes as a loyal and equal partner through so many years, has retired to a modest little home in Prince Rupert where [106] he is still the friend and counsellor of many of the native people who find their way to his hospitable campfire. [107 blank]

Conditions, Habits and Customs
Before Christianity Was Introduced

Before the Gospel was preached by the Missionary, the natives were ignorant, superstitious, degraded, wild and cruel.

Their homes in the different villages were, as a rule, built right along the beach. This location was found to be so convenient for the loading and unloading of their canoes. Each home would consist of a large one-roomed house, and would be built sufficiently large to accommodate several families. Houses would vary in size but as a rule from six to fifteen families would occupy each house. The walls consisted of one thickness of split cedar boards, and the roof was made from two thicknesses of cedar bark, which was made sufficiently tight to be waterproof. In the centre was left a large square hole which was to act as a chimney, the fire being made right in the centre of the room on the bare earth. During the winter, straw would be spread on parts of the floor for beds, changing it twice during the season.

During the summer season, very little clothing was worn. The high class Indians wore a blanket, which was tied around the waist with a belt. These blankets were made from the wool of the mountain sheep and were roughly woven on wooden frames by the women. The lower class were not allowed to dress as those of higher rank, their clothing always being according to and suitable to their station. Instead of blankets, robes made from the hides of deer and mountain sheep would be [109] worn. These skins were well tanned and then sewn together until of sufficient size to take the place of a blanket.

During the winter the higher class would wear robes made from expensive furs, such as marten or lynx. The chiefs would select sea-otters or foxes. Of course, in those days furs were really of no value to the natives, as there were no purchasers. It was not until the arrival of the Hudson's Bay Company that their furs were traded. Winter clothing worn by the lower class would be made from the commoner fur-bearing animals, such as groundhogs and mountain sheep or deer. Each person in both classes was always the happy possessor of two suits for each season — one to be worn for ordinary purposes and the other for special occasions only.

As a protection from rain and snow, a special mat made from the inner bark of red cedar was worn. This was woven very closely and tightly in order that it be absolutely waterproof and sufficiently large to cover the entire' person. A waterproof hat was worn, too, which was made from the roots of spruce.

Instead of wearing socks and stockings, special straw was gathered, which when dried was soft, and it was then wrapped around the feet. Over this straw covering, moccasins were worn, which were made from the skins of animals. Leggings were worn, and they, of course, were made from the fur skins. During the sleeping hours they were used as covering, and on top of that was placed a cedar mat made especially for the size of the bed. A pillow was used, made from moss and fine straw. [110]

In the early days, no food other than that provided by nature, was ever used by the natives. Each season provided a plentiful variety in its turn. Very often during the winter season food became exceedingly scarce, so that there was great danger of starvation amongst the tribes, there being perhaps only a few dried salmon remaining in each family. This article of food was then so precious that small pieces, a few inches square, were cut and one piece handed out to each child.

Everybody was anxiously looking forward to the middle of March when the oolachan on the Naas River began to appear. About that time whole tribes moved up there by canoe, making their camp at various points along the river. Each morning special expert hunters would go out in their canoes, hunting for hair seals. The first one killed was opened in the canoe; if oolachan were found in the stomach, that was taken to be a sure indication that the small-fish, as they are often called, were not far away. When the news was carried to the different camps on each side of the river, there was much rejoicing. A few days later the fish would surely be seen in millions.

However, during the days of waiting, all the women would be busy making baskets out of spruce roots, some of them large enough to hold a hundred pounds. These baskets were to be used by the men in carrying the fish on their backs from the canoe to the pen where they were all deposited. While the women were busy making baskets, the men spent their time in cutting cordwood, which was necessary for the cooking of the fish. [111]

Great excitement prevailed amongst the tribes on the first day that the oolichan appeared. Shouts of rejoicing were heard from the different camps for many miles along the river. This shout realty meant in words, "Now our time of danger is over; these fish are our salvation." They named these fish "Alumandkum," {*haldmawt*} meaning salvation. The run would last about three weeks, and during that time there would be very little sleep. Men, women and children were all busy at something. Just as soon as the fish appeared, the river would be alive with whales, porpoises, and large fish of all kinds which were following them, as were also different birds, such as eagles, crows, ducks and seagulls, the latter kind being present in clouds — many millions of them. These birds would eat the fish both by day and night, and their chattering was so great that nothing else could be heard along either side of the river.

The first cooking of the oolichans had to be done according to certain rules in a very special way. A special woman was chosen. She must be middle-aged, very sedate and solemn. On her head was worn a big Hydah hat, while on her hands were mitts. About fifty oolichans were brought to her and put on a wooden rack, which was placed over a special fire made of spruce bark. This fire must not be blown while the fish were cooking over it, for if it were, a north wind would surely spring up and, coming down the Naas River, would prevent the canoes from facing it, which would thus be unable to catch any more fish. After the fish were browned on one side, a clean cedar mat was placed [112] alongside the fire, and then all the people were called in. As the rack was turned over on the mat, all who had entered the house gave a big shout, exclaiming "Lowaa," which means "Great honor to the oolichan." As soon as the fish were browned on the other side, they were placed on the mat which served the purpose of a dish, and the woman who had done the cooking divided the fish according to the number of persons in the house. She then would order each one to honor the fish while eating it, so that there would be no scarcity of the run. Each fish was to be held flat in the hand; it had to be broken in two and eaten very hot. No one was allowed to cool it in any way by blowing on it with his breath. A breach of this rule would surely bring a storm. After eating the fish, no one, however thirsty he might be, was allowed to drink a drop of water. That would cause rain to descend and thus spoil the fishing.

Just imagine the load of anxiety on the minds of all those hundreds of people, who were out catching fish on that day. In about two weeks the general cooking began. During this time, all the fish caught had been deposited in one place, where it had become quite stale and somewhat tainted. Fish in this state was preferred, in order that more oil could be extracted. Neither porcelain nor iron kettles were used. Special wooden boxes were prepared, which were large enough to hold four hundred pounds or more. There were several fires made in each fish-house, the number being regulated according to the families living there. The fish were cooked by means of redhot stones, which were placed in the box. These stones were of a special kind, [113] and could only be gathered from one place, called Lak-wun-maslik, now known as Red Bluffs. These particular stones could stand a greater degree of heat than any other kind. Long wooden tongs were used to pick up the hot stones and place them in the box. This had to be repeated three times before the fish were cooked. The oil was then skimmed off the top and refined by boiling again with smaller hot stones until quite clear. This oil would then be poured into a box and stowed away ready for sale. Perhaps there would be about four gallons of oil to one cooking from four hundred pounds of fish.

The boxes used as containers were made from cedar wood. They were neatly made and tightly put together so that there would be no leakage. The tops fitted tightly and were fastened down with yellow cedar bark. Each box had handles made from red cedar boughs. Quite a large number of boxes were filled during the fishing season. It was the aim of each family to have sufficient for their own use and a certain amount left over to sell.

Oolichan grease, as it was called, was considered by all the tribes everywhere as a great luxury. It was eaten combined with berries, sea-weed, fish-eggs, clams, dried halibut, salmon and potatoes. This grease was, and is still, considered to be as essential to the native as butter is to the white man.

Oolichan were caught by means of long poles made specially for that purpose. These poles were made of red cedar, with about three feet of the bottom part somewhat flattened. In this flat part sharp wooden [114] nails, made from the hardest part of spruce limbs, were inserted about an inch apart, each needle being tightly placed with spruce gum. Just as soon as the oolichans commenced to run, canoes manned by four or five persons were ready to haul in the fish by means of the poles. There were usually two men at the bow combing in the fish, while the rest of the crew would be paddling.

The modern way of catching oolichan is by means of long nets which are placed in the water when the tide is flowing out, and held firmly there by means of two large poles driven in the bottom of the river. One net will hold two ton of fish, and a good day's catch will amount to eight tons. Cooking is no longer done by using red-hot stones. Instead, a large wooden boiler, having a heavy sheet-iron bottom, is used, and this is placed over a fireplace which is built of rocks and clay. By this method sixteen gallons of oil can be extracted in one day as against four gallons cooked by the old method.

The next food in season was herring spawn and seaweed. To obtain this food. men, women and children would camp out at various points where it was most plentiful. There were certain bays known to the native where the herring spawned in very large quantities. This was gathered from kelp and sea-weed. When well dried in the sun it was packed in boxes and stored away for future use. Any surplus was traded off amongst the Naas people and also amongst the Upper Skeena tribes.

After this came the gathering in of the sea-weed. As with the herring spawn, so with this food, there were special places where nature provided a bountiful [115] supply. Dundas Island was particularly noted. After being dried in the sun the sea-weed was picked up and made into cakes of about one and a half inches thickness, and then laid in boxes that would be the exact side. This article of food was considered to be very valuable. One cake would last a long time, When wanted for use, a small quantity would be cut off and chopped or cut into very fine pieces and then boiled. Sometimes it was mixed with salmon eggs or fresh clams. This food, too, was considered to be a very superior dish, especially amongst the interior people, who were always willing to give a high price in order to obtain it.

The inner bark of the hemlock (*kasheoo*) was also considered a very strong food, and it was in much demand during the winter. A good hemlock camp was selected, when many families would congregate there and stay until sufficient of this food had been obtained. A good clear tree was felled and denuded of its bark, while quite juicy. This would be in the month of June. The women would gather all the bark and scrape the inner portion with a special knife, until it became as thin as paper. When the scrapings were sufficient for one cooking, a fire was made. This was accomplished by digging a large hole in the ground and building the fire in the centre, on which were placed several stones. When these were thoroughly heated, the fire was all taken away, leaving there the hot stones only. Branches and leaves were then placed on top of the hot stones, and on top of this were placed the hemlock scrapings. It had to be spread very evenly, being very particular [116] not to have one part thicker than another. For a top covering was placed a cedar mat in order that escaping steam might be prevented. Water was poured all round the edges to cause steam and start the cooking process. That was left all night. In the morning the covering was taken off and the hemlock was found to be cooked to a pulp. It was then placed on a large flat board and hammered until it became so pliable that it could be moulded by the hand into any desirable shape. As a rule it was made into square cakes about half an inch thick. These cakes were placed on top of a long rack where they remained until perfectly dry. They were then packed in boxes where it would keep in perfect condition indefinitely.

When required for use a small portion of the cake was broken off and soaked well, then pulled into fine pieces, which were eaten combined with oolichan grease, or with the grease mixed with snow and made into ice-cream.

Wild fruit of all kinds, of which there was an abundance, formed quite an important part of the native diet. The names of the different fruits are as follows:

Wild Crabapples (Malkst ~ *malkst* 78). Wild Cherries (Clyah ~ ?? *scon* g96). Cranberries (Met ~ *dahdee* 70). Elderberries (Lawls ~ *lo'ots* 58). Red Huckleberries (Withlaaks *maay* 1369 *wüłeekx* 2111 *wüłeekxs* 70). Wild Black Currants (Wahkel ~ *waakyil* = highbush 71). Blueberries (Mahalth ~ *mihaał* = dwarf mountain 67). Salmonberries (Magawkst ~ *magooxs* 1379, ma<u>k</u>ooxs 86). [117] Wild Strawberries (Magooldt ~ *maguul* 75). Wild Raspberries (Nahshoo ~ *naasik* 83). Solal (Jawest ~ *dzawes* 63). Soapberries (Ash ~ *'as* 61). Chokeberries (Domeet ~ ?? *hallochalk* = choke cherries g96). Saskatoons (Gem ~ *gyem* 574, 756).[25]

Above all the berries, soapberries {*'as* 61} were prized the most. They were thoroughly dried and made into square cakes. When required for use a small piece was broken off and placed in a pail containing water. This was well stirred with the hand until it became a thick, foamy mass, and looking similar to soapsuds; hence the name "soapolili". In taste it was bitter, similar to quinine, and it was considered a good tonic. Today these berries are prized as much as ever. One bundle, which contains six cakes, sells for three dollars. In the old days, one bundle would be valued for no more than twenty-five cents.

Chokeberries only grow in the interior, and were always considered to be the cheapest of all fruits. This kind of fruit was very largely used at the potlatch feasting, and it being of a very dry nature, was always eaten combined with Saskatoon berries and oolachan grease.

---

[25] {j Updates spelling and sources for more information come from John Dunn, <u>Sm'algyax Reference Dictionary</u>, *Nwana'a lax Yuup* ~ <u>Plants of the Gitga'at People</u> #s 60s-80s, and Harlan Smith's <u>Ethnobotany of Gitksan</u>, beginning with g#.}

The salmonberry was the only kind grown that could not be preserved in any way. They were then, and are now, considered very delicious, gathered and eaten white fresh from the bushes. At the present day, these berries are eaten by the white population as a substitute for strawberries. [118]

Superstitious or Old Heathen Beliefs

Without exception, the Indians all believed in One as the Creator of all things, and this One lived far away somewhere in the sky.

They believed that He was always present and knew all about their doings; that for their good deeds they would be rewarded, and punished for all offences both in this world and after death. If, during a journey, a storm should arise they would offer a sacrifice to this Being in the shape of food of any kind, and at the same time offer up a prayer for protection and safety for the rest of the journey. The sacrifice when offered was burned, and the smoke was supposed to take the petition away as it ascended.

In like manner, when far away from home they would ask for success in their undertaking, they also offered sacrifices. They also believed in One who was an evil spirit, and who was continually trying to cause them to do evil.

They believed that if a man lived a good life and did kind deeds, that he would live in happiness somewhere, and be rewarded. While if a man lived a bad life and cared only to be selfish, mean and cruel, he would be rewarded accordingly and have no happiness evermore.

Medicine Man or Conjurers

"Medicine Man," so called, is wrongly named. Properly speaking, the name applied should be conjurer, or Indian doctor, and this applies to either man or [119] woman. In certain families this art was preserved from one generation to another, Anyone outside those families wishing to become a doctor must claim relationship. All the songs in connection with this practise have been handed down for hundreds of years. Each doctor had what he called "soul hunters." These soul hunters might perhaps be the head or feet of a mink, owl, eagle, hawk, or the tooth of a wolf, etc. These were all kept in a big bag, together with some paint powder of their own manufacture, which was to use on their hands and faces during the performance. They claimed that when a person was sick that sickness was caused by the absence of the soul. These articles were then brought out of the bags and laid around the head of the patient while all the conjurers sang their songs and at the same time drumming and beating the boards.

During this performance the soul is being hunted and brought back again. Should the patient fail to recover, it was because the soul could not be brought back or caught. It might be underneath a steep mountain, or in the deep water, or in some other out-of-the-way place, too difficult to get at.

The cause of the soul taking its leave of any person was fright, and wherever this took place, the soul stayed. When the soul was recovered it was placed inside a hollow bone which was made from the leg of a grizzly bear. This was tied with a string and hung across the conjurer's chest. Both ends were securely covered with the inner bark of cedar in order that the soul might have no chance of escape. This article was named the "soul trap". The conjurer would then call [120] all the relations together and inform them that the soul always good news both to the patient and his friends. The news soon spread through the village and all would rejoice that their alarm and anxiety were gone.

At the time appointed, the house was crowded with people to witness the ceremony — special songs were selected and sung — two or three extra conjurers were called in to take part. As a rule, the sick person would be on his feet again and as well as ever in a few days.

On the other hand, should the conjurer fail to find the patient's soul, he would abandon all hope and give up in despair, dying in a few days.

It was wonderful what power a conjurer had over the sick. Is there any wonder that they had such implicit confidence in him, obeying him in every detail? A conjurer not only had power to restore the lost soul, but he claimed to have power to take away their souls at any time. Knowing this. all Indians lived in constant fear of him.

I remember one time when Rev. T Crosby was very ill at Fort Simpson. An old conjurer, named Neas-beans, went into the mission house and said, "Don't you be alarmed. Sir, I found your soul last night lying in the gutter all covered with filth. I got my stick and poked it, rolling it over into a dry place. You need not be afraid that you will die; in a few days more you will be well again. Sure enough at the time specified the old man took the soul to the mission house and was desirous of placing it on Mr. Crosby's head. [121]

In order to be a conjurer, a person must be thoroughly qualified. In the first place he had to undergo starvation. For a certain number of days he had to stay in bed with only a mat or bearskin for covering. During that time he was neither to eat or drink. All through the night he was taught how to start his songs and how to use his rattle. His sleep was to be taken during the day. At night all the other doctors had to be with him — nobody else. These conjurers were fed at the man's expense and they would remain until they were able to declare that he was as competent to practise as themselves.

The fee charged by any doctor would depend upon the circumstance of the patient. If poor, a small fee only was expected, but if wealthy the charge was made accordingly. A medicine man, or Indian doctor, never made nor used any medicine of any kind. Any of the natives who understood the art of making medicine from roots and bark were never doctors at all. In one large village there might be forty doctors, but out of the entire population perhaps only one person understood the making of medicines.

Gambling

The Hydahs from Queen Charlotte's Islands were the first to introduce gambling to the natives on the mainland. There were only two gambling games, which were known as Lahal and Xshan. *Lahal* was played by two rows of men, each row having an even number of [122] players. Each man staked a certain amount of money to the man kneeling opposite. The two rows had to kneel facing each other. Each one had a stick in his hand with which he beat a board in front of him, keeping time by singing a gambling song. During the game the row that was playing would beat the boards, while the other side looked on. Two men in that row would have a bone in each hand during the performance and the other side who were watching appointed one man to guess which hand held the bone. Every miss counted one stick passed over to the other side. There were twenty sticks altogether. If the man were a poor guesser and missed twenty times, the game was over. But if during the game he guessed wrong occasionally, the other side would take their turn in guessing. When the game was finished, each one would put up more money and start over again.

During the whole game, singing was kept up to keep time. The hideous noise made was to confuse the guesser and also to put life into the game. Sometimes a man was sleeping in. A professional gambler might win a few hundred dollars in a few hours. For instance, the value of one canoe staked might mean $200.00 or more.

Xsban is a game similar in many ways to the other, but it was played quietly. There was no singing and as a rule no one even had to speak or make any noise whatever. Ten sticks were counted instead of twenty. There might be any number in each row and each man played the game with the one opposite. No one took any notice of his neighbour's actions. Each man looked [123] out for himself. Two of these gambling sticks were marked in a special manner, one being different from the other. One of these was the special one to be guessed. These two were hidden inside two bundles of soft cedar bark. They were then turned over and over until the man would call out "Ready". The guessing would then begin. If the guesser were correct the first time, then the man opposite would take his turn at guessing and the other side would hide the sticks. Whenever there was an even missing on both sides it was called a "tie" and the game would begin over again. But if the man on the one side missed ten, he was the loser. This was the older game.

The writer has seen a bag of these gambling sticks that have been handed down for six generations. The oldest people were fond of this game. They would go all day without food in order to keep at it. The game of Lahal was mostly indulged in by the young people.

In the northern part of British Columbia, the Potlatch always takes place in the winter time. On the death of a chief, his successor, before claiming the chief's place, his title, his honor, or his name, must give a potlatch. The successor of the dead chief must be either his brother, nephew, or niece.

In order to have a big potlatch, quite a large sum of money is required. The amount may reach the sum of two or three thousand dollars. This means that a [124] man must work very hard for three years or so and save most of what he earns for this coming event. He will deny himself every comfort, so that he may have a big display. The entire cost is not carried by one man, however. The members of the crest to which he may belong, club together and contribute *their* share towards the big feast, but the host himself contributes the largest share. The sum total gathered does not mean that it is all cash. Canoes, rifles, horses, cattle, etc., are all counted in. The more money that he is able to spend on the potlatch, the greater is the honor conferred upon him.

To hold a potlatch and fail to give satisfaction to all the people is a standing disgrace to him for life. When preparations are complete, then an invitation is sent to all the different tribes. After they congregate, the ceremony begins. This feast usually lasts from three to six weeks or longer, according to circumstances, and during that time there is feasting every day and dancing every night.

At certain times during the Potlatch, blankets and cotton are torn into strips, each person present receiving a piece. At these times, too, various kinds of food are distributed, and each person takes home with him whatever he has been given. Rifles, clocks, trunks and canoes are chopped up and burned before the crowd. Even money has been known to be thrown into the blaze.

When the potlatch is ended, the giver is a very poor man and suffers for want of both food and clothing for many weeks afterwards. He takes his cedar mat [125] and single blanket which he places on the ashes alongside the fire, and there he lies. Doing this acknowledges that he is suffering from the potlatch, all because he wanted to gain honor.

As a rule, the potlatch must be carried on by one crest. For instance, a wolf crest will give a potlatch to all the other crests of the different villages excepting that of the wolf, but all the wolves of the village where the potlatch is held will help the wolf who is the giver of the potlatch. The same is true of the eagle, blackfish and crow.

The word Potlatch is taken from the Chinook meaning "to give". But the real meaning is much more than that. When a man gives a potlatch he is really banking, for when a potlatch comes off in another village he fully expects to receive more than what he gave himself at his own feast. Suppose, for instance that he had given two blankets to one person, and he in turn gave a potlatch, three blankets would have to be given in return instead of two.

The real potlatch, conducted in the early days, before the whites came, was very different from the modern feast. There were rules and regulations to govern every move and these were strictly adhered to. The feasting period then lasted for about three months. There was no cash in those days — all gifts were in kind — mostly furs. There were rules to guide the dances, the whole of the feast, and the young people.

During the potlatch the wisest and best speakers were chosen to give lectures for the benefit of those who had come together to enjoy themselves. These lectures [126] taught them how to respect themselves and to honor those who were in authority as their chiefs. The young people were instructed to lead pure lives and shun all forms of evil. A certain number of men were appointed to inform the chiefs should any of these rules be broken during the feast. When the potlatch broke up all returned to their homes feeling that they had received help and encouragement.

But alas' How different is the Potlatch of today. Amongst the natives it is the root of all evil and the big mountain of sin against which the missionaries have to fight.

In these days. any man of the common order may give a potlatch providing he is rich enough. He need not wait until he has a large sum of money to expend. If he can manage to save one hundred dollars or a little more, he is entitled to give a feast even if not conducted on a large scale. This feasting is merely an excuse to carry on all kinds of sin. At such times the laziness, filth and every other evil is indescribable. Immorality among the young people and drinking of whiskey or home-made intoxicants are two outstanding features.

Mixed with the potlatch of today is the white man's dance, which to the native is a great attraction and the source of much evil. On any mission where this feasting is practised God's work can make no progress. Those who attend these gatherings lose all interest in religion and religious teaching. The day school is affected also, for the majority of the children follow the crowd, anxious to see all that transpires. It can readily be seen how this affects their training and future life. How [127] much discouragement and uphill work the missionary and teacher have to face.

Yet there are many intellectual whites who uphold the potlatch, and consider that the natives have a right to enjoy themselves in this way. It is quite evident that they only see the surface and have no conception of the undercurrent. If the government only realized that the potlatch is ruination to the progress of the Indian and is leading the young people on to destruction, I feel sure that they would adopt more stringent measures to enforce the Indian Act.

Totem Poles

A totem is a tall cedar post or tree, sometimes 50 feet high or more, according to the rank of the person for whom it is intended. A totem pole is in reality a monument erected to the memory of a dead chief. The head of any village always claimed to have the highest pole. A totem is always ornamented with the carving of many grotesque figures of animals, fish or birds, which give the history of the one who erects them. Each tribe was divided into families which took for their coat-of-arms or crest, some animal, fish, or bird, such as the wolf, bear, crow, eagle, and black-fish. The carvings on the totem show the descent and intermarriages of these families. Whatever figure is carved at the top of the pole represents the name of the crest to which that pole belongs. For instance, if the carving be a bear, that pole belongs to the bear crest, and all [128] the different figures carved below that represent the history or tradition of that crest, as handed down from generation to generation.

It was law amongst the Northern Indians that the totem to be erected should be the exact length. If the law was violated, due punishment was meted out. An instance of this happened on the Naas river where one of the chiefs had a totem pole complete and raised. During the ceremony it was discovered that the length exceeded the allowance. When the chief was informed that the pole was too long, he refused to listen, therefore he was shot right on the spot.

The cost of the totem was enormous, for when the pole was raised it was necessary that the big feast or potlatch was held, and for this gathering a large sum of money was expended. Any neglect on the part of nephew or son to erect a totem pole in memory of an uncle or father, if chief, would be a standing disgrace in that family forever.

Dances

(1) The Peace Dance.

This belonged to the chiefs and higher class of Indians. If there were any disturbance, dispute, or fighting amongst the different tribes, the chiefs would meet and call together the different parties connected with the quarrel. The chiefs would then dance before them and scatter eagle feathers down over their heads. After that the spokesman declared before all that peace [129] now reigns, and that any person guilty of causing trouble again would have to be dealt with according to the law and punished severely.

(2) The Wild Dance.

This dance belonged to all both high and low. When a man wished to be promoted in the ranks it was necessary that he go through the wild dance. He would go through the village from house to house smashing everything that he could find. All the other wild dancers joined in the march. He was perfectly nude and marched with a big club in his hands. The greatness of his power was reckoned accordingly to the number of articles he had smashed. For nearly two weeks he would march through the village three times a day, and at the end of that time he gave some kind of Potlatch to all the wild dancers. After that he was considered to be one of them and willing to keep all their rules.

(3) The Dog-Eater Dance.

This is similar to the wild dance, except that live dogs are eaten.

(4) The Man-Eater Dance.

This dance belongs to the high chiefs, and was introduced to the Northern coast by the Kitamaate and Bella Bellas. This dance was more of a secret nature than any of the other dances, and all who belonged had power to make rules and control all the other dances. During a performance they would bite off pieces of flesh [130] from each other's arms but no outsider would be touched. Suppose a man-eater chief were living in the same house with common people and death were mentioned in his presence, he would start the same dance over again, and perhaps keep it up for two or three nights. If it were really necessary to mention "death" the words "Salmon berries" was used instead. During the man-eater dance, the chief who acted as man-eater would be fed by every family in the village. Before a family would begin their meal a very small piece of the first course would be taken to the man-eater and dropped into his mouth. This was repeated by every family and was considered to be the greatest honor the man-eater could have. The rule was that he had to taste the first of everything and any neglect on the part of any family to adhere to this rule would result in the dance being repeated again and the death of the party who had omitted his duty.

Quite a number of years ago, at the time when Bella Bella Mission was just starting. Dr. Thomas Crosby and the writer were in a man-eater chief's house there right in the hottest time. We saw several persons come in during the day and drop a piece of food into the chief's mouth. Before starting our own meal and after we had asked the blessing, I suggested to Dr. Crosby that we ask the chief if it would cause any offence for us to eat and not offer him any, as the custom was. His answer was, "No, you are not included in the 'band.' "

A few weeks afterwards this same chief was converted in our meetings and was the first to put his name down for a fifty-dollar subscription towards the building of a new church. His name was Kanchit {Humchit ?}. [131]

Indian Marriage

In the early days there were two kinds of marriage ceremonies, one amongst the chiefs and high classes and one amongst the people.

When a chief or a person belonging to the high class would take to himself a wife, his tribe and the tribe of the woman would meet together and have a sham fight, which would last perhaps for half a day.

When a marriage took place amongst the common people, the man would go into the house of the woman he intended to have and stay all night. That was the announcement.

During the sham fight stones and clubs were used, and although several persons might be cut, bruised or hurt in some way, nobody complained or had his feelings hurt, as this was not considered real fighting. This blood being shed was to remind the contracting parties that the marriage was solid and was not to be treated lightly. It was expected that the married couple do their utmost not to bring disgrace upon their friends. They were supposed to respect and honor them as long as they lived.

Except in very rare cases, marriages amongst the high class were always known to be true and lasting, even if they lived to a very old age.

During my very early mission work at Bella Bella, I was privileged to witness a marriage ceremony amongst the chiefs of that tribe, which was quite different from that of the Tsimpsheans. After the marriage had been announced publicly in the head chief's [132] house, the couple left for their own home and behind them walked all the chiefs and young people carrying an Indian box. On reaching the house, this box was opened and out of it was taken a blanket made from the inner bark of the yellow cedar, which was presented to the new wife by the chiefs. In making this blanket, it had gone through several processes, leaving it soft , and wooly. Square Indian coppers were fastened on the outside of this blanket, covering every bit of space. This, of course, made it very heavy — the weight being over one hundred pounds. This has to be worn by the bride for about ten days. The chief told her that, as she felt the weight of this resting on her shoulders, so she must accept the heavy responsibilities of married life, and never treat her marriage lightly. Since she had accepted the responsibility she must do her utmost to carry it out by staying at home, advising and assisting her husband in every possible way.

At the marriage feast amongst the Tsimpsheans, after speeches had been made and advice given to the marriage couple, the father of the tribe made his speech, when he endowed certain gifts to his daughter. It might be part of his hunting ground, or some of the lakes where he hunted beaver, or a canoe loaded with different kinds of gifts. The husband then would be fully privileged to hunt and trap on these grounds as long as they lived together. If at any time the woman should go astray, the best councillors on her side would go to the house and talk to her, reminding her of the blood that had been shed on her marriage day and that it was her bounden duty not to forget it. [133]

Training of Children

In the early days before civilization, the natives were very particular in the training of their children. Every evening just before dark, when everything was quiet, it was the duty of uncles and grandfathers to gather the children around them for instruction. They were required to sit perfectly still in a certain position until the instruction was finished {*daxsmwan* = mind, obey, literally 'act like flounder bottom fish'}. They did not even dare to move the head on one side. They were taught that when old enough to earn their own living, they were to depend on themselves and not on their parents or friends — whether fishing or hunting, they were to be industrious, securing all kinds of food possible. Laziness, they were told would bring them poverty and disgrace amongst their people and cause them to be a laughing stock to everybody.

On the other hand, to be industrious, meant that they would command self respect and honor, and always have plenty and thus be ready to alleviate any distress amongst the unfortunate.

Each child was trained for what they considered him to be best adapted, as for instance, canoe makers fishers trappers, hunters, singers and speakers. Particular stress was laid on cowardice. They were taught to be brave and fearless, so that during any battles fought in which they would have to take part, they would prove themselves to be skilled fighters.

During the winter months, their bravery was tested in the following manner. On the coldest mornings when the cold north wind was blowing a gale, and the sea [134] water had turned into ice, the chief sent orders to each before day-light to have all young people and children roused from their sleep and sent into the icy sea water for a cold bath.

On coming out of the water, and as they proceeded to the chiefs house each one received a few lashes on his back and chest by two chiefs who had been appointed to stand in the path and wait for them. This was considered to be the hardening process. After entering the house, each one received a fur robe and after a good thawing out, a small gift was presented to every one by the chief and one of the appointed speakers made a speech. This was to encourage them all to be strong and honor their tribe.

Any young person or child, failing to go through this performance brought a slur on himself and the whole family. And, as a rule any of these failures, never made any success in life, nor was ever promoted by his tribe to be a leader in any way. Promotion to a higher standing in the heathen life was given during any feasting occasion when all were at home. A potlatch followed, at which all who claimed by tradition to be their ancestors were invited. Presents were given them and perhaps two out of the number would be chosen to bore one or more holes in the ears, the number of holes represented their title and were given in order that they might be the successors to their Fathers and Uncles when grown up. The lower class could only claim one. The higher class were further distinguished by having a hole bored through the nose at the tip. In times of war these marks have often been the salvation of some of the prisoners. [135]

When it was seen that these prisoners belonged to the higher class, their lives were often spared and great kindness was shown them. If possible, they were sent back to their homes. A reward was given by the friends of the prisoner perhaps several hundred dollars worth of furs.

Warfare

Before Christianity was introduced by the missionaries, fighting amongst the different tribes was quite common. Often all the tribes through the Northern part of British Columbia would be in a turmoil. The chiefs belonging to each tribe would select their best men to act as leaders so that when the warfare actually began there would neither be misunderstanding nor confusion.

Spies were sent out in various directions some months before the fighting began, upon their return a report was given to their chiefs in their assembly and if approved, plans were made accordingly. The length of time required for preparation would depend on the nature of the intended attack. For instance suppose Queen Charlotte Islands were the object of attack, then many months of preparation were required before they could commence their journey. Several well experienced pilots were required, as the tribes of the interior were quite ignorant of navigation in open waters. Neither did they understand any thing about the lay of the villages and countries over there hence the need for these experts. When battles were fought on a less [136] extensive scale, very little preparations were required. War was never declared amongst the Indians because of any desire to acquire more territory, nor because of any trouble caused by disputes. War was merely a means of retaliation for what had transpired amongst their forefathers many years before. Each crest, whether a wolf, a bear, or an eagle, kept themselves together as a regiment, choosing the best man from amongst them to be their leader. Regulations regarding diet and mode of living were strictly adhered to during the war periods.

It is interesting to note with what skill and craftiness plans were made by the leaders to ensure victory. Take for example, the scheme thought out by the Bella Bellas. It was said that they were the most powerful tribe of the south. The other smaller tribes near by, such as the China Hats, Bella Coolas, Tailioms and Kimsquits, had no peace. They lived in constant fear of an attack from these warriors. At last the Bella Bellas devised a plan whereby they could retaliate. Instead of having a potlatch right in Bella Bella village they selected one of the islands right at the entrance of Rivers Inlet. On this island, they built a big house making it large enough to accomodate hundreds of people. When the building was finished and all their plans complete, cordial invitations were sent out to all the tribes around that locality to attend a Potlatch on this island. The date was set for the time when they were expected to arrive. The reception was to take place in the new building as they arrived, on the first day of the feast. The welcome song and drum could be [137] heard before they entered. Each chief preceeded the the {ok} tribe to which he belonged. There were two doors. An outer and an inner door It was arranged so that only one person could enter at a time. Above the inner door there was a trap and the entrance was dark so that nothing unusual could be detected. But just when the person expected to step inside the building, the trap came down and killed him instantly. His body was then thrown to one side and the next person to follow whether man or woman, shared the same fate, until the whole tribe was exterminated. During this time the drum and the song of welcome had never ceased. The men who were outside in charge of the canoes were the only ones to escape. Hundreds of bodies were piled up inside the building and all were cremated in the woods the next day. To day that island is known as "Slaughter Island". From that time to the present the Oweekeenos have been noted as the weak tribe. Take another example; About 90 years ago a big battle was fought between the Kishpeat tribe in the interior, and that of Legiac, the largest tribe amongst the Tsimpsheans.

After their plans had been completed about 200 war canoes started off from Port Simpson to travel up the Skeena River to Kishpiax village, a distance of about 230 miles. In order to deceive the people, the canoes were loaded with boxes supposed to be full of dried seaweed, fish eggs, and ollachan grease for trading purposes, but which really only contained stones, sand, and moss, each box being weighed and filled according to the weight of the genuine article supposed to be there. [138]

The Interior Natives were always very anxious to obtain any salt water food from the coast, and they were willing to pay any price for such. The Tsimpsheans, knowing this, expected their bait to be effective. When the canoes landed at Kishpiax, the people there met them in a friendly way and received them into their homes as friends and traders. Two or more of the canoe loads with their crew were taken into each house. By the time that the last canoe was unloaded, the fraud had been discovered and fighting began at once. All the women and children who could get away ran into the woods to hide.

Legiac, chief of the Port Simpson Band, had brought with him an umbrella, which in those days was a great curiosity. The interior natives had never seen one. Legaic knew this, so he stood up in his canoe, opening and shutting this umbrella several times. This seemed such a wonderful thing that the few old women who had remained in the village shouted with all their might to those in hiding, "Come and see this wonderful thing." They named it "tzow," meaning "to bring both darkness and light on the earth." Everybody rushed from the woods to look at this umbrella, and, of course, all were taken prisoners.

A rope of cedar was put through the holes of the lips of the older women to keep them safe, while the children and young girls were tied up and put in a canoe. In those days the only article of clothing worn as a covering for the body was a fur robe. As the women were being caught, their robe was the first thing to be caught hold of, then any woman who was not too [139] much ashamed to run, would escape behind the village right behind where the church now stands. Several escaped thus, but the majority, on loosing their robe, dropped right on the ground and were captured at once. It took two days to burn the dead bodies in front of the village.

Before leaving, the enemy set fire to the village. One stump of a totempole, partly burnt then, still stands today.

After the battle was over, and the canoes had departed those who were still left in the village expected to find quite a stock of salt water food in the boxes left behind and were looking forward to a big treat. Much to their disgust and disappointment, not a particle of food was to be found. As they opened box after box, nothing was to be seen but dirt, sand or stones. The majority of the prisoners were sold as slaves to Alaska tribes, and to Hydahs of Queen Charlottle Islands. The remainder were kept on Legaic's premises and were his own slaves.

As a rule, all slaves among the Indians along this Northern Coast were shamefully treated by their master. Their only food consisted of the remains from any meal from the family table. Their clothing was very scant, and they were exposed to all kinds of bad weather, and were employed to do the very roughest kind of work. When a slave died there was no funeral. A stone was tied to his neck and his body was then cast into the sea. When Legaic secured these slaves from Kishpiax, he commenced to build a very large house at Metlakahtla, the work being done by these slaves. [140]

Part of it was built underground, and to do this meant and immense amount of labor. Many tons of earth had to be taken out before the excavation was sufficiently large. This part of the work alone occupied more than one year.

When Mr. Duncan moved away from Fort Simpson he selected this very spot as a building site for the Mission premises, but before commencing, this large hollow space had to be filled in. Today this part of Metlakahtla Mission containing about five acres is known as Mission Point.

When very young, I remember the Hydah's coming over to Port Simpson from Queen Charlotte's to trade with the people there as usual. Two days after their arrival, a big fight took place right on the beach. Just in front of the Hudson's Bay Company's Fort. The Hydahs were so feeble that only a few were left to return home. The majority had their heads cut off by the Tsmpsheans and were piled up on the beach. For two or three days afterwards, as the tide came in and washed the beach, the water was red with the blood from the dead bodies lying there.

Another fight which lives in my memory was fought on the Naas River, and this time whiskey drinking was the cause. It happened during the small-fish season. One of the Naas Chiefs invited all the other tribes who were gathered there for the oolachan times to a whiskey feast. Everyone became intoxicated and all began to fight. This fight lasted for two weeks, several of the Interior people were killed and Fort Simpson lost three chiefs. [141]

The following year, the Tsmpsheans, out of revenge, started for the Naas to have war with the people there. As they were passing Kincolith Mission, the Missionary in charge there, Rev. R. Tomlinson, called them in, advising them that the best way of settling the matter was to get the Government to do it for them. They agreed to this, providing the Government would settle the trouble in the Indian way. They wished no settlement made in the white man's way. The Government agreed to settle the trouble. A gunboat was sent up — blankets, guns and other valuable articles were given to the Tsmpsheans, and they then had a peace dance, which lasted for two nights. This was the last fight that ever took place amongst any of the different tribes. Previous to this battle, the only weapons used in warfare were the bow and arrow, spear and club. The head of the spear was made out of bone and the club was made from the hind leg of the cariboo.

Before white man's laws were introduced amongst the Indians, and before Indian Agents were appointed by the government to enforce their laws, they were governed by laws of their own.

Each tribe had a number of men elected to act as Councillors with the chief. Whenever any rule was made, all the people in each village had to agree before enforcing it. On approval it was to be strictly obeyed. Any violation of the law was duly punished. There [142] were laws to govern hunters, marriages, dances, war, and everything pertaining to the public. Violation of any law was punishable in various ways. For example; in a case of stealing, which was rare, the person, if caught, was punished by being roasted to death. If a murder had been committed, payment in goods was required, or the life of the murderer. If a hunter happened to trespass on another hunter's grounds, it meant that he had to forfeit his life.

Only a few years ago, some of the families belonging to the Kishpiax tribe, were trespassing on the Stikine ground. They were caught. As they did not return to their homes at the usual time, their friends became alarmed. Search was made, and in spring their bodies were found at the bottom of the lake, each one — men, women and children — with a stone tied around the neck.

Any dancers who violated the dance law were tried by the man-eaters privately, and condemned to death.

It is not known how the natives acquired the knowledge of canoe making. The Hydahs on Queen Charlotte Islands were the first Indians who made really good canoes, and this workmanship was all natural talent. These were called War Canoes, and were built ten fathoms in length. Canoes of this size would hold fifty people besides their cargo. The old people say that they remember their great grandfathers making [143] canoes, but how this knowledge was first acquired, remains a mystery. Cedar was the kind of wood chosen to build a canoe. The log selected would be about 18 feet in diameter. A canoe of that size would easily hold four tons. It was always made in one piece. Sometimes smaller ones were made that would hold two tons, and a smaller size still that would hold one and a half tons, besides the necessary crew. The trees selected were of a special kind, and were only found on the north end of Queen Charlotte Islands. In olden times it was necessary for a man to go through certain ceremonies before going out to hunt for the tree. He would spend a certain number of days fasting, and he would drink nothing but sea water in order to cleanse his system and have good luck. For a certain number of nights he would sleep separate from his wife. He would be on the floor, having his back close to the fire, and lying on the one side all night. He would then start for the woods and after felling a tree and finding it sound, he would offer a prayer of thanksgiving to the great spirit. On his return home, he would call all his relations and give them a feast, when there would be a general rejoicing amongst them all. He would next ask his nephews to go out with him to give assistance with the work. The first thing was to get the correct shape from bow to stern, and after that the hull had to be burnt out. This meant a good deal of labor and careful watching. It had to be watched very carefully both day and night. When this process is completed, the entire crest went to the woods to haul out the canoe to the village, where it was to be finished. [144]

Each of these hands had to be paid. The next day the canoe was partly filled with water into which red-hot stones were placed. When the boiling point was reached, the canoe was covered with mats in order to keep the steam in. As soon as the canoe would spread easily, to just the beam required, the water and stones were taken out and the canoe was then ready to be used. This was one winter's work.

Long before steamboats navigated the coast, all the different tribes travelled long distances by these war canoes. It was a very common event to travel from Queen Charlotte Islands or from Fort Simpson down to Victoria. In crossing Hecate Straits, Milbank Sound, Queen Charlotte's Sound, and Gulf of Georgia stormy weather had often to be encountered, so it was very necessary that the canoes should be of the best workmanship and very sea-worthy. But no canoe ever travelled single handed; they always went in bands. This method was to prevent other tribes from attacking them in passing other villages on their way down. Each canoe chose an experienced man to act as captain. He had to be a man of sound judgment regarding the weather and in selecting suitable camps. In fact, he was held responsible for the entire crew. He had to be obeyed in every detail.

All the bands would camp together and after the evening meal, before retiring for the night, all the fires were to be extinguished in order that no enemy could detect the camp during the sleeping hours. Half of the crew kept guard all night alternately and the women and children would be isolated by themselves [145] in some other part of the wood. This precaution was taken in case of any attack.

In order to prevent the canoe from splitting during the journey, great care was necessary. When not in use during camping hours, as a means of protection from the hot sun, cedar mats were used as a covering and over this water was frequently sprinkled quite freely.

Smaller canoes, capable of carrying two tons, were used in navigating the rivers — such as the Stikine and Skeena. When the Hudson's Bay Company established their different trading posts in the interior, buying furs from the Indians, they had no other means of obtaining their supplies than by these freight canoes. Later on when the gold mines were discovered in the Omineca and Cassiar districts, hundreds of canoes were in demand to carry both passengers and freight. Some years later the Hudson's Bay Company replaced the canoes by stern-wheelers. A journey on these boats was considered luxurious compared to the open canoe where passengers were always exposed to all kinds of weather. And then, later still, the river boat was superceded by the railway, which was the greatest improvement of all.

Names and Traditions of Indian Villages

From Headwater of Skeena River to the Coast and up North to Naas River.

Kish-ga-ges is the farthest Indian village on the Skeena River and is situated at the junction of that river and the Babine. [146]

It is said that sea gulls used to congregate on one of the mountains close by, and build their nests in great numbers. Because of this, the people of that place have always been known as the Sea Gull, or Kish-ga-ges tribe.

Sixty miles below Kish-ga-gas, is the Village of *Kishpiax,* situated on the right bank of the Skeena, at the junction of that river and the Kishpiax. Tradition says there were no people of that name until a man named Yaal, came from Kitzequela to escape punishment after having murdered one of his fellow-men while gambling. This man walked on and on until he discovered a small river. Along this river were many ravines, and to his delight he was able to take refuge there, where he remained safely hidden for many years. His tribe had given him up for lost, and had almost forgotten him, when one night he surprised them all by appearing amongst them.

He called his relatives together and told them what he had discovered. He told them that he had good news. That this river where he had been hiding was full of salmon during the summer months — so full that anyone could pick them out of the water with the hand and cure and smoke any amount. Also that the ponds and lakes were alive with the beaver, and the valley was so thick with all kinds of fur-bearing animals, such as mink, marten, lynx and foxes. The mountain sides were covered with groundhogs, and the mountain tops were alive with mountain goats and cariboo. Everything could be killed without any effort.

This good news moved the hearts of his relations [147] and they were easily persuaded to follow him to this wonderful discovery.

They left secretly during the night, and in the morning it was found that about a dozen houses were empty and nobody knew where the people had gone. When they reached their destination and saw the ravines, they called it "The Hiding Place".

And as they settled and multiplied there they became known as the people of the hiding place, or Kish-pi-ax. So the name Kishpiax really means "a hiding place".

As these people increased and extended the village they became the wealthiest and strongest tribe on the river. They found that Yaal had not exaggerated his report in the least. Of furs of all kinds they had in abundance. The walls of their houses were lined with furs and they had fur robes to wear of every description. Regarding the salmon, Kishpiax River was filled to overflowing with every kind.

in those days no salmon net was ever thought of. Instead of this a salmon trap was invented, by a few of the wiser ones, and was used after they had cleverly dammed the river in two places. In order to dam the river, the people were formed into two divisions the chiefs taking the lead. Material for this purpose was collected during the winter and hauled to the place selected for the dam. Stone axes were used to hew the logs and stone hammers were used to drive the piles across. Each hammer weighed a hundred pounds so some strength was required to wield those hammers. The women prepared and made all the rope requires [148] to tie the dam together, of cedar bark.

For the salmon traps, they softened some spruce roots, and then, when soft and tender, split it up into lengths exceedingly fine almost as fine as paper, which they used to fasten the finer parts of the salmon trap together. When all the necessary salmon traps were completed, the chiefs of each crest would own one, and those belonging to that particular crest, would be permitted to take all the salmon they wanted from that trap free. According to traditions, these traps were set in special places, and at a certain time from one another. They were not to be moved and were handed down from one generation to another. During the heavy run of salmon the traps had to be visited twice a day. A watchman was stationed at each dam, and gave a special call to the people, when the fish were running very thick. If this were neglected the weight of the fish would break these salmon traps and carry them away. In a few days after a heavy run, many millions of fish were caught in these traps.

When it happened occasionally that an early freshet came, it would carry away the dam and the salmon traps. This meant a famine amongst them for that year, and the women would wail and mourn for they realized the serious situation.

Tradition of Hazelton (*Kit-un-maht*)

Hazelton is situated at the junction of the Skeena and the Bukley Rivers and was formerly known as the [149] "Forks of the Skeena". The Indian name for Hazelton is Kit-un-mahts, which means "The People who spear the salmon by torch-light". The people living here, had an advantage over all the other tribes, as this was a centre place.

From there trails led to the Omineca Mines, Babine, Hudson's Bay Company's Post, Hug-wil-get Village, Kish-ga-gas, Kul-do and Kishpiax. During the excitement of the Omineca gold mine discovery 45 years ago, all the freight canoes from the Coast and all the gold seekers landed here. So the Kish-un-mahts were the first Interior Indians to come in contact with the white men and to copy their manners and mode of living. They built log cabins, planted potatoes, and vegetables and learned how to work like a white man.

In a short time the whites had part of the townsite surveyed for themselves, the rest of it was a reservation. The name was then changed and given the name of Hazelton. This name was chosen because of an abundance of Hazel nuts growing in that locality.

Later on as the place grew, the government appointed officials to administer the law.

No missionaries had then been amongst them.

Many white men had to submit to the Indians in order to save their lives. One trader, who lived at the Forks was stabbed by a scalping knife while standing outside his store. Bye and bye the missionaries came along. The English Church established a mission and a church.

As the years passed, the Methodist Church sent out a Medical Missionary, Dr. HC Wrinch. A fine [150] well-equipped, up-to-date hospital was built nearly two miles above Hazelton, at what is known as "Two Mile Creek".

As the population increased the Methodist Church sent a minister to make his headquarters at Hazelton, holding services there, and at several other appointments and mining camps in the district.

In the early days all transportation was done by canoe. Cost of freight was very, very, high.

The usual size of the freight canoe used was capable of carrying two tons, beside a crew of five men. During the summer, each man was paid fifteen dollars and the price of the canoe was also reckoned as the price of one man. The provisions for the trip would amount to another fifteen dollars making the total of $105.00.

In the spring and fall, when navigation was more difficult the cost was greater. Then twenty dollars instead of fifteen was paid to each man, making the total for these trips to be $140.00.

The Skeena River is considered a very difficult and dangerous river to navigate. The canoes were often in great danger, and the freight was often lost or badly damaged which, of course, was a dead loss to the owner.

When the freight reached Hazelton, it was distributed to different posts to which it was assigned. Men, women and children were engaged to pack the goods even as far as Omineca mining district, also Babine and Kish-ga gas. [151]

Traditions of Kitzeguclas

Kitzeguclas is situated on the left bank of the Skeena, half way between Hazelton and Kit-wun-gah: The population is mixed, some being descended from the Hug-wil-gets {Hagwelgat Dené} and some from the Kit-un-maht (Hazelton.)

Because of this they were never united in anything that they undertook to do, and have always been noted for quarrelling and disagreeing amongst themselves never listening to, nor obeying and respecting their chiefs. Consequently it had always been difficult to make a success of any undertaking they had ever planned. This trait is still prominent to-day. For instance, a few Christian people, after much consultation with their missionary, decided to move away from the old heathen village and form a new settlement seven miles above, where there was plenty of splendid land for agricultural purposes. New houses, also church and mission house were erected. Land was cultivated and for a short time all were happy and content. Soon however the old spirit began to crop up. A few of the old heads wanted to rule the place and everybody in it. The result was, the village was almost deserted. Some returned to the old village and others went elsewhere, thus hindering the mission from making further progress.

Tradition says that during Noah's flood one of the big mountains from Asia floated away and landed just where the village stands to-day. As this big mountain travelled along it knocked others down, thus leaving [152] a valley behind, which stretches as far as the eye can see. The name of this mountain is Kitze-ugia, and the tribe living there have always been known as the "Kitzegulas" which means the peaple of the Kitz-uela mountains.

Tradition of Andancaul

Andancaul is situated on the right bank of the Skeena River, almost five miles below Kitzeguela village. It was formerly a large fishing camp belonging to the Kit-wun-gah tribe. Behind this camp is a very high hill — the highest on the Skeena.

The name of this hill is Andimaul, meaning the "Seat of Native Astronomers". The top of this hill was a specially selected place for the astronomers {*gyamget*, literally 'moon reader'} belonging to the different tribes to gather together on an evening watching the sun sinking away on the mountains. By watching the sun in the spring of the year, and again in the fall, they claimed to be capable of discerning just what the coming season would bring forth.

In the spring, they could tell whether berries were going to be plentiful or scarce, and whether there would be a good run of salmon or otherwise. Also whether the summer would be hot or cold, wet or dry. In the fall, they knew what kind of winter to expect, whether severe or mild and whether a light or heavy fall of snow, also whether any epidemic would be prevalent. One branch of the "Grease Trail," extending from the Naas, led right past this seat on the hill, and along [153] this route travellers were continually passing and re-passing.

Today any traveller passing by may see several little spots, here and there, which it is claimed to have been worn away from constant use as seats by these astronomers in the olden days.

When sitting there in consultation and each one agreed, then a messenger was sent to all the different tribes warning the people and telling them what they might expect to happen. At the present time astronomy at Andimaul is a thing of the past. This place is now a fishing camp only for a few families from Kitzeguela who have made it their home, and as they joined the Salvation Army this is now a small Salvation Army settlement with an officer in charge.

Tradition of Kilselas People

Many hundred years ago, tradition says, there was no human being living at Kit-se-las. But one day, a man named Nahmauksque, came over from Kit-a-maat. He followed the Kit-a-maat river until he came to the lake, and from that he followed the creek which flows from the lake until he reached the Skeena. The name of that creek is *Gitsum-ovdzack*, which is now known as the Copper River. He then followed the Skeena up on the same side until he came to a small stream, which was packed full of salmon, so he decided to build a little house for himself on this location. He walked further, looking for some other discovery, when [154] to his great surprise he found a big dam. Above this dam was a good-sized pond, nearly as large as a lake. This location pleased him so much that instead of building at the salmon creek as he had intended, he resolved to build his house here, and began at once. After completing his house he returned to Kit-a-maat and told his relations of his wonderful discovery. This news was told to his relations only, and not to outsiders. On his return, he took along a few of his relations and gave each one a location. *Nah-mauksque* was the head chief, and the village was named Gil-akzauksh by him. The population increased, and for many years all lived together in peace and harmony. They had no idea of any other people living along the river, either above or below them, except those living at Kit-sum-kalum. After enjoying peace and quietness all those years one night their peace was all upset by a very sad and sudden occurrence.

That night a chief was killed while sitting in his own house during the early part of the evening. His name was *Gwanaque*. A bow and arrow shot from the outside entered his heart and killed him on the spot. After extracting the arrow, they examined closely, but failed to recognize to whom it belonged. It was very roughly made, and they knew that it neither belonged to Kit-a-maat nor Kit-sum-kalum.

The tribe belonging to the chief who was killed, decided that this arrow was to be kept and preserved until they could discover from whence it came.

For many years after this happened, whenever there was a big gathering, this arrow was brought out and [155] passed from one to another, trying to find out any information that would lead to its discovery. Each time they failed. But one day during the springtime a large crowd of gamblers arrived from Kit-sum-kalum and Kit-a-maat. After spending some days there enjoying their games, they were all assembled for the last game in the house of the head chief, Mah-mawksque. This being the closing game, it was the most important day of all, and there was a crowded house. Amongst the number of those who were looking on were two strangers who were noticed at once. These two had not been present at the other gatherings.

Both these men were noticed to have their hand and part of their garments over their mouths. The head chief, Nah-mauksque, ordered that this, being the last last gathering, the arrow should be passed, not missing any person.

These two strangers were seated almost at the door, and were thus the last to have the arrow passed. On examination, the stranger whispered to his friend, "This is my brother Benumgueltque's arrow". This whisper was heard by the man who had handed him the arrow, and at once he called out to the whole crowd: "This man says that this arrow belongs to his brother, Benum-queltque."

This caused so much excitement that everyone rushed from his seat trying to capture these two strangers, but they, being near the door, had made good their escape. They were seen at quite a distance running fast towards the dam, one of them carrying the arrow in his mouth crosswise. But before the water was [156] reached, those following them discovered that they were beavers. Both these beavers jumped into the water, the one with the arrow in his mouth keeping it there.

Then in the middle of the pond they came up once, and on going down again, struck the water with their tales, which was a sign that they would come up no more.

The tribe thus discovered that their chief had been killed by a beaver, also that the two beavers on entering the house where the gamblers were assembled had covered their mouths with their hands and garments in order to escape detection by hiding the big front teeth. Immediately the tribe held a consultation to consider what would be the best course to pursue. They decided to cut the dam into two parts, in order to exterminate the beavers.

By adopting this method and killing off every beaver, they felt sure of killing the murderer of their chief amongst the number. This was tedious work and took a long time, but at last their task was completed and their efforts rewarded by killing off every beaver, even the king himself, the last one to come out of the dam, was amongst the number.

Strange to say, when the king made his appearance he was quite conspicuous, with numerous human faces covering his body. On each paw, on each eye-lid, on each ear, and on his body, were these tiny human faces to be seen. This tribe who killed the beavers are today known as the Eagle tribe, having Kit-kon {*Githawn*} as the name of their head chief. Their totem poles have always been distinguished by having the carving of the [157] beaver king, just as he was seen at the time. The special blanket belonging to the chief, was painted in the centre with the beaver king. At the time this happened, the Kitselas tribe had no knowledge of any other human beings living up the river. The only thing noticeable to them was in the springtime, during the high water, when they saw some cedar bark rope and poles belonging to fish traps floating down the river, which were washed ashore in some of the eddies in the canyon. These were picked up and examined and were found to be similar to their own. Prom this they concluded that some people must be living up the river somewhere, but just how far they had not the remotest idea.

Heat-git-lob made a trip quite a distance above the canyon and built a camp trapping and hunting. Not one of that company ever lived to return home again to tell the tale of what hapepned during their stay there. It was then that the others concluded that some other tribe did live not far distant who had murdered their own people.

Search was made and continued for many days without any success. This happened in the winter time. Early in the following fall, what appeared to be a very strange log came floating down, and was first seen when just above the canyon, with a person sitting on it. That person was paddling and trying to effect a landing there above the village. Everybody seemed excited; men, women and children all ran out to see the sight, all anxious to know who this strange person could be. [158]

What had appeared in the distance to be a log proved to be the half of a cotton tree canoe. Just as soon as the canoe touched the landing a young woman jumped ashore. Her name was *Shumagooldt*, and was the niece of *Healgitlob*.

This is her story:

"One night while in the camp when all were sound asleep, a number of men came in, killing every one except me. I was taken as a slave. First I was blindfolded, so that I might not find my way if I attempted to escape.

"During the first day's travel we crossed a creek which was called Anskaadsk, because we had to wade across. The following day we reached another creek, which we had to wade also. This they called Kshgwun-boyausk, because there were so many mosquitoes. The next day we arrived at a village. Behind this village stands a little mountain which is shaped like a heart, and is called kit-wum-gah.

"When summer came around and the berries were ripe, the women packed up and moved across the river lo their camps, which are on the mountainside just opposite the village. They chose me to look after the camp on the bank of the river while they all went up the mountain to pick berries. They were to be away several days. So, while alone, I resolved to do my utmost to try and escape. The cottonwood canoe in which we had crossed the river, lay on the beach, half of it in the water. My strength not being sufficient to push the canoe entirely in the water, I tried to cut it [159] in two with a sharp rock. This rock I changed several times each day.

"But my work was very slow. After working several times each day for a few days, my aim was accomplished, and the half that was already in the water I quickly filled with ballast in order that the cut end might be high, and thus avoid the water rushing in. I then Jumped in with my paddle and, as you see, have reached my home and people in safety."

The Kit-se-las people, after hearing Shumagoodlt's story, discovered that their theory regarding the floating poles, rope, etc., that they had seen, was correct. At once they held a council and decided that a number of them should go up and visit Kit-wum-gah to demand peace and a settlement for the murders they had committed.

Shumagooldtd was to be their guide on the journey. After three days' journey they entered Kit-wum-gah village. A peace dance was held during their first night's stay there. Both sides agreed to the settlement by which there was to be no more murder or war between Kit-wum-gah and Kit-se-laa.

Mountains, creeks and lakes where they had been accustomed to trap and hunt were handed over to the Kit-se-las people as a token that there would be no more murder nor ill-feeling existing between them. The names of the chiefs on both sides were exchanged, and songs belonging to these chiefs were exchanged also. This was all done in accordance to their laws and customs. [160]

The Kit-wun'gah chiefs declared before the chiefs of Kit-se-las that no other tribes from the coast should come up and trade with them. This privilege of trading was extended to the Kit-se-las tribe only. This arrangement was strictly carried out for hundreds of years. It was not until the white man made his appearance and the missionary came that this taw was changed. Legaic's tribe, Kishpaclauts, through intermarrying with Kit-se-las, were the first people from the coast to trade with the Upper Skeena.

Kit-se-las people, as they increased, divided themselves into two distinct tribes, each bearing a different name. The tribe who chose to live on the left bank of the river was named Kit-lac-tzauks, which means "people living by a ravine," and the tribe who chose the opposite bank was named Ki-tzaalth, meaning "people living on the edge of the lake".

Spook-Shute, or Port Essington

Spook-shute was formerly a camping place in the fall of the year for the Tsmpsheans when on their way home from the Upper Skeena after spending the summer months there drying salmon for their winter use. Hence the name Spook-shute means a "fall camping place". The main reason for camping here was to wait for suitable weather to pass *Gid-um-naghi*, now known as Point Lambert. Tradition states that the chief, *Gid-um-naghi*, lived in the water at that point under the rock, controlling the power of both water and wind. [161]

Whenever he did not feel pleased, he would not allow any canoe to pass that point. He would cause a strong wind to rise very suddenly, making the waves dash furiously around the point, and thus swamp the canoes. Before leaving Spook-shute, the occupants of each canoe would prepare what they called "Oomgawksh," which means an offering. This consisted of pieces of salmon meat. wrapped neatly in some of the soft, inner bark of red cedar, and as they approached the point, the captain of each canoe signaled to his crew to paddle very softly, making no noise of any description, while he would cast this offering into the water to appease the wrath of *Gid-um-naghi*. While doing this he would offer prayer to him, asking for protection and guidance so that they might reach their destination in safety.

It is said that any canoe passing that point without honoring the chief always came to grief. In 1793, when Vancouver, the discoverer, was anchored in the bay here, he gave the name Port Essington. Nevertheless, "Spook-shute" has never died out. Some of the tribes still use that name occasionally, and there are gasoline launches known by that name also.

In 1872 the Hudson's Bay Company built a trading post here. At that time Port Essington was nothing but a wilderness, not even Cree Indians living here. The steamer, *Otter,* brought up the lumber all the way from Victoria, also twelve workmen to erect the building. At that time the writer was acting as cabin boy on that steamer under Captain Lewis. There was considerable trouble in getting the lumber landed. Much ice was in the river and in spite of two anchors, the [162] steamer drifted down to Point Lambert twice. This was in the month of January.

Six months later we made our second trip and brought McFeak, the trader, to take charge of new post, also goods for the store which by this time had been erected, and all was in readiness to commence business.

One year later, Mr. Robert Cunningham, trader, moved up from Inverness and built a store here also. The news soon spread up the river and down the coast that two new stores had been built at Spook-shute, and were paying better prices for furs. This was quite an attraction and before long, all the different tribes began to congregate here to trade off their furs. In those days, no cash was paid. Instead the Indian would load up his canoe with goods of all kinds, and feel quite satisfied, returning home again with the feeling that he had completed a great business transaction between the trader and himself.

Even the Alaska Indians had heard the wonderful news, and they too, soon proved the truth of the report by taking the long journey and bartering their furs at Port Essington.

At this time the Omineca gold mine began to open up, and great excitement prevailed all over the country. Miners came here in hundreds from Victoria and the States. Some came all the way from the old country. Three steamers sailing from Victoria were kept busy. Their names were, the *Otter, Isabel*, and *Emma.* The two latter were special, running to accommodate extra passengers and freight, all bound for the Omineca Country. As Port Essington was the gate-way to the [163] Inkrive, they all had to camp here, often weeks, at a time, until freight canoes could be obtained to take them and their goods up the river as far as the Forks, now known as Hazelton.

Before Port Essington was established, passengers were landed at the mouth of the river at Wil-thautk meaning the place of slide and known to the whites as Woodcock's Landing. The modern name is Inverness.

As the miners were passing up and down the river, making Port Essington their stopping place, they left hundreds and thousands of dollars behind. This was undoubtedly a big uplift to the new town just sprung up. It may be of interest to say something of the wealth acquired by one man, Jamieson, just returning from the Omineca district where he had spent one year. During that time, he discovered a creek which he named after himself-Jamieson Creek. He travelled down to Victoria on the steamer *Otter,* on his way to England. As I was cabin boy on that boat, he came to me one day asking for four soup plates. He put those plates on the table and filled two of them with large, gold nuggets. The other he piled high with gold dust. This was to show all the passengers on board the richness of his newly discovered creek.

As the Kit-sum-kalum and Kit-se-bas tribes passed up and down the river in their canoes on their way to Naas for the oolichan fishing, they were impressed by the progress that was being made at the new town of Port Essington. They carried the news home to their friends. This led them to council together, and both bands soon decided that it would be to their interest [164] and that of their children, to move down to the mouth of the river and make Port Essington their home This was not accomplished without opposition. Quite a number of the older people had very strong objections to the change. They were afraid that if they left their old heathen ground and all their heathen rites and the Potlatch behind, these things would be lost forever, and they themselves would always be the laughing stock to the tribes. However, the young people were determined to make a start. First one family then another came down in their canoes and camped on the beach. Small log houses or shacks were built and soon three quarters of the people were living here. They were not slow to discover that to live down here was not an easy way to obtain a living. When not hunting, they were employed by the traders doing various kinds of work. And now those old chiefs and people who had been so strongly opposed to move, began to feel lonely, so they too, decided to cast in their lot with the rest.

About this time a few of the Kit-se-las people who had been living for sometime at Met-la-kah-tla and had become Christians through Mr. Duncan's teaching came to Port Essington to visit their friends, after hearing the report of their settling at the new place.

Metlakahtla

This village is situated on the Tsmpshean Peninsula fifteen miles south of Port Simpson and about five miles north of Prince Rupert. This is known as one of [165] the most ancient villages belonging to the ten tribes of Tsmpshean nation.

The meaning of Metlakahtia, is the inside passage of the Kit-kaht-las.

During war time in the olden days, it was not safe to travel outside in the open waters. The Hydahs from Queen Charlotte's Island were always on the watch; They, knowing the time when the Kit-kahtla tribe would be journeying north on their way to Naas oolichan fishing. For this reason, they always chose the inner passage, so kahtla really means, the inner passage of the Kit-kahtlas.

Each of the ten tribes had its head chief, and each tribe was divided into several crests, with a chief to represent each crest.

This chief would choose the wisest and bravest men from their tribe. For instance, one man would be chosen to act as adviser for war, another would be chosen to plan out peace and settlement after war.

One who was able to form words and tune, would take the part of musician. This man, with his eyes shut. and a stick in his hand, tapping the floor to keep time. would compose a few pieces very quickly, the learners sitting around as he might dictate. These songs would include War dance. Peace dance, and the head chiefs Reception dance. The words for each song were always appropriate for the part chosen.

The head chiefs, in order to be wise, had to listen to advice of these men in council for he was responsible to the whole tribe for their welfare.

Battles were fought often. Indians from Alaska, [166] Queen Charlotte's Islands, Bella Bella, Bella Coola, Kit-a-maat and even from the Upper Skeena were all united in their attacks on Metlakatla. Fortunately, this village is situated on high ground so that whenever a battle was planned by these other tribes, their canoes were easily seen long before they approached Metlakahtla. This gave the inhabitants time to prepare for an attack. The Tsmpsheans at that time being such a powerful nation always gained the victory.

Whenever war was declared amongst the different tribes, it was not because of any desire on their part to acquire more territory, nor because of trouble caused by any dispute. It was merely a means of retaliation for what has transpired amongst their forefathers many years before.

Each crest, whether a wolf, a bear or an eagle, kept themselves together as a regiment, choosing the best man from among them to be their leader. Regulations, regarding diet and mode of living were strictly adhered to during the war time periods.

Women and children were always to be protected and taken captives.

Metlakahtla was the winter village for the Tsmpsheans, while the lower part of the Skeena was where they made their summer home.

During the spring time, they moved up to the Naas river, where they lived during the oolichan fishing. [167]

Port Simpson

It was in the year 1831 that the Hudson's Bay company first established a trading post at Port Simpson. A barge and a schooner loaded with goods, together with a number of men and their families, sailed from Columbia river bound for the North.

The first location which they selected was at the mouth of the Naas river, now known as Graveyard point, a few miles above Kin-kolith, where they built a fort, several dwellings and a store. They only remained at that post for two winters. The cold weather was so severe, that scarcely any business could be done during that season of the year. Their ships had to anchor out a distance, it being impossible for them to discharge their freight. All this trouble caused them to decide for a better and more suitable location. The site then chosen is now known as Port Simpson.

At that time it was merely an Indian camp and stopping place. Legaic, one of the head chiefs of Kish-pac-lot's tribe invited the company to build on this bay. One of the leading men who superintended the erection of the building, was named Simpson, hence the name of the settlement became Fort Simpson, which in later years changed again to Port Simpson.

A large fort was built, covering several acres. The Fort was square and the two front corners were built each with a bastion in which cannon were stationed facing the village.

At three different times the Fort was attacked by [168] the Tsmpsheans, and these cannons used in defence were the salvation of all who were living inside the Fort.

The staff who were living inside the Fort consisted of a doctor, school teacher, two salesmen, two managers and forty common hands. Each man was always armed, ready for any emergency, and each had to take his turn in guarding the gate from morning till night. Then during the night two were appointed as guards for the whole Fort, each one taking his turn for a certain number of hours. Every half hour he would ring the Fort bell and in a loud clear tone call out, "All's well". These precautions were necessary in order that all who were living inside the Fort could feel that they were perfectly safe to enjoy their night's rest without danger.

Only one Indian at a time was permitted to enter for trading purposes and unless he had furs to show was not allowed to pass even then. On no account was he permitted to trade inside the store. He presented his furs through a small opening, where a salesman attended to his wants. Cash was not used. A land otter, for instance, might be exchanged for a tin cup; a beaver skin for a common cotton shirt, or a mink for one bunch of leaf tobacco.

Quite often the Hudson's Bay Company have saved the Indians from starvation. When the winters were long and severe, native food became very scarce. They had then no means of obtaining food in quantities sufficient to last for any length of time. There were no nets for catching fish, Salmon were caught by a basket which was tied to a stick and then dipped into the [169] water. Oolichan, or small fish were caught by means of long poles of red cedar made specially for that purpose.

It was the Kitamaats who first introduced the nets to the Tsmpsheans, but as the price was high then, only a very few of the chiefs were able to own one. As time passed on, the entire tribe saw the great advantage of using these nets, and they were not satisfied until they were rich enough for their use to become general.

A few years later, all the other tribes began to notice that the Hudson's Bay Company at Fort Simpson was the centre place for trading and thus the place became a source of great attraction. The natives from Alaska, Queen Charlotte's Islands, Skeena river, Kit-kahtla, Kit-kahia, Kit-amaat and Naas river, all headed for Fort Simpson just as soon as their hunting trips were over, their canoes being loaded with furs — martens, beavers, sea-otters, lynx, mink, wolves, bears, fishers and every kind of fur imaginable.

Fur values in those days could not be compared with present-day prices. For instance, a very common blanket known as the potlatch blanket, was exchanged for ten marten skins. The blanket might be worth two dollars or less, and the marten skins about ten dollars each, so it can be readily seen how the poor native was treated in a bargain. Mr. William Duncan, who was the first Protestant missionary to come North, and who was sent out from England by the C.M.S (Church Missionary Society) was the first man to tell the natives that they did not receive one-quarter the value for their furs.

The furs, when bought, were shipped by the [170] Hudson's Bay Company down to Victoria twice each year, early in the spring and late in the fall. They owned a steamer named the *Bearer,* which was the first, and, in those days, the only steamer plying the Pacific Coast. A few years later the *Beaver* was replaced by the *Otter,* another Hudson's Bay boat.

The journey from Victoria to Fort Simpson was then a very different matter from what it is today. The fuel consisted of wood and it had to be replenished at different points along the way. At the first suitable stopping place, all hands went ashore armed with crosscut saws and axes. Then a sufficient quantity was cut to last until the next suitable camp was reached.

Swanson Bay, now noted for its pulpmills, was at that time noted for the great quantities of hemlocks growing there, and as that was the only kind of wood used for steam, the boat never failed to stop there both on the up and down trips, taking away as much as she could conveniently carry. The captain of the *Otter* was named Swanson, hence the name of that camp became known as Swanson Bay.

There was no lighthouses in those days, and no buoys were to be found on the whole coast. The captain was simply guided by his chart and compass. At dark they always anchored. There were no passengers travelling either up or down, therefore neither grumbling nor complaining could be heard because of these delays and long trips.

No business of any kind was conducted along the coast other than the three Forts owned by the Hudson's Bay. One was at Fort Rupert, on Vancouver Island, [171] one at Bella Bella, and the other at Fort Simpson. These stores received their goods by this boat twice during each year.

The length of time taken to reach Fort Simpson from Victoria would be about three weeks or so. Note the difference now in these days. Steamers leaving Victoria for Prince Rupert arrive at that Port in thirty-six hours or even less.

Naas River Tribes

On the Naas river, there were formerly five large villages occupied by the Naas tribes, who earned their living by trapping and hunting, oolichan fishing and catching salmon.

The names of the villages referred to are as follows:

Git-gwanwok — Place where people sleep.
Git-an-gidah — Place where people comb oolichans into the canoe.
Git-lahouse — People of the sand.
Git-wunsil — People of Lizards.
Git-lak-damaks — People of a pond.

The inhabitants of these villages all speak the same language and are known as "Nishgas". While these people are a distinct tribe from the Tsmpsheans, yet they understand and speak each other's language quite readily.

During the oolichan fishing, when the Tsmpsheans were on the Naas at their camps, they would invite [172] the Nishgas down to visit them where they would be entertained for several days. Friendly feasts were given, as was also a Peace Dance, where all agreed to live in as peaceful and harmonious manner as was possible. Should any dispute or friction arise, the trouble was to be settled by arbitration. The fact was welt known to the Tsmpsheans and other coast tribes, that the Naas river belonged solely to the Nishgas, but at the same time all knew that during the oolichan fishing the river was thrown open to anyone belonging to the other tribes who cared to fish there. Even the natives from Alaska came. When the whites first entered the country bringing in their whiskey, which was sold to the Indians, much trouble was caused among all those tribes on the Naas river. Fighting and bloodshed were common, there being no law to prohibit or punish offenders.

After Mr. Duncan came to Metlakahtla as a missionary, he visited the Naas river and informed the people that the law must be enforced on the Naas as well as at Metlakahtla or Fort Simpson — and if the law were broken, he would send a canoe up with his constables to bring down the guilty ones to Metlakahtla for trial. This, he told them, was for the good of the country as well as for themselves.

Mr. Duncan was the first missionary to visit and preach to the Naas river Indians. For a number of years he fulfilled his promise in administering the law to all the tribes living there. [173]

Tradition of Kit-Sum-Kalum People

The formation of the rocks at Kit-sum-kalum Canyon, lay in tiers, and tradition says that the first village discovered there was built right on the topmost tier. Hence the name, Kit-sum-kalum, which means, "people living on the ridge".

Two chiefs belonging to the Naas river, named Neasyok and Neas-kaal, with their families, left their own homes and began wandering about in search of some better location where fishing would be much easier, and where they could secure good hunting ground.

After many long wanderings, climbing mountains and journeying through valleys, they discovered a small lake perfectly round, and at the bottom lay a quantity of pure white sand where small trout could be seen from quite a distance. At this spot they decided to locate. They gave the name "Dapm-queth-al-altkt," which means a lake perfectly round.

These people continued to live at this spot for many generations. In the springtime they found it quite easy to spear all the salmon they wanted, the sandy bottom preventing the fish from hiding, and the clearness of the water enabling them to see just where the salmon were. In those days the spears used were made from the horns of mountain goats, also from a piece of the leg bone of the grizzly bear.

During the winter months, Neas-yok and Neas-kaal used to go off hunting bears in their dens, as well as trapping beavers and other furs. [174]

When going on one of those winter journeys they made it a rule never to eat any snow or ice to quench their thirst. They believed that if they indulged in this, their constitution would be weakened and they would be unable to stand any fatigue or hardship, or to keep up the pursuit of any animals they were trying to follow, and thus be unsuccessful. This rule has been kept from one generation to another amongst the hunters until the present time.

As a substitute for snow or ice, when their thirst needed to be quenched, they selected a small nice round pebble the size of a marble, which was kept in their mouth as they journeyed on through the snow on their snowshoes. This pebble was handed down and passed on to the different generations, at the same time gradually increasing in size, until at last it became too large to be placed in the mouth. It was then laid aside and placed at the back part of the house where Neas-yok lived. As this pebble increased to a considerable size and became solid enough to be stationary, Neas-yok, when tired, would go and rest his back by this stone. Today that stone still stands. It has been examined and measured by prospectors, and is ten feet high and eight feet through. One side faces the Naas and the other side, the Kit-sum-kalum river, thus forming a dividing line between the Naas people and those of Kit-sum-kalum.

But while this stone forms the boundary line between those two tribes, all those on the Naas descending from Neas-yok, are allowed the privileges and rights of the Kit-sum-kalum tribe right up to the present time. [175]

After a number of years had elapsed, the descendants of Neas-kaal separated from those of Neas-york. Neas-kaal followed the stream, until he found a lake very much larger than the one where they had been living so long. The Journey was still continued, and at last another lake was discovered larger still than the two previous ones, and here was situated a large village, inhabited by many people, all busy drying their salmon, this being the summer time. This village was built right on the ridge of the topmost tier. All the houses belonging to chiefs were built partly underground. One of the chiefs entertained Neas-kaal and all his people.

After the meal, Neas-kaal was called outside by his host, who showed him the village and the dam across the Kit-sum-kalum river, and all the salmon traps connected with it. He gave him instructions how to build a dam and how to perfect it during high water.

At last night came on and everybody went to bed. During the night while Neas-kaal and his people were sound asleep, the rest of the inhabitants took their departure. In the morning, Neas-kaal and his party awoke to find themselves the sole occupants of the village. With surprise and fear they moved from house to house wondering what was going to happen, and hoping they would find some life somewhere. But nothing was to be seen except a few dried salmon in each house, which had been left behind for Neas-kaal and his people, and a quantity of feathers which covered the ground all through the village. The floor of each house, too, was covered with them. They came [176] to the conclusion after a thorough examination, that the inhabitants of this village had been robins, and the man who had entertained and instructed them in every detail, was one of these birds. Neas-kaal and his people occupied the village and followed out the instructions given him.

They built a dam and salmon traps exactly as he had been told. This was the beginning of salmon traps being made and used amongst the upper river tribes. Any one visiting Kit-sum-kalum village today may see the hollows in the ground all through the ancient village, and each one is called the "Robin Chief's House".

The End

Ligeex High Chief Dynasty

The chiefly line of the name+title Ligeex has spanned centuries to maintain its preeminence among Tsimshian of the of the Eagle crest, as illustrated by his ~ their unique claims, events, confrontations, and privileges during the Fur Trade era of the first half of the 1800s.

Introduction

The antiquity and character of chiefs, and, in particular the high chief, of the Coast Tsimshian of northern British Columbia have been largely misunderstood by academics.[26] Each held and holds a hereditary name that is regarded as immortal by Tsimshian and their North Pacific neighbors, but it is often difficult to separate out the series of actual human holders, although the actions of each served to exalt or tarnish the fame of that name.[27] For natives, however, the *adaawx*, a sacred history precisely told by the head of a "house" (matriline) possessing its leading hereditary name, indicate that the titled name of Ligeex was held by a succession of Eagle crest (matriclan) leaders of the Gispaxlo'ots (People of Elderberry), which, through his efforts, became the foremost tribe in historic times (Marsden ms, Marsden and Galois 1995).

This name is first mentioned in *adaawx* referring to events about five hundred years ago, but the most famous bearer, known as Old Ligeex, was active about 1800-1840 during the peak of the land-based fur trade (Robinson 1996).[28] The impetus for this dynasty seems to have been the dispensing of membership in spiritual guilds or secret orders (known as *wiihalaayt*) inherited by the founder from his *Wutsdaa* (Bella Bella Heitsuk) father but wrongly attributed by Marius Barbeau to Old Ligeex of three hundred years later.

A chief bearing the name of Ligeex, apparently about 1830, was the originator of the secret societies among his band. These fraternities of mutually helpful craftsmen and raiders were his own device to break down the resistance of hostile clan chiefs opposing him and to bring about his domination among the northern tribes. They progressed the more easily among the Kwakiutls for the lack of opposition, in the absence of clans.

---

[26] Tsimshian is an ethnonym deriving from *ts'm* 'inside' and *ksyaan* 'Skeena River'. Basic sources on the Tsimshian (including Southern, Gitksan, and Nishga) include tens of thousands of manuscript pages by the Tsimshian chief William Beynon (Gwisk'aayn). Another important source on the Ligeex line is Homer Barnett (1940).

[27] In keeping with its importance, the name Ligeex has no easy translation. Among Tsimshian, the more important a name, the more interpretations it has in order to consume time and energy. According to native sense, the name means "impassability, invincibility, impenetrability, what cannot be overcome." The Ligeex spelling used herein was approved by literate Tsimshian for publications used in tribal schools and by the Tsimshian Language Authority. Europeans have spelled this name as Legaic, Legeek, Ilegauch, Illgayauch, Legaeek, or, recognizing its cohesiveness, the Illegaich Gang, but all versions have been standardized herein.

[28] In this generally garbled account of this dynasty, Old Ligeex is called Legaik 2, but IV would be more like it (Robinson 1996).

The potlatch, an ancient system of native transactions and social entertainment, everywhere became the vehicle of new ambitions of conquest, prestige, and power (Barbeau 1990: 765).

In the normal course of North Coast diffusion, such guilds had been spreading from Bella Bella, speakers of a Northern Kwakiutlan or Wakashan language, to the south and to the north, where they had already been placed among the Southern Tsimshian. By intermarrying at Kitamaat and Wudsdaa, Ligeex was able to bring these orders into the Tsimshian heartland to add to the prestige and fame of his house.

However, the murder of Old Ligeex's designated heir in May of 1839, precipitated a bitter rivalry between his own brother and nephew (sister's son, later baptized as Paul), both with claims to matrilineal succession.

Several academics, however, mostly relying on the records of the Hudson's Bay Company (HBC) trading at Fort Simpson, though built on land donated by Old Ligeex, have denied evidence of his primacy. Behind their arguments, moreover, lurks a misunderstanding of Tsimshian leadership, wrongly assuming a consistent royal imperiousness appropriate mostly to European monarchs. While impetuous and ambitious, the Ligeex line were neither tyrants nor autocrats, but rather successful negotiators skilled in the selective use of force.

For Tsimshian, a chief has, minimally, two contrasting management styles. Inheriting an unblemished pedigree from a long line of prior chiefs in the matriline, each holder of a famous name was expected to be "skilled in all things, energetic and ambitious" (Garfield 1966: 17). Overall, chiefs were "able leaders, good speakers, haughty and proud before strangers, and humble and generous toward tribesmen. The ideal leader was an able organizer and speaker, and a model of good taste and conduct" (Garfield 1966: 27). From a native perspective, a chief had to prove wisdom (*'wii ho'osxw*), kindness (*ammagoot* = "good heart"), and strength (*daxgyet*) in order to gain respect (*antɫx'ooms*) (Gitsegukla History1979: 37).

The Tsimshianic language family is composed, in the interior, of Nishga (Nisga'a) on the middle Nass River and Gitksan of the upper Skeena River and, downriver, of Canyon, Coast, and Southern Tsimshian. Since hard and fast boundaries are a convention only in state societies, as elsewhere in the world, Tsimshian border zones were, at least, bicultural and bilingual. Southern Tsimshian leaders were as fluent in Wakashan as Tsimshianic, while Gitksan knew Athapaskan and Nishga used Tlingit. Some of the Tsimshian chiefs spoke Haida and/or married there. Such dynastic marriages united the chiefly families along the entire coast, overarching differences of town, tribe, or parent language.

Viola Garfield, the classic Boasian Tsimshianist, estimated thirty Tsimshian tribal chiefs, each heading the major house of the tribal town (Garfield 1966: 26). While immortal names conferring rank were and are almost always male; in the absence of a close male heir, a woman could and did "carry" the name and was accordingly treated as a "man."

Before Christianity, each leader had four named spiritual aspects, often distinguished as sm "real." As *smgigyet* ("real people") house chiefs, they coordinated summer economic activities and conducted feasts and namings; as *naxnox* dancers, they sponsored and/or performed in fall masked ceremonials. As *smhalaayt*, with a carved frontlet on the forehead, a woven blanket over the shoulders, and a raven rattle in the hand, they initiated young people into ritual roles of the crest. As *'wiihalaayt* leader of one of the four secret guilds, they ritually confirmed the royal rank of children and adults" (Halpin and Seguin 1990: 279).[29]

Beneath these chiefs, several hundred lineage and house heads managed the societal routines and made up the nobility. Each tribal chief was advised by a council of these nobles, together with craft and resource specialists such as shamans, carpenters, carvers, painters, musicians, composers, herbalists, midwives and astronomers (MacNeary 1976: 156; Miller 1992). With the advice of these specialists, overall efforts were coordinated by the chief of the leading house of that town.

Since each Coast Tsimshian tribe functioned in terms of its constituent ranked houses, all territories and trade routes were controlled by the house chiefs. Both water and land routes were owned and defended by a house, although marriages among royalty forged trade alliances to provide access to a variety of desired resources.

In general, coastal towns specialized in various kinds of seafoods and marine goods (dried cockles, clams, grease, dried candlefish, seaweed, dried herring eggs, shells) traded to interior chiefs in return for prestigious furs, hides, and copper. Throughout the coast, potlatches relied heavily on such inland pelts, particularly of marmot.

Along with marital ties, such alliances were strengthened by exchanging names and privileges, by feasting, and by ceremonial displays. At strategic locations along inland trails, chiefs built feast houses where friendship-making (*ne-amex*) rites (a kind of halaayt ritual) could be held to warn against poaching.

The crucial importance of trade for Tsimshian society is further indicated by the use of seven numbering systems to readily specify the type and quantity of goods involved.[30] As merchants, Tsimshian were seasonally mobile, arguing against the proposition that seasonal rounds were post-contact phenomena in the Northwest. Based on archaeological surveys of Vancouver Island, Inglis and Haggarty (1987) suggest that the prehistoric density of town sites there indicated local control (ownership?) of all local resources, which were harvested by residents and circulated only through trade. After European epidemics and dislocations destabilized the Nuchahnulth population, however, survivors began a pattern of seasonal movements to harvest available resources in various locations.

Extensive archaeology along the Skeena River and Prince Rupert Harbor indicate occupation for thousands of years leading to historic Tsimshian (Coupland 1988, MacDonald 1979, Matson and Coupland 1995). In particular, a dense concentration of town sites along Metlakatla Passage indicates a thousand years of joint winter residence by a dozen Coast Tsimshian tribes. In the spring people moved to the Nass for the candlefish run, rendering their trade mainstay of oolichan grease. In summer, towns moved to their territories along tributaries of the Skeena River until they all gathered together at Fall Place (*spaksuut* = "Fall place", Port Essington) for festivities before wintering back at Metlakatla.

---

[29] For Marjorie Halpin and Margaret Seguin (1990), their Tsimshianic spellings have been updated.

[30] These counting systems are distinguished as 1) general, 2) animal or flat (as pelts), 3) humans, 4) long objects, 5) canoes, 6) people in canoes, and 7) unit measures. See Dunn, *Sm'algyax*, 1995: 38-40.

Each year, summer was devoted to economic activities under the leadership of the chiefs of four crests – matrilineal clans forming semi-moieties of Orca-Wolf and Raven-Eagle (Miller 1978, 1981a, 1981b). Crest celebrations, hosted by chiefs, were potlatches, when the *adawx* of the household was recited and displayed on carved poles (Miller 1989).[31] During the winter, chiefs assumed their priestly names and hosted dramatizations of their *halaayt* privileges, mostly elaborated visits to Heaven. The autumn gathering was devoted to presenting wonders, enactments of an encounter between an ancestor and a supernatural spirit (*naxnox*).

After 1830, Tsimshians relocated to a trading post and then an Anglican mission, adding to the three social classes of nobles, commoners, and slaves characteristic of the entire Northwest Coast Culture Area. Thus, historically, Tsimshian developed a fourth class of royalty, tribal chiefs who arose from the ranks of the former town leaders when heirs were placed in charge of either old or new locations. To reinforce their increased rank, royalty received initiation into one or more of the guilds and claimed new crests combining humans traits with fabulous creatures (Halpin ms., 1973, 1978, 1994).

During 1787 to 1805, the fur trade was ship-based and concerned with sea otter pelts, so coastal chiefs had the advantage, particularly the Kitkatla Orca named *Ts'ibasaa*, who served as Southern Tsimshian high chief. Another leader in an advantageous position was *Txagaaxs* ("World Raven," also named *'Wiiseeks*) who became a rival of Ligeex until killed during the 1836 smallpox epidemic. With the shift to beaver pelts during 1805-1825, Old Ligeex came into his own by maximizing his links with the interior.

Seeking a land base, the HBC built Fort Nass in 1831, but the site was too exposed to freezing winds. There, in particular, Ligeex benefited from the marriage of his daughter *Sudaał* to Dr. John Frederick Kennedy, physician and resident trader.[32] For two years, she talked to her father about a better locale until he offered his camp "At The Wild Roses" for Fort (Port) Simpson, built in 1834 (Meilleu 1980, Grumet 1975, 1982). By 1840, when Old Ligeex vanished from the record, the other Coast Tsimshian tribes had each founded a neighborhood there in lieu of Metlakatla. By claiming a monopoly over the entire Skeena River, as well as ready access to the HBC, Ligeex rose to prominence over all the Tsimshian royalty, based not on his might but rather on his generosity by sharing these resources with his fellow chiefs.[33]

---

[31] A traditional chief had a moral and religious obligation to transform chaotic cosmic energy into socially useful power by being a conduit for it down through his spine, ceremonial cane, or totem pole, which, above all, was the "deed" to "his" rank, name, house, and territory.

[32] One source said that her mother was a Haida wife of Ligeex, but every other authority indicates that her mother was Nishga. If her mother (and very identity) had been Haida, the HBC records would have been very different. Instead, Haida traders at the fort often had to be guarded and escorted during their visits. Barnett (1940 #1: 8) gives her name as Ashigiumk, with a son called Taawiis, who went with his father after the wife died. Matthew Johnson (Barnett 1940 #1: 49) recalled that Kennedy supplied his father-in-law with the first shingles, pants, and other trade specialties ever seen among the Tsimshian, including a gun before firearms were banned. At Fort Simpson, Ligeex was "boss" of the young men cutting firewood and gardening for the traders (1940 #1: 57).

[33] In the most explicit statement about the nature of this monopoly, Matthew Johnson told

Outsiders, of course, saw mostly his imperious aspect, particularly his brilliant military strategies. As Chief Heber Clifton noted (Barbeau and Beynon, 1987b: 69):

> Ligeex was a most ferocious warrior and he had no respect or feeling for anybody, just like his Eagle warriors, mostly all Gispaxlo'ots. He was dreaded by all. Women from other tribes used his name in their nursery songs to instill fear into their children. The Ligeex warriors were a vicious group.

Among the Tsimshian themselves, however, the Ligeex title was specially honored because of its succession of able managers, potlatch hosts, *halaayt* initiators, dynastic marriage brokers, and war lords (Garfield 1939: 201-204, Miller 1997: 86-87).[34]

In contrast, academics have consistently misread statements from Henry Tate to Franz Boas about the history of the Ligeex line (Boas 1916: 510), which need to be reconsidered carefully. In particular, because it fit with European notions of chronology, a false link was made between the Kitamaat origin of the name and the Ligeex six generations back from 1888 who painted his claim on a Nass River cliff. Therefore, the introduction of the Ligeex name, probably about five hundred years ago, was distinct from the momentum provided by the European fur trade, about 1750, to move that name into primacy. What Boas actually wrote was this:

> "Thus the highest in rank among all the Tsimshian chiefs was Ligeex, the chief of the Eagle group of Gispaxlo'ots. His family alone had the right to perform certain ceremonials corresponding to the highest secret societies of the Kwakiutl. Tradition says – and it is undoubtedly correct – that an Eagle woman of the Gispaxlo'ots tribe eloped with a Kitamaat chief (the tribe of Kwakiutl affinity inhabiting Gardner Channel), whose family assumed membership in the highest ceremonial society. After her return to the Skeena River, the woman was given the name *K'amdmaxł* ("ascending the mountain with a costly copper"). The name Ligeex is said to be a Kitamaat name (perhaps from *la* = "to go", *-eg.a* = "behind" ?).[35] The chief of the tribe took it after the

---

Homer Barnett (1940, notebook #1: 31), "Ligeex made a law that only one canoe per house, to control trade with Hagwilget." In other words, Ligeex regulated the trade for all the Tsimshian, specifying that each house, roughly a crest-based matriline, could send one and only one canoe to trade upriver along the Skeena with the Tsimshianic Gitksan, who in turn traded with the Athapaskan Wet'suwet'en (Bulkley River Western Carrier) whose towns included Hagwilget. Each house and canoe, of course, paid a tariff to Ligeex for this regulated access.

[34] Ligeex's vital role in the *halaayt* initiations of elite children appears in Volume 12, text 179, The Halait And All The Different Kinds Of Halait, taken by William Beynon in 1937 from Julia White and Mrs R. Tate, now at the Butler Library of Columbia University, also Reel 3 of the set by Microfilming Corporation of America, 1980.

[35] According to Chief Gordon Robinson of Kitamaat (1956: 24-26) the name Ligeex means "overland traveler" and was assumed by Jasee (ts'si), a Gwinhuut Raven chief at Kitamaat whose own name had been given by his Eagle father and means "Eagle Claws."

previous hereditary chief's name, *Nisbalaas*, had lost its standing, because the bearer had been killed by a chief of the Raven clan and his head put up in the house of the latter."

Three paragraphs later – after describing Ligeex intermarriage with the Kitkatla royal Orca house, links with the Gitando, and remarking "I have also been told that the Gispaxlo'ots had the privilege of trade with the Gitksan, which they maintained successfully against the Hudson Bay Company until the later purchased it in 1866" – Boas added "The Ligeex who ruled about one hundred and fifty years ago (the sixth back from the year 1888) had his figure painted on a vertical precipice on Nass River, a series of coppers standing under his figure."

With greater precision, Matthew Johnson,[36] chief advisor to the Ligeexs in the early 1900s, told Homer Barnett that the grandmother of Ligeex I married the Kitamaat chief, while their daughter married Hamdziit, a leading Heiltsuk (*Wutsdaa*, Bella Bella) chief (Barnett 1940, notebook #1: 44). Thus this matriline became doubly empowered from the south by a Kitamaat name and Wutsdaa guilds from fathers whose paternal role in this matrilineal society was to extravagantly advance the public career of his children.[37] Moreover, Heiltsuk chiefs had a tradition of memorializing their fame by having a "portrait" painted on a rock face.[38] Through his mother's Eagle crest, Ligeex was also allied with the *Gwinhuut* Fugitive Eagles of the Alaskan Stikine and Tlingit, along with the legendary Haida princess named Omen. His crests included both the Frog Hat, held on his head by two members of his father's clan, and a cane topped by a Frog, together with the Beaver Hat, which was held on Ligeex's head by a member from each of the four crests to show that Ligeex "was the highest in rank among all the clans" (Boas 1916: 267, 272, 512). For Tsimshian, this public act of cooperation among the four crests is regarded as proof of his primacy.

Moreover, Ligeex had many *naxnox* and *halaayt* privileges uniquely his own. One *naxnox* involved two enormous hands that reached down from the roof and lifted a man toward Heaven, while another, called Crack of Heaven, was a mask that made the house divide in two, move apart, and rejoin. His *halaayt* names included *txagaxsm laxha* (Heaven Body), *hanatana*, and *gaguliksgaax* (Boas 1916: 513, 556; Barnett 1940, notebook #2: 21-22, 1942).[39] Needless to say, these feats were spectacular beyond those of other chiefs.

---

[36] Johnson was born 5 November 1855 and so was 85 when he worked with Barnett in 1940.

[37] Dr. Emmon Bach, a linguist formerly at the University of Massachusetts at Amherst and now at the University of Northern British Columbia, worked on the Kitamaat version of Northern (Kwakiutlan) Wakashan with Jeffrey Legaik, who died in 1976.

[38] A Beynon text (microfilm reel 2: 111-128) places this painting on the Nass, but another or duplicate also exists on the Skeena (where I have seen it) across from Port Essington, most likely sponsored by Old Ligeex to assert the claim to his Skeena trade prerogative. The original Skeena artist's name was *Dzumks*, although *Gaya* of Gitlaan later refurbished it. The basket Dzumks stood in and the rope used to suspend it were purchased from a Skidegate Haida chief, who made the trip home and back in eight days, for five coppers and five slaves.

[39] Barnett (1940, notebook #2: 20-21) lists five wonders and eight masks.

The men called Ligeex participated in dynastic marriages; Old Ligeex married very well (Marsden and Galois 1995: Figure 2). Before 1800, he wed Maskgaax (*Meksgaax*) of the House of *Saxsa'axt* of the royal Gitwilgyoots, who had sea otter beds and traded with the Masset Haida. One of their sons married into a Raven house of the Gits'iis, then married *A'maa'tk*, a sister of *Nisnawaa*, a leading chief of Kitselas from the House of *Senaxaat*, trading with Kaigani Haida and *Gwinhuut* Tlingits. One of their sons married a royal Gitzaxłał Raven with trading privileges into the Tongas Tlingit. After 1800, Old Ligeex allied with *Nts'iitskwoodat*, a niece of *Sgat'iin*, a Wolf chief of the upper Nass River. One of their daughters was *Sudaał*, who married Kennedy of the HBC, and another wed *Txagaax*, the former rival. This third wife lived well as a trader until dying in the 1836 smallpox outbreak, when the HBC provided her coffin and grave. At his apogee, Old Ligeex married *Nasełiyoontk*, also known as *Ksmgyemk* (Lady Sun), of the Kitkatla royal Orca house of *Ts'ibasaa* (Hale), who, in turn, wed Ligeex's eldest sister (named *K'amdmaxł* for their mother), and their Eagle son, Ligeex's heir, was named *Hatsksnee'x* (Long Fin).[40]

Through trade and ritual exchanges, the Ligeex received enormous cedar canoes from Haida Gwaii (Queen Charlotte Islands noted for huge cedar trees) to transport large loads of trade goods along the Skeena.

The keepers of the gateway to the furs of interior Gitksans and Athapaskans were the Kitselas at the Canyon of the Skeena. Their royal house was founded by a Fireweed from legendary Temlaxam (Prairie Town) with extensive kin ties. Later Githawn (*Githoon*, Salmon Man), a famous chief, founded an Eagle royal house there, fostering alliances with Ravens upriver among the Gitksan. Each spring, the Kitselas formally opened the annual trade with the Gitksan; only then could Old Ligeex impatiently begin his monopoly.

To circumvent this ritual requirement, Ligeex several times tried to vanquish the Kitselas and upriver towns. During one foray, he arrived in front of Kispayaks using the first umbrellas as a *naxnox* display to lure these townspeople into an ambush, which was brutal but indeterminant. Instead, over time, Ligeex used his own and other marriages, along with feasts, to regularize a successful alliance with the Kitselas.[41]

Yet, for all his preparations, Old Ligeex's well laid plans went awry just before he died about 1840. From 22 to 29 May 1839, a skirmish between Tsimshian and Skidegate Haida rocked Port Simpson. Among the many casualties was probably the designated heir to Old

---

[40] Today, Northwest natives are well aware of such parallels between the dynastic marriages of European and of Tsimshian noble houses. Royal Tsimshians specifically equate their own houses with others like the English House of Windsor, although their own, of course, are far older. It is to their benefit that Canada, unlike the US, honors such noble statuses.

[41] Similarly, Barbeau and Beynon (1987b) also include the origin of his crests of the Gunhuut (*Gwinhuut* "fugitives", including Tlingit) branch of the Eagle semi-moiety from a conflict with the Ravens at Laxsail, Alaska (: 31-35), the origin of the Ligeex name and halait privileges from the Kitamaat and Bella Bella Heiltsuk (: 62-65, 69-75), his revenge against the Haida (66-68), conflict with the Kitselas (: 84-85), series of four ascendancy potlatches (: 92-94), chiefly contests (: 95-111, 118-126), staged cremation *halaayt* (: 116-117), and attempted murder of William Duncan (: 206-209). Other texts refer to actions by Gispaxlo'ots royal houses (: 213-235).

Ligeex, leaving the succession uncertain. When the old chief died a year later, his own brother (*Hatsksnee'x*, the proper name for the heir) and nephew (probably a boy) vied for the position with equal matrilineal claims.[42]

During this fierce rivalry, *Ts'ibasaa* tried hard to humiliate the boy, who was sagely protected by *Xiyoop*, his Eagle spokesman and guardian who once purchased the Cormorant Copper from the Haida with his own resources to best the Kitkatlas.

In time, the boy himself seems to have taken the name *Xiyoop* and continued to prove he measured up to his responsibilities. In keeping with family tradition, he married a Kitselas woman named wałk,[43] who had lived for four years in Victoria and could advise him about the ways and supplies of European fur traders.[44] He became a skilled warrior and plotted to confirm himself as Ligeex by massacring Skidegates in revenge for the lost heir. As Ligeex, he had a special house built where these Haida would be invited to a feast, trapped, and killed. Instead, however, at its completion, Niswiksunash, Gitlaan chief, threw eagle down on him in public, thereby forcing him to remain peaceful.[45] In 1865, his rival uncle was taken by the Gitando to be the Eagle chief named *Sgagaweet*.

Meanwhile, other major changes were taking place. Sponsored by the Church Missionary Society, Evangelical Anglicans, in 1857, William Duncan, a lay missionary, arrived from England. After devoting a year to learning Tsimshianic from *Clah* inside the fort, he began preaching in Ligeex's own house until they had an angry falling out when Duncan persisted in ringing his bell during the enforced silence of the *halaayt* initiation of a Ligeex daughter. In 1862, to protect his converts, he led them to found a wealthy cooperative community back at

---

[42] Old Ligeex, his brother, and his nephew should have all been Eagles through their mothers (also a sister of the brothers in terms of the nephew), yet this Uncle has what appears to be the Orca name of the heir to the royal house of Kitkatla, whose premier name was Ts'ibasaa, until he exchanged this name with a ship captain for that of Hale. Such a link to this foremost Orca house is reinforced by the intense rivalry between *Ts'ibasaa* and the boy Ligeex in the 1840s.

[43] Barnett (1940 #1: 32, #2: 27) says she was the daughter of *Eks*, a man who died from miscalculating the amount of poisonous root to eat during ritual purging in preparation for halibut fishing.

[44] Barnett (1940, notebook #1: 27). While *Wałk* was on a visit to Port Simpson, the future Paul Ligeex decided to marry her, but she was warned that he was "mean" when drinking so she refused and escaped on the *Beaver*, the Hudson Bay Company steamship to Victoria, founded in 1849, where she stayed for four years, benefiting from contact with Sir James Douglas, first governor after a long career in the Hudson's Bay Company. When she returned north, Ligeex had reformed so they married. He called together the other chiefs and reported what his wife had told him about Victoria, proposing an expedition there, which took a month in 1854, opening a whole new trade network that, unfortunately, provided the route for the rapid spread of the 1862 devastating smallpox pandemic. See also Bolt (1992).

[45] The downy white feathers of eagles or swans were and are scattered at native gatherings to enforce peaceful intent. Such eagle down was a pledge of legal and moral action free from any treachery. Antonia Mills (1994) aptly titled her book on the Wet'suwet'en Athapaskan neighbors of the Gitksan, *Eagle Down Is Our Law*.

Metlakatla, where Ligeex joined them and was baptized Paul Legaic I (Murray 1985, Usher 1971, 1974). After two decades of success, however, differences with an imposed Anglican bishop drove Duncan and most of his converts to New Metlakatla in Alaska, seeking religious freedom under United States protection.

Frustrated and shamed after his Haida plot went askew, his councilors advised the soon-to-be Paul to join Duncan's community of Christian converts, where his primacy was still valued. At Metlakatla, all the houses looked the same so everyone would be equal before God, yet Paul was allowed to have a house larger than the others because of his rank. Named *Walp Hawhaw*, it bore a lion head carved at the end of its ridgepole and a sign written by Duncan, "This is the Lion House."[46]

While Paul played a prominent role in the Christian community until his death, over time, Duncan himself usurped the primary role of Ligeex, as evidenced by his oratorical fluency in the native language, his care and welfare for the community, and his constant industry – all traditional marks of chiefly status (Usher 1974: 109). Indeed, he was explicitly called "Chief".

After Paul joined Metlakatla, his councilors at Fort Simpson made his nephew *Awx* his surrogate among the traditional chiefs until his inheriting of the Ligeex name in his own right when Paul I died in 1869. As he assumed the English name Paul Legaic II along with the elite name title of Ligeex (Brock 2011: 205, 207), he hosted and, in return, was feasted by other First Nations since highest prestige comes from outside the local community. In 1869, at Fort Simpson, he was feasted by Kaigani Haida serving pilot bread and molasses, and Paul, in response, hosted whiskey feasts. At the end of 1870, he has stockpiled gifts and goods for a major potlatch, inviting Tlingits, Kitkatlas, and others. In February of 1871, Paul gave away all that he owned, including elk skins, 60 coppers, and 710 trade blankets.

As Ligeex, Awx married a Kitkatla woman and potlatched a new-style milled lumber house when their first child was born in 1872. After his wife died, he moved to Victoria, where he died, perhaps also known as Paul. When he died in 1891, his tribe gave away $800 in rifles, $650 in blankets, and $150 in clothes, in addition to new coats, shirts, pants, and stocking to those who attended to the body. In challenging response, the Gitando gave out $3000. In 1892, a marble monument to the entire Legeex line was set up at Port Simpson, where it still stands as an utterly unique marker among Tsimshian royal name titles.

The Ligeex title next passed to Marite (Martha, *Wułish*), a niece of sixteen, who died of measles two years later. In 1895, through his mother *Diiks*, sister of Paul I and wife of Taylor Dudoward, William Kelly inherited the Ligeex name until he died 29 September 1933. In lieu of a clear succession, the Gispaxlo'ots formed a committee of fourteen members to perform the powers of this chiefship[47] until in 1938, his son William Kelly assumed the name by right of his

---

[46] Barnett (1940, notebook #1: 53). The native word used here for lion (*hawhaw*), originally referred to a mighty spirit power until Duncan used it in a bible song about Daniel in the Lion's Den, still being sung. Since Matthew Johnson (notebook 1: 46) also reported that Duncan jailed natives who cut down their totem poles because they attracted tourists, he may have had a similar reason for labeling such a "curio," although respect for Paul was such that he was one of the few partners Duncan allowed into his private trading company.

[47] The Gitando also laid claim to some of these Ligeex powers because they had buried two

father adopting him as a nephew (sister's son).[48]

Against this historic native record and continuing Tsimshian regard for this great chief, several academics have argued against any primacy of the Ligeex line nor any claims to a Tsimshian chiefdom, despite two thousand of years of interactive winter occupation by allied tribes at Old Metlakatla. In particular, written reports mentioning other natives trading along the Skeena are taken as denials of any Ligeex monopoly, but this view is ethnocentric. Native sources are clear that anyone could trade along the Skeena, provided that they paid a tariff to Ligeex for this privilege. Thus, while these other traders may have been seen, their payments to Ligeex were not.

In one *adaawx*, a Nishga Wolf Chief named *Łitux* went overland and traded so successfully with the Gitksan that he had to attempt to come down the Skeena after the spring thaw. Forewarned, Ligeex sent word to his Eagle clansmen at Kitselas that this Wolf "was eating out of my food box." Intercepted, Łitux's canoes were smashed and his goods confiscated. Later, in consequence, revenge battles were fought on the Nass until peace was restored.[49] Yet, this Nishga's offense was not that he traded, but that he had the bravado to evade the tariff.

Nevertheless, Donald Mitchell (1983: 60, 62), relying on existing records from Fort Simpson, has argued that the Tsimshian had "a tribal level of social complexity and that to characterize it as a chiefdom is to misinterpret its significance for an understanding of cultural evolution."

These thirty years record at least 32 different trading excursion up the Skeena River. Seven refer only to Tsimshian trading; ten identify the traders as Gispaxlo'ots... and 15 make specific reference to Ligeex as the trader.... It seems clear that Ligeex and his group, the Gispaxlo'ots, did monopolize the Skeena River trade and that they did so for at least 30 years... It seems undeniable that Ligeex and his people – the Gispaxlo'ots – had some kind of exclusive right to carry the fur trade up the Skeena River and into the interior. It also seems obvious that Ligeex was or became the individual of highest rank among the Metlakatla Tsimshian lineage heads. In this sense he was the "principal chief" of the Tsimshian although he may not have attained this status until the 1840s.

But the contemporary observations of Fort Simpson traders make it seem most unlikely that Ligeex headed a political unit that could in any useful sense be termed a chiefdom. He ruled over no group but his own, and even there his hold seems fragile. In short, there was no chief and I would argue that the Tsimshian case provides us with no evidence of a Northwest Coast chiefdom.

Similarly, after another intensive study of the written record, Jonathan Dean (1993, 1994,

---

prior Ligeexs.

[48] See Barnett (1940, notebooks #1: 55-58; 2: 6-10, 16); Johnson explicitly said (Barnett 1940 #1: 58) that George Kelly was the fourth Ligeex he knew, listing as prior Paul, Awx, and Mather (?), which accounts for a present rival claim.

[49] See *Conflict at Gits'ilaasu*, Teachings of Our Grandfathers (*Suwilaay'msga Na Ga'niiyatgm*) 6 (Prince Rupert School District 52, 1992f).

ms.) determined that at Fort Simpson three chiefs were most prominent: Neshoot of the Gitzaxłaał, Txaqaaxs (Wiiseeks) of the Ginaxangiik, and Ligeex of the Gispaxlo'ots, but only Ligeex survived the 1836 smallpox epidemic, in part because he was vaccinated by the HBC. As noted above, however, Old Ligeex finally coopted these very chiefs through strategic marriages.

While Ligeex reportedly enjoyed a 'monopoly' in this time, this cannot be understood in Western terms, as a complete shutdown of all but Gispaxlo'ots commerce, but <u>might</u> have consisted of nominal control. Even after the rise of Ligeex in 1840, strangers from the Interior continued to use the Skeena to bring trade down to the fort, and the Nass river valley also continued as a very important venue. Beginning in the 1850's, the managers at Fort Simpson employed Neshaki – a Nishga noblewoman – to conduct the trade and transport furs from her village at Caxatan, and she continued to freight for the Company on the Nass after Ligeex left to join William Duncan at Metlakatla in 1862. By the middle 1860's Neshaki was even operating on the Skeena River, in Ligeex's 'backyard' (Dean 1994).

More specifically, in an unpublished study of the career of Ligeex, Dean suggested that Ligeex became more famous in memory after the name lapsed and the Gispaxlo'ots would not reciprocate with feasts, gifts, and potlatches, using past glory to justify present inactivity (Dean ms.: 20).[50]

Yet living memory among all the Coast Tsimshian, particularly as enshrined in the *adaawx*, makes it clear that the matriline of Ligeex high chiefs contributed to their overall cohesion during the trying times of the fur trade, Duncan's mission and flight from the Anglican bishop, and the imposition of Anglo-Canadian law and bureaucracy. Today, as all British Columbia First Nations prepare for their long overdue land claims and treaties, the name of Ligeex continues to be invoked as reminder of the superior leadership so characteristic of the Tsimshian from ancient times.[51]

Motivation

Lastly, the Ligeex climb to the top should be considered. While all chiefs were driven to excel, this line did more. Several hints indicate why. First, they were vastly and well connected. *Hamdziit*, the father of I, was a high ranking Heitsuk, a tribe so known for their supernatural

---

[50] Dean (ms: 20) made that charge that during the 1862 smallpox outbreak, "Had Legaic been the international specialist and the foremost chief as often portrayed, he should have taken steps to stabilize the situation (in spite of, or perhaps, because of, the smallpox) as semo'iget [*smoogyet*, real person, chief = "the real one who protects the people"] and *wihalaayt* ['*wiihalaayt*', great priest], whose *raison d'etre* was to master temporal and natural powers." As the *adaawx* indicate, however, the Ligeex succession was then in disarray from smallpox and rival claims.

[51] During my twenty years of fieldwork, Ligeex was always mentioned with such respect that people say the title is "too heavy" for anyone alive now to carry. The man who made the most current claim for this name died in January of 1997.

powers that they are sometimes called wizards or enchanters. Second, the *Gwinhuut* Eagles were a royal house but small, so they probably tried harder. Third, the primary *Gwinhuut* Eagle chief among the Gispaxlo'ots before Ligeex was *Nisbalaas*, who became eclipsed. Boas wrote that a later Nisbalaas had been beheaded by Ravens (Boas 1916: 355-370).[52] Thus, to overcome this shame, the Ligeex name was advanced at a time of great stress and managed to overtake all rivals. Four, like Chief Seattle, the early Ligeexs served as an intertribal war lord for concerted Tsimshian engagements. Over time, military success led to loyalties that advanced this name among all the other chiefs.

At apex, Ligeex provided an orderly system to channel the flow of furs, power, and largesse so that these other chiefs could expect to benefit from his generosity and skill as an effective manager. Other chiefs had other prime specialties, such as *Ts'ibasaa* opening the winter ceremonial season or Sgagaweet leading the cannibal *halaayt*. Yet when outsiders were involved, all united behind Ligeex.

Acknowledgements

Study of these disparities between academic piecemeal and Tsimshian holistic treatments of Ligeex owe much to conversations with Susan Marsden, Viola Garfield, John Dunn, Christopher Roth, Ernest and Lynne Hill, Ray Fogelson, Marjorie Halpin, Jonathan Dean, and Chiefs Tom Brown and John Clifton.

References

Adams, John
  1973 *The Gitksan Potlatch*. Population Flux, Resource Ownership and Reciprocity. Holt, Rinehart, and Winston of Canada, Toronto.
Barbeau, Marius
  1951 Tsimsyan Songs (with 75 song texts). *The Tsimshian: Their Arts and Music*, Proceedings of the American Ethnological Society 18:97-157. JJ Augustin, NY.
  1990 *Totem Poles II*: According to Location. Canadian Museum of Civilization, Hull. [1950]
Barbeau, Marius, and William Beynon
  1987a *Tsimshian Narratives I*: Tricksters, Shamans and Heroes. John J. Cove and George F. MacDonald, eds. Canadian Museum of Civilization, Mercury Series, Directorate Paper 3.
  1987b   *Tsimshian Narratives 2*: Trade and Warfare. John J. Cove and George F. MacDonald, eds. Canadian Museum of Civilization, Mercury Series, Directorate Paper 3.
Barnett, Homer
  1940 Data from Port Simpson and Hazelton. University of British Columbia Special Collections. 3 notebooks.
Boas, Franz
  1902 Tsimshian Texts, Nass River Dialect. DC: Bureau of American Ethnology, Bulletin 27.
  1916 *Tsimshian Mythology, Based On Texts Recorded by Henry Tate*. Bureau of American

---

[52] This disaster may have included the massacre of virtually all Gispaxlo'ots chiefs, giving Ligeex even greater incentive to advance by lavish potlatching.

Ethnology, Annual Report 31 For 1909-10: 29-1037. DC.

Bolt, Clarence

1992 *Thomas Crosby and the Tsimshian. Small Shoes for Feet Too Large.* University of British Columbia Press, Vancouver.

Brock, Peggy

2011 *The Many Voyages of Arthur Wellington Clah. A Tsimshian Man on the Pacific Northwest Coast.* University of British Columbia Press, Vancouver.

Coupland, Gary

1988 *Prehistoric Cultural Change at Kitselas Canyon.* Canadian Museum of Civilization, Ottawa.

Dean, Jonathan

1993 'Rich Men', 'Big Powers', and Wastelands ~ The Tlingit-Tsimshian Border of the Northern Pacific Littoral, 1799 to 1867. University of Chicago: History PhD.

1994 "Those Rascally Spakaloids ...": The Rise of Gispaxlot Hegemony at Fort Simpson, 1832 to 1840. *BC Studies* 101: 41-78.

ms.   "My Canoe Was Full of People - But It Capsized - & all the People Lost but Myself ...": The Rise and Fall of Legaic, 1840 to 1865.

Dunn, John

1995 *Sm'algyax ~ A Reference Dictionary and Grammar of the Coast Tsimshian Language.* University of Washington Press for the Sealaska Heritage Foundation, Seattle.

1979 Tsimshian Internal Relations Reconsidered: Southern Tsimshian. *The Victoria Conference on Northwestern Languages.* Barbara Efrat, ed. British Columbia Provincial Museum, Heritage Record 4: 62-82. Victoria.

Garfield, Viola

1939 *Tsimshian Clan and Society.* University of Washington Publications in Anthropology 7 (3): 167-340. Seattle.

1966 The Tsimshian and Their Neighbors. *The Tsimshian and Their Arts.* University of Washington Press, Seattle.

Gitsegukla

1979 Gitsegukla History (*Anawkhl Gitsegukla*). By the Band Council.

Grumet, Robert

1975 Changes in Coast Tsimshian Redistributive Activities in the Fort Simpson Region of British Columbia, 1788-1862. *Ethnohistory* 22 (4): 295-318.

1982 Managing the Fur Trade: The Coast Tsimshian to 1862, *Affluence and Cultural Survival*: 26-39. 1981 Proceedings of the American Ethnological Society. Richard Salisbury and Elisabeth Tooker, eds. West Publishing Co, St. Paul.

Halpin, Marjorie

ms. Masks As Metaphors of Anti-Structure.

1973 The Tsimshian Crest System: A Study Based on Museum Specimens and the Marius Barbeau and William Beynon Field Notes. University of British Columbia, Anthropology Ph.D. Dissertation. Vancouver.

1978 William Beynon, Ethnographer, Tsimshian, 1888-1958. *American Indian Intellectuals*: 141-156. Margot Liberty, ed. Proceedings of the 1976 American Ethnological Society. West Publishing Co., St. Paul.

1994 The Structure of Tsimshian Totemism. A Critique of the Boasian Paradigm for Northwest Coast Art," *Culture* 14 (1): 5-16.

Halpin, Marjorie, and Margaret Seguin
  1990 Tsimshian Peoples: Southern Tsimshian, Coast Tsimshian, Nishga, and Gitksan. *Northwest Coast.* Wayne Suttles, ed. Handbook of North American Indians, Volume 7: 267-284.
Inglis, Richard, and James Haggarty
  1987 Cook to Jewitt: Three Decades of Change in Nootka Sound. *"Le Castor Fait Tout":* Selected Papers of the Fifth North American Fur Trade Conference, 1985: 193-222. Bruce Trigger, Toby Morantz, Louise Dechene, eds. Lake St Louis Historical Society, Montreal.
Kroeber, Alfred
  1923 American Culture and the Northwest Coast. *American Anthropologist* 25 (1): 1-20.
MacDonald, George
  1979 Kitwanga Fort National Historic Site, Skeena River, British Columbia, Historical Research and Analysis of Structural Remains. Parks Canada: Manuscript Report 341.
  1984 The Epic of Neḵt: The Archaeology of Metaphor: 65-81. *The Tsimshian: Images of the Past, Views for the Present.* Margaret Seguin, ed. University of British Columbia Press, Vancouver.
McNeary, Stephen
  1976 Where Fire Came Down, Social and Economic Life of the Niska. Anthropology Ph.D. Dissertation, Bryn Mawr College.
Marsden, Susan
  ms.   Controlling the Flow of Furs: Northcoast Nations and the Maritime Fur Trade.
Marsden, Susan, and Robert Galois
  1995 The Tsimshian, the Hudson's Bay Company, and the Geopolitics of the Northwest Coast Fur Trade, 1878-1840. *The Canadian Geographer* 39 (2): 169-183.
Matson, Richard, and Gary Coupland
  1995 *The Prehistory of the Northwest Coast.* Academic Press, San Diego.
Maud, Ralph
  1982 *A Guide to BC Indian Myth and Legend. A Short History of Myth-Collecting and A Survey of Published Texts.* Talonbooks, Vancouver.
Meilleur, Helen
  1980 *A Pour of Rain: Stories from a West Coast Fort.* Sono Nis Press, Victoria, B.C.
Miller, Jay
  1997 *Tsimshian Culture. A Light Through the Ages.* University of Nebraska Press, Lincoln.
  1978 Moiety Birth. *Northwest Anthropological Research Notes* 13 (1): 45-50.
  1981 Moieties and Cultural Amnesia: Manipulations of Knowledge in a Pacific Northwest Coast Native Community. *Arctic Anthropology* 18 (1): 23-32.
  1981 Tsimshian Moieties and Other Clarifications. *Northwest Anthropological Research Notes* 16 (2): 148-164.
  1984 Introduction, Tsimshian Religion in Historical Perspective. *The Tsimshian and Their Neighbors of the North Pacific Coast.* Jay Miller and Carol Eastman, eds. University of Washington Press, Seattle.
  1984 Feasting with the Southern Tsimshian: 27-39. *The Tsimshian: Images of the Past, Views for the Present.* Margaret Seguin, ed. University of British Columbia Press, Vancouver.
  1989 An Overview of Northwest Coast Mythology. *Northwest Anthropological Research Notes* 23 (2): 125-141.
  1992 North Pacific Ethnoastronomy: 193-206. *Earth and Sky ~ Visions of the Cosmos in*

Native American Folklore. Ray Williamson and Claire Farrer, eds. University of New Mexico Press, Albuquerque.

Mills, Antonia
 1994 *Eagle Down Is Our Law: Witsuwit'en Law, Feasts, and Land Claims.* University of British Columbia Press, Vancouver.

Mitchell, Donald
 1981 Sebassa's Men: 79-86. *The World Is As Sharp As A Knife, An Anthology in Honour of Wilson Duff.* Donald Abbott, ed. British Columbia Provincial Museum, Victoria.
 1983 Tribes and Chiefdoms of the Northwest Coast: The Tsimshian Case. *The Evolution of Martime Cultures on the Northeast and Northwest Coasts of America.* Ronald Nash, eds. Department of Archaeology Publications 11: 57-64. Simon Fraser University, Burnaby, BC.

Prince Rupert School District 52 (Vonnie Hutchingson, Susan Marsden)
 1992a   *Na Amwaaltga Ts'msiyeen*: The Tsimshian, Trade, and the Northwest Coast Economy. Teachings of Our Grandfathers (Suwilaay'msga Na G̲a'niiyatgm) 1.
 1992b   *Adawga Gant Wilaaytga Gyetga Suwildook.* Rituals of Respect and the Sea Otter Trade. Told by Henry Reeves. Teachings of Our Grandfathers (Suwilaay'msga Na G̲a'niiyatgm) 2.
 1992c   *Saaban.* The Tsimshian and Europeans Meet. Told by Dorothy Brown. Teachings of Our Grandfathers (Suwilaay'msga Na G̲a'niiyatgm) 3.
 1992d   *Fort Simpson, Fur Fort at Lax̱łgu'alaams.* The Teachings of Our Grandfathers (Suwilaay'msga Na G̲a'niiyatgm) 4.
 1992e   *Ndeh Wuwaal Kuudeex A Spaga Laxyuubm Ts'msiyeen.* When the Aleuts Were on Tsimshian Territory. Teachings of Our Grandfathers (Suwilaay'msga Na G̲a'niiyatgm) 5.
 1992f   *Conflict At Gits'ilaasu.* Teachings of Our Grandfathers (Suwilaay'msga Na G̲a'niiyatgm) 6.
 1992g   *Na Maalsga Walps Nislgumiik*: The Story of the House of Nisłgumiik. Teachings of Our Grandfathers (Suwilaay'msga Na G̲a'niiyatgm) 7.

Robinson, Michael
 1996 *Sea Otter Chiefs.* Bayeaux Arts, Calgary.

Sapir, Edward
 1915 A Sketch of the Social Organization of the Nass River Tribes. Canadian Geological Survey, Museum Bulletin 19, *Anthropological Series* 7.

Seguin, Margaret, ed.
 1984 *The Tsimshian: Images of the Past, Views for the Present.* University of British Columbia Press, Vancouver.

Tsimshianic Oral Literature

Probably the oldest continuing traditional literature in Canada if not the world, Tsimshian epics – recorded by native scholars such as William Beynon and Henry Tate working with academics – have been vilified in provincial court, then, most honourably, redeemed by the Canadian Supreme Court in a 1998 legal case involving LAND claims (see Leslie Hall Pinder). The experience has been unique in the humanities, though not in the annals of colonialism.

The Tsimshianic language family, speakers of a linguistic isolate, perhaps related to the Penutian stock, consists, in the interior, of Nishga (Nisga'a) on the middle Nass River, and of Gitksan (Gitxsan) on the upper Skeena R, and, near the ocean, of Coast and of Southern Tsimshians. Coastal Tsimshians recognize four paired clans (semi-moieties) called *Ganhada* (Raven) and *Laxsgiik* (On Eagle) or Gispwudwada (Orca, locally called Blackfish, Killerwhale) and Laxgibuu (On Wolf). Inland [b] Gitksan and Nishga use Frog for Raven, and Grizzly or Fireweed for Orca.

Neighbours to the north were Tlingit, to the west Haida, to the south Wakashan speakers, and to the east various Athapaskans. For millennia, these nations interacted through trade, warfare, ceremonial exchanges, and royal intermarriages, effectively overarching differences of town, tribe, or parent language to blend oral motifs and themes.

Tsimshianic distinguishes two basic narrative types known as *maalsk*, 'tellings,' or *adaawx,* more culturally dense, rich, nuanced, and owned accounts that Natives call 'history', although 'sacred history' better conveys their many other-worldly aspects, as Claude Levi-Sirauss made famous with the minor example of Asdiwal.

Stylistically, both narratives use repetition to underscore a main theme; to build momentum, rhythm, balance, or suspense; and to lull an audience while the narrator plans ahead. While the plot is familiar to listeners, subtleties in the word choice, along with rephrases and refrains, have provided the basis for aesthetic judgments. Text has sometimes varied with song, particularly when claiming privileges to music.

Tellings have no restrictions on time, manner, or person speaking or hearing them. They are general tales that can have moral as well as entertainment value. Many involve their trickster Raven (*txamsn*), also known as Giant (*wiigyet*), who does good by both intent and mistake as well as by providing a singularly negative example. Ravenous in his appetites, he tricked the original owners out of the sun, moon, stars, tides, freshwater, and other necessities.

Indeed, ownership has been a primal feature of the Tsimshian universe and distinguishes these 'tellings' from 'sacred histories', where many details of place, creativity, and individuals are manifested as the hereditary property of a noble house, the basic unit of North Pacific cultures.

A house is simultaneously a cedar plank building, its membership traced through mothers and sisters, its landed estate frequented by named ancestors, and its crests – artistic treasures consisting of hats, masks, regalia, songs, dances, and other means of display – specifically explained in terms of a name in a sacred history. [1140] Each name serves in the way that 'Arthur' does for the "Matter of Britain", providing a tag for events, neither solitary nor unique as with Euro-Canadians, but, according to First Nations, as exemplary and worthy of repeated emulation through subsequent generations.

Tsimshians say that people are given to names rather than the reverse because the names are immortal and each benefits a 'holder' who treats it with respect by leading an honourable and generous life. Moreover, names are said to 'live again' in another mortal body, recursively interweaving past, present, and future within an overall context of immortality. Thus, Native history is a progressive viewing of glimpses of the divine to benefit an ongoing community through public events such as feasts, ceremonies, and potlatches. So vital is this mortal/immortal connection that during and after devastating European-derived epidemics, in the absence of suitable heirs, names were passed on to pets such as dogs or to arms, legs, and other body parts of overburdened 'holders'.

Tsimshians also say 'names feed people' because each is firmly grounded in a portion of the landscape, conferring rights to all its resources. These rights were and are witnessed at validating public events to make them 'legal,' with a new totem pole providing that 'deed,' as long as that holder and name generously share that bounty with household members and with many guests. In this manner, the immortal sustains the mortal to benefit their shared prestige.

Because the highest-ranking name holders were and are invited to every feast and potlatch, they were in a position to hear all the major epics recited in public. Their role, however, was to witness rather than to record or judge these 'other' *adaawx* for only the master of a house had the unassailable right to recite its epic, personally or, for greater prestige, via a 'hired' narrator.

While sacred histories primarily validated ownership to crests, many of these were shared among a duster of houses whose ancestors participated in the same epic events, setting them off as a subset within a clan to create clusters such as Gispwudwada (Orca, Grizzly, Grouse, Mosquito, Stars, Sun, Fireweed), Ganhada (Raven, Frog, Sculpin, Starfish), Laxgibuu (Wolf, Bear, Crane, Owl), and Laxsgiik (Eagle, Beaver, Halibut, Octopus).

Native moral and religious law demands respect toward all forms of life. Thus, while humans might use parts and pieces of other beings, the entire body could be used only by members of that particular species. *Adaawx*, therefore, carefully interdict any abuse of living things or their articulated skeletons, their source of eternal vitality, which were burned to assure reincarnation. Indeed, a primary duty of any chief, as with the leader of any species, wm to become so 'evolved' as to channel such vitality down his spine (or its representation in totem pole or cane) to fructify the land of his people.

Beginning with the actions of divine Heaven (*laxha*) in a stark and wet world that is obviously post-glacial, the most ancient *adaawx* span at least 12,000 years. Later ones sort themselves out as overlying episodes that happened relatively close to each other. Because of the past glacial conditions and present watery environment, flood stories reappear throughout the full chronology.

Any version is told from the perspective of one house so it is both personal and laudatory, reporting triumphs always but defeats rarely. Each is thoroughly 'grounded' in its claimed, consumed, and imagined landscape.

By about 8000 BCE, obsidian was being traded from Mt Edziza, north of the Stikine R, throughout northern British Columbia and the Alaska panhandle. Established towns and trails (c3000 BCE), today paved as modern highway, spread trade goods throughout the region. This trade included exotic goods supporting a ranked society much like that of modern Tsimshian.

Armour, weapons, and fractured bones from graves indicate increasing warfare. Trophy heads and rod armour imply ripples of influence from the Old Bering Sea complex (c1000 BCE) on both sides of the Pacific, which in turn had connections with Shang China (c1600 BCE), suggesting an ancestral foundation for the cultures of the Inuit, Aleut, and northern Northwest Coast.

Abroad range of foods began to narrow toward the use of shellfish (c1000 BCE), then salmon (c500 BCE). Coinciding with this specialization, concern with ranking restricted the access to any resource as corporate property and encouraged its more intensive production, under the supervision of that leader, to benefit not just individual but also house, town, and clan prestige.

Plank houses and towns grew larger (c500 BCE), indicating population increase, and complex woodworking tools elaborated the form-line art style for which Tsimshians are famous. Social rank was indicated by differences in house size and imported goods, with the greatest house in the centre of the front row, as in historic times.

Tlingit ancestors (cAD 200) in the shadow of Asian military strategies applied them to Tsimshians, who in turn used them on Haida and various Wakashans. Slavery was almost surely one of the motivations for these attacks, adding extra labour for the elaboration of chiefly prestige.

Particularly significant among the 15 or more overlying episodes are the descent of Raven, the visit undersea to Nagwinaks, the revenge of the Heavenly Children leading to the founding of the great city of Temlaxam, the wars of Medeek (Grizzly) over hundreds of years, and the rise of Metlakatla from 1,800 years ago until the 1830s, when Tsimshians moved to the trading post at Fort (later Port) Simpson run by the Hudson's Bay Company, entrenching strong tribal chiefs by lavish generosity at potlatches to intensify rivalry and confrontation so as to sort out overall chiefly rankings. From these tests, the Eagle crest of the Gispaxlo'ots tribe elevated the Kitimat-derived name of Ligeex to Coast Tsimshian 'high chief'.

Religious beliefs shifted when, about AD 1800, a series of Athapaskan prophets called Bini ('mind') preached a blend of European and traditional beliefs, until William Duncan, an Anglican lay missionary, settled among Coast Tsimshian, learned their language, and created a cooperative Christian community that still exists in Alaska.

Today, *adaawx*, as a basis of clans (*p'teex*) and heraldic crests, continue, while *naxnox* (masked wonders) and *halaayt* (elite privileges vested in four guilds) do not. In other words, the realm of women survived well through the power of narrative, while the realm of men did not, except as recast in biblical, Christian, particularly Anglican, ways.

Further reading: Marius Barbeau and William Beynon, *Tsimshian Narratives* I: Tricksters. Shamans and Heroes, *Tsimshian Narratives* 2: Trade and Warfare, in John J Cove and George F MacDonald, eds, Canadian Museum of Civilization, Mercury Series, Directorate Paper 3,1987; Franz Boas, *Tsimshian Mythology*, Based on Texts Recorded by Henry Tate, Bureau of Am Ethnology, Ann Rpt 31: 29-1037, 1916; Jay Miller, *Tsimshian Culture, A Light through the Ages* (Lincoln: U Nebraska P, 1997).

Jay Miller

A

Please Help Wipe Out Typo Gnomes

Comments & Corrections Welcome

Sold @ Amazon.com